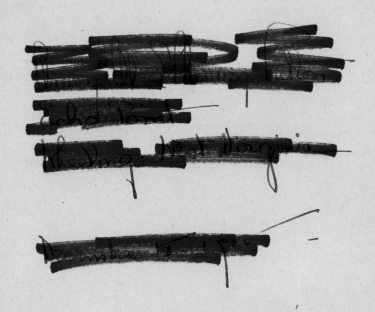

Echd Point

Wheeling West Virginia

THE LIFE OF
ELBERT H. GARY
THE STORY OF STEEL

THE LIFE OF
ELBERT H. GARY
THE STORY OF STEEL

BY

IDA M. TARBELL

AUTHOR OF "LIFE OF ABRAHAM LINCOLN," "HISTORY OF
THE STANDARD OIL COMPANY," ETC.

D. APPLETON AND COMPANY
NEW YORK :: LONDON :: MCMXXV

PREFACE

A year and a half ago the publishing house of D. Appleton & Company invited me to prepare a Life of Judge Gary, Chief Executive Officer of the United States Steel Corporation. The project had already been discussed with Judge Gary and a promise secured from him that if I would undertake the work he would turn over biographical data already gathered, and open to me the records of the Corporation.

So unusual an opportunity was not to be passed by a writer who for twenty-five years has been dealing with one or another phase of contemporary business and industrial history. Judge Gary belongs to a group of powerful men who in the last fifty years have led in the creation in the United States of what we call Big Business. The most conspicuous of these leaders have been the elder Rockefeller in oil, the elder Morgan in banking, E. H. Harriman in railroads, and in the earlier half of the period Andrew Carnegie in steel. These men of undoubted financial and commercial genius typified certain attitudes of mind toward business and were the sponsors of practices and an etiquette essential to understand if we are to have a realizing and helpful sense of the actual development and meaning and potentiality of Big Business.

v

Judge Gary is a leading figure among them, not because he is the head of the country's greatest industrial corporation, but chiefly because he has been a leader in developing a code of business practices, an attitude of mind radically at odds with that of the powerful at the time he became a factor to be reckoned with in their world.

From his entrance into steel, he held that the prevailing code was essentially wrong and also impracticable—bound to destroy rather than to establish a corporation. The unusual degree of success he has had in bringing his associates and competitors in the steel industry to accept his policies is the most significant story of the American business world of the last twenty-five years.

The story is written in voluminous records—government hearings, investigations and examinations of the Corporation; sworn testimony in court; written correspondence; technical and controversial literature; the daily newspaper comments; the files of the Bureau of Safety and Sanitation; the minutes of the Finance Committee and the Board of Directors. All of this important source material, printed or in manuscript, is in the open library or under lock and key at the Corporation's headquarters, and as promised has been freely opened to me. Whenever I have found in it references to reports or letters which it seemed to me might illuminate a doubtful point, these have always been cheerfully unearthed and exhibited to me whatever the expense of time and trouble.

The unique Industrial Museum of the American Steel and Wire Company at Worcester, Massachusetts, the technical collections on wire and steel of the Congressional Library and the Carnegie Library of Pittsburgh

have been found useful. Other sources consulted have
been the Roosevelt papers in the Manuscript Department of the Congressional Library of Washington; records of the Federal Trade Commission in the matter of
"Pittsburgh Plus"; and the full correspondence of
President Harding, Secretary Hoover and Judge Gary
regarding the abolition of the twelve-hour day.

I have been helped in my effort to understand these
records by many persons associated with Judge Gary
in the development of the Corporation, including officers, members of the Finance Committee, and presidents and executives of the subsidiary companies. I
have also talked with many of his competitors and with
persons connected with various government investigations and prosecutions, among them Mr. James Garfield, Secretary of Commerce and Labor under President
Roosevelt; and Mr. George W. Wickersham, Attorney-
General during President Taft's administration.

Judge Gary himself has been generous in taking time
to discuss with me the events of his life, to explain his
professional policies and principles and his relations
with his contemporaries, among whom are some of the
most important figures in the industrial and business
life of the country in the last twenty-five years. These
conversations have been an interesting and illuminating
experience. It was possible to voice freely to Judge
Gary my own points of view, to express whatever doubts
I may have had of a particular policy or performance,
to be listened to respectfully and to talk the matter out
in that impersonal and unbiased spirit which so many
of his associates and competitors consider one of his
most remarkable characteristics.

It will be seen from this summary statement that the

facts in this book are drawn from the most authentic sources, in many instances unpublished and hitherto inaccessible.

The responsibility for the interpretations made rests solely with the author.

IDA M. TARBELL.

CONTENTS

ILLUSTRATIONS

THE LIFE OF
ELBERT H. GARY
THE STORY OF STEEL

THE
LIFE OF ELBERT H. GARY

CHAPTER I

THE BACKGROUND

THE sons and daughters in the early American family were usually of opposing minds—stay-at-homes and pioneers. There were those among them who loved the fields their father had cleared, the cabin he had built, the trees he had planted, the community of which he and they were a part, and they asked nothing better than to carry on where they were born. There were those who had the lust of adventure in their hearts, the call of the beyond in their ears and who pushed ahead into the forests, clearing new fields, breaking prairies, building new cabins, planting new orchards, founding new communities. The sons and daughters of each group repeated the story.

Without the pioneer the early American settlements would have remained a fringe along the Atlantic coast and the great forests and plains which stretched back, mysterious and dangerous, would have remained untracked; without the conservers of the footholds made, the settlers would have bred a race of nomads. The adventures and sufferings, the adaptions and victories of these two types of American settlers make the history of the opening and developing of this country.

1

Dip into the story of almost any one of the white families catalogued in the census of 1790 as numbering at that time over one hundred persons; trace their migrations and their settlements, and you will find that the original group has spread like a fan north and south and west from the parent foothold.

Take the New England Gary family. They first appeared on this side of the Atlantic in 1638 when Arthur Gary, a man then thirty-nine, married and the father of two boys, both born in Hertfordshire, England, as he had been, is named among the freemen of Roxbury, Massachusetts, a member of the first church and a supporter of the Roxbury grammar school, said to be the first free school established in this country.

Soon after Arthur Gary and his wife settled in Roxbury a third son was born to them, Samuel. The three boys grew up in the settlement, and all three died there, leaving behind them reputations as substantial, useful citizens. William, the oldest, became a deacon in the church and deputy to the general court of Massachusetts; Nathaniel, the second, a successful planter; and Samuel, the third, a soldier in King Philip's War. It was the planter alone who left children—eleven of them, three of them sons. And for all three Roxbury turned out to be too small, though their pioneering was not far and was, so to speak, thrust in their faces.

The New England colonies soon saw the necessity of acquiring lands back from the coast as rapidly and as peacefully as possible; among the early purchases of the Massachusetts Bay Colony was a tract some fifty miles long and ten miles wide, extending from Worcester County, Massachusetts, down into Connecticut. This tract had touched the imagination of the Roxbury people and they had obtained the grant of a township from the general court. Soon after, thirteen of their residents were sent to "spy out" Woodstock as the new possession was called, one of these thirteen being Nathaniel Gary, the oldest of Arthur's three grandsons. Although Nathaniel Gary settled in Woodstock he wanted more land than it afforded him, and in a few years set himself to help in developing a second plantation, that of Pomfret.

He did well in the new undertaking, securing a deed for five hundred and fifty acres, a tract known until this day as the Gary Neighborhood. He not only had land, but he had importance in the new settlement, an importance shown by an unusual privilege accorded him, the right to build in the highway near the church for himself and his family a house "to sit in on Sabba'-days"—a small house, tight and warm, with benches and an ample fireplace. Here on Sunday mornings a fire was kindled by those who first came, and here Mr. Gary, his family and his friends thawed out their chilled fingers and toes after their cold rides over the hills of Pomfret, before entering the meetinghouse, which their curious piety required should be fireless.

Nathaniel's brothers, William and Samuel, soon followed him to Pomfret and they, too, built themselves into the neighborhood as substantial planters and public servants. All three left families. It is with a grandson of Nathaniel that we are concerned—Josiah, who died in Pomfret in 1790. Seven sons and seven daughters of the fifteen children born to Josiah and Sarah Sprague Gary, his wife, were at his funeral.

Among these seven sons was one William, by all accounts a lovable fellow, a man of scholarly tastes, a teacher for many years—known as Master Gary. Indeed, Master Gary established at Pomfret what may be called the first Gary School. But he was more than a schoolmaster. He was an active citizen, serving year after year as tax appraiser, on juries, wherever needed.

William Gary was not more important in the community than his wife, Lucy Perrin, a woman of the best Massachusetts antecedents, a masterful woman of character and ability, particularly prominent, as was her husband, in the Methodist Church.

Both the Garys and the Perrins had been supporters of the Methodists from their first coming to Pomfret, joining the movement no doubt, as so many others in New England were doing at that time, as a protest not only against the spiritual lukewarmness and suppression but the shocking indifference to drunkenness and immorality shown by the established New England churches. Both families had freely opened their homes to the circuit riders and missionaries of the new sect, and both had become faithful observers of its severe discipline.

Like all early Methodists they were particularly concerned with the spiritual condition of their children, urging them into the church and sacrificing gladly when a son decided for the ministry. It was a matter of rejoicing to William and Lucy Gary that they could "raise" not only a son—Charles Wesley, their oldest—but a nephew for the ministry. The latter, indeed, became one of the prides of the church in his day—the youngest candidate ever received by the denomination, it is said. The counsel with which his uncle, the schoolmaster, sent the fifteen-year-old preacher on his way is a credit to his good sense, as the fact that the boy himself kept it alive is to his:

"Never pretend that you know much, George, for if

you do pretend, the people will soon find out that you are sadly mistaken; neither tell them how little you know, for this they will find out soon enough.''

Along with these two young students for the ministry in the Gary family was another son, Erastus, born in 1806—a good Methodist boy but not one to whom the call to the ministry came. It was the land that called Erastus Gary—more land than Pomfret offered, for by this time in the division and subdivision of the original Gary plantation, the farm of each had dwindled to a small plot. Erastus, on coming to manhood, found himself with only thirteen acres. It was too little for him. Moreover, he revolted against the conditions under which the land must be worked in Connecticut—a fresh crop of stones each spring as certain as the grass itself. Again, there was little or no chance for a young farmer in Pomfret to piece out his income by outside labor, as was the practice in those days. The town had been losing population for several years, because of its failure to attract new industries, as many other Connecticut settlements were doing. Life had become hard and meager for most of its people, and there were some distasteful features for a spirit as vigorous and independent as that of young Erastus Gary. Then, there was an irritating and humiliating intolerance, even some contempt, for the church of his family. But stronger than the dissatisfying conditions at home, was the pull of the West. A new name, alluring, tantalizing, was in his ears. He could not forget it—Illinois. Wonderful tales were told all through the East of that vigorous young state—tales of cleared land, the prairie—great stretches of it, without a rock or a tree—nothing to do but put in your plow. And the quantities you could buy with a few dollars! It all went to disquiet him more and more with the few acres and the annual stone crop.

A hundred and twenty-five years before, the same tales, the same call, had come to the youth of New England from New York, New Jersey, Pennsylvania—fifty years later from the Shenandoah Valley, from Kentucky; but there were new musical words luring them now—Michigan, Indiana, Illinois.

It became too much for Erastus at last, and he persuaded the Reverend Charles to buy his thirteen acres. Then, with money in his pocket—it probably amounted, with what he had been able to save, to something like one thousand dollars—he started westward.

How would he go? There is a tradition in the Gary family that he went by horse or carriage as far as St. Joseph on Lake Michigan and then by canoe to Chicago. He was not curious about new methods of transportation or anxious to make his journey in the quickest and most comfortable way, if that was what he did. More likely, he made his way from Pomfret to Springfield and thence to Albany by coach along the broad way which had been in use for decades now. If he had been as enterprising and eager for information as he showed himself later, he would have taken the railroad at Albany. The year before there had been opened between that town and Schenectady the first iron road in this country—about twenty-one miles long. I cannot believe that he would have let that experience slip him. And at Schenectady he could have taken the Erie Canal, which for six years now had been the great highway across the state to Buffalo. From Buffalo he could have followed by wagon or on horseback down the lake to Cleveland, or he could have taken a schooner or a steamer and gone to Detroit, and thence by horse, have made his way to St. Joseph, Michigan.

But the significant thing is not how he got there, but that he actually went to the place for which he started. Many a pioneer in those days changed his objective en route. Charles Cleaver, who has left us one of the most fascinating records we have of pioneering to Chicago in this period, did not start from New York for Illinois, but for Canada; but he met so many travelers who told him tales of the fertility and promise of the Illinois land, that he and his party, after a little reconnoitering, entirely changed their minds. Erastus Gary went to the place he started for, and in the fall of 1831 landed in Chicago.

The town was not much to see in those days. Twenty to thirty log farmhouses scattered westward from the mouth of a river over a low and swampy prairie; a bare log church in which in turn three or four denominations worshiped; several rough boarding houses, frequently called hotels; five or six general stores and a post office, just opened to receive and care for the mails which were brought in on horseback once a week from the East, as well as now and then from the South, and for which the settlers came from a hundred miles or more in every direction.

But if the new town was rough and unkempt it was bursting with life—the feel of its future was in it. Traders, explorers, settlers, government agents filled not only all the beds of the new town but the floors of its houses, night after night. Schooners were already coming from Buffalo and Cleveland and Detroit. There was talk of the government improving the harbor—of canals and railroads from the East to the West. The town was lifted, too, from the ordinary commonplace of a pioneer settlement by Fort Dearborn and the government agency—well-cared-for places, with gardens and trees, kept up as befitted government possessions even if far from civilization.

Now Erastus Gary might have taken the land which he had come West to buy, in the present city of Chicago, but when he came to look over the swampy district he saw nothing there for a bona fide farmer. He was no speculator; he wanted a sure thing—land where he could raise things, land within a reasonable distance of this town, which he felt sure was to grow, and from which he reasoned that railroads would run westward. And so he started westward, where the railroad was to go; and finally some twenty-seven miles from the city that was to be, he selected a section—six hundred and forty acres —selected it with the care of the man wise in lands, seeing to it that there was timber—a lot of fully one hundred acres—and springs and sunshine, and a running stream near by. The location of that original piece of Gary land in Illinois is admirable proof of the wisdom and caution of the new strain that had come into the state.

The young man's next move was equally provident, and quite characteristic of one reared in the "Land of Steady Habits," as Connecticut was then called. He had found his land and staked it out, but it was too late for breaking sod and building. Instead of loafing in Chicago, as any single man might well have found excuse for doing, he made his way back to St. Joseph, Michigan, where he had heard of a school that needed a teacher. In the spring he and three fellow-travelers paddled back to Illinois in a dugout they had made themselves.

But he did not come back to peace; for scarcely had

he begun his work on the new tract when rumors of Black
Hawk's invasion of northern Illinois stirred the scattered
settlers west and south of Chicago. All the women and
children of that part of the world were hurried at once
to Fort Dearborn for safety; while every man able to
bear a gun—Erastus Gary among them—joined the mi-
litia. The next three months he spent as one of the guard
of the fort. The only serious Indian scare which Erastus
Gary remembered while on duty there turned out to be
an approaching flock of sheep! It was not Indians which
finally drove the refugees from the fort, but soldiers sent
by the government to protect them. In July, the first
steamer that ever tied up at a Chicago dock brought a
company under General Scott to reënforce the fort.
When it was noised abroad that they had brought Asiatic
cholera with them, the refugees quickly fled to their homes
—less afraid of Indians. By August all reason for fearing them was gone; Black Hawk and his warriors had
been driven beyond the Mississippi.

Young Gary now went to work in earnest on his claim,
building a log house, breaking land, buying stock. He
needed help and sent for a younger brother, Jude, selling
him one half of the land. So hopeful did the prospect
look to the brothers that they persuaded their mother,
Lucy Perrin Gary, now a widow, and their brother, the
Reverend Charles Wesley, to leave the home on Gary
Hill in Pomfret and join them. A little later the Gary
colony was increased by the coming of Jesse and Warren
Wheaton, two brothers, one of whom had married a sister
and the other a niece of Erastus Gary. Together they
made a fine group of hard-working men and women, of
similar tastes, traditions and ambitions.

From the start, Erastus Gary and his relatives did

well. A settlement was growing up beside their farms—
Warrenville, a good town to-day. Erastus bought a
tract to the north and started a sawmill. Here the Reverend Charles Wesley settled, helped build a church,
became the backbone of the community. The settlement
is still called Gary's Mill. Seeing that the railroad, which
he believed a certainty, would probably go to the northeast of Warrenville, Erastus Gary bought five or six hundred acres in that direction and let it lie. He believed
in land. He used to tell his sons that it was the only
thing for which a man could afford to run in debt.

Growing acres, growing crops, growing stocks, but little money; and Erastus took good care of the little that
came to him. There is a family tradition that he disapproved of the use of sugar in doughnuts; but if the
doughnuts did not get sugar, the tradition is equally
strong that he never failed the church or the needy—a
"liberal giver" he was called, and there are documents
to prove it. When he died in 1888 there was found among
his possessions a box full of uncollected notes—records
of moneys loaned over forty years, of which his sons
knew nothing, and which it looked as if he had never even
attempted to collect. Somebody needed the money more
than he did, so he let the notes lie. It is to be expected
that a man of such a nature—thrifty, able, generous—
would win confidence and affection, and Erastus Gary
won both. This was effectively shown in 1839, at a moment when the settlers of DuPage County—as the part
of Illinois to which he had come was called—were deeply
disturbed over the validity of the claims which they were
cultivating.

These claims were to unsurveyed lands belonging to
the United States. This fact emboldened "claim

jumpers" and "land sharks," as speculators were called, to pester the genuine settlers. The men of DuPage County were not of the kind to be fooled with by this sort of gentry. The news that a land pirate of any description had set up his camp on one of their claims was enough to bring out a group of sturdy, mounted citizens to run him out of the county, and they were none too gentle in their methods.

They could take care of this kind of nuisance, but they were intelligent enough to see that a much more serious threat to their properties was bound to come when the government finally should lay its lines. It was evident that these lines could not possibly agree with their own, for in locating they had taken in timber, water and prairie that pleased them, without regard to the square or rectangular form of their claims. The result was often tracts of fantastic irregularity. It was certain that when government surveys should be made, claims would be found to overlap. What was to be done?

They worked out as fine and sensible a piece of mutual agreement for forestalling trouble and settling the future inevitable difficulties as one often sees—the DuPage Society for Mutual Protection. In it they bound themselves to "deed or redeed" to one another, according to rules which they laid down in their charter, whenever the government survey did not agree with their line or lines. Each settler was at once to turn in a description of his claim to the general land office and if disputes arose between them, the claims were to be turned over to a board of arbitrators appointed from among their number.

The DuPage County Society for Mutual Protection also put into its charter an effective method of dealing with those who would not accept arbitration. They outlawed the recalcitrant who attempted to seize upon any part of any other person's claim, or infringe in any way on the lines which they had laid down. He was "deemed a dishonest man"—"no better than a thief or a robber" —"not entitled to the protection of their union." He sometimes failed to get even the toleration of his church. An influential member of the church at Gary's Mills, where the Reverend Charles was a power, refusing to deed back ten acres of a claim, which by the rules of the Union belonged to somebody else, was called before the church board and finally expelled, because "a man who refused to perform an act of justice was not fit for membership."

It is proof enough of the position that Erastus Gary held in this body of resolute and just-minded citizens that he was made one of the three arbitrators to adjust claims and outlaw aggressors. This was the beginning of a long series of services in looking after the law and order of the county which for thirty years or more he rendered. During this long period he served as a magistrate—Justice Gary he came early to be called—his reputation was as solid for fairness and honest dealings as for thrift and honesty.

Ten years passed in this strenuous work of settling and community building. Erastus Gary was thirty-six years old and still unmarried. And then, luckily for him, he found a woman of his own kind, one who by tradition, spirit, and ambition was admirably fitted for his mate.

In 1839 there had settled on a farm of 160 acres, about two miles west of the Erastus Gary farm, a family by the name of Vallette.

The Vallettes were French in origin, and had been in America for over a hundred years, the first of the name

being John Vallette who in 1702 had received a grant of
land in Newport, R. I. The Vallettes had married into
important New England families. The grandmother of
Jeremiah, our Illinois pioneer, was a Hammond, a de-
scendant of one of the first settlers in Hingham, Massachusetts; his mother a Bissell of the distinguished Connecticut family; his wife a Mott, who traced her line
directly back to Adam Mott of the New Haven Colony—
all leading names in the founding and developing of New
England. A romantic tradition follows the grandfather,
for he was known as Captain Vallette, and is supposed
to have been an officer in the French army.

The migrations and experiences of the Vallettes in the
new world, though not of as long duration as the Garys',
were essentially like theirs. They had been active pioneers, prosperous farmers, good citizens, good soldiers.
The same influences that had worked on Erastus Gary
had led Jeremiah Vallette to migrate to Illinois from his
farm in Stockbridge, Massachusetts; and he and his family took hold of the settlers' problems in much the same
way.

There is saved in their family a series of letters written back to New England, telling of the new country and
of their experiences in settling. They give a glowing
picture of the land—its prairies beautiful with flowers
and rich with berries of all descriptions—its melons big
and luscious, to be had by "dropping the seed into the
sod after it is turned over"—its "black, mealy soil" and
the crops they could raise from it—the drove of cattle
and hogs they fatted on the cheap hay and rich ranges.
That is, the Vallettes were happy and hopeful in their
change from Massachusetts to the prairie.

In the Vallette family was a young woman of nineteen,

Susan Abiah Vallette—Abi they called her—well educated for her time—a teacher, a Methodist, sober, industrious, charming. She took her place in the social life of the community to which Erastus Gary belonged. The two constantly met at services held in their homes when the circuit rider passed—at camp meetings and singing schools—at "bees" and "raisin's"—and quite naturally Erastus Gary soon found himself deeply drawn to the girl. But whatever she may have felt, she held herself bound. As happened so often to a girl in pioneer migrations, she had left a lover behind her—a young man studying for the Baptist ministry. He was to come for her but put it off, as he had been doing for a long time before she left New England, making excuses—he had not finished his studies—his "liver was bad!" He put it off too long, for a year after Susan Vallette came to Illinois, she began to find reasons why he should not come just yet. *Her* health was bad—she was in no haste to marry. "If he writes he will not come this fall"—as Susan had suggested—"I should rather think they will never have each other," wrote her sister to one of the family back home; and she added, "she would have as bright prospects for settling in life as she has now, if he does not come"—which probably meant that Erastus Gary was pressing his suit, and judging from the tone of the references to the delaying Baptist minister in the family letters, he was receiving the support of the Vallettes.

At all events "W. L.," as he is called in the correspondence, followed his betrothed's suggestion, and did not come out in the fall of 1840; and, as her sister had foretold, they "never had each other," for in October of 1841 she married Erastus Gary—a happy thing for both of them—so they both thought to the end of their days.

Susan A. Gary

SUSAN A. GARY, THE MOTHER OF JUDGE GARY, TAKEN
WHEN SHE WAS ABOUT THIRTY-EIGHT YEARS OF AGE

Erastus Gary

ERASTUS GARY, JUDGE GARY'S FATHER, AT SEVENTY-
NINE YEARS OF AGE

The young couple began life together in the log house Erastus had built ten years before, on his farm at Warrenville. It was a snug and comfortable home—big living room with great fireplace—bedrooms and outside kitchen, young fruit trees and vines near, and all around the prairie, radiant with flowers in summer, white with snow in winter. There was heavy work for both of them —there were dangers and excitements. The Indians were no longer feared, but wolves and wildcats prowled at night and rattlesnakes crawled by day. Terrific storms of wind and rain swept over them and in winter biting cold settled down. Their anxieties in illness and separation were real enough, yet the Garys were free from the poignant loneliness and fears of hundreds of families in Illinois at this date, who had settled in neighborhoods which had never "built up." They at least had physicians and neighbors—their own families within reach.

Life was full for the young couple, and it had the dignity which the definite serious purpose of the pioneer gives. These two recognized themselves as community builders. They felt that the future intelligence, piety, order, prosperity of the new community were in their and their neighbors' hands. Neither Erastus nor Susan Gary ever wavered in giving a full measure of strength to the severe social, moral, and religious creed which they learned in New England and of the soundness and rightness of which neither throughout their lives had any doubt. Men and women go far when convinced that they are following a faith which is not only for their own highest good but for the highest good of their family and of their community.

If it had not been for the railroad, Erastus and Susan Gary would probably have lived their lives out at Warrenville; but in 1846—fifteen years after he had come to Illinois—the railroad, which we have seen had decided Erastus' first location west of Chicago, became a certainty.

It is difficult for us to-day to realize the stir and hope which the opening of canal or railroad brought a community in those days. Erastus Gary knew something about it. He had seen the entire commercial life of the East changed by a canal. He was nineteen years old when in 1825 the first boat passed from Buffalo to Erie through the "big ditch"—4 feet deep, 40 feet wide—old enough to read understandingly in the *Hartford Courant* —Pomfret's chief journal—of the four barrels of Lake Erie water brought to Albany on that boat, and of the impressive ceremony of their pouring into the Hudson, thus uniting, so Governor Clinton declared, lakes and ocean.

The proof that Governor Clinton was right was immediate. Trade with the West beyond dreams followed at once. Boston saw with alarm that New York was taking away her long established place as *the* port of the new world. Philadelphia had cold chills over the rapid growth of Pittsburgh, for it was easier for merchants to go up the Hudson, through the Erie canal, down Lake Erie and across the portage to the Alleghenies, and thence to Pittsburgh, than to follow the highway over the mountains. The whole trade and travel of the country was dislocated by the opening of the Erie Canal, and Erastus Gary read how, to meet the situation, business men and state legislatures demanded canals, and more canals. They wanted to connect every river, bay, lake, in such a way that they, too, would have free access to the ocean.

When the rage for canals was at its height, a new transportation excitement broke in, to puzzle and chill the advocates. "Why build canals?" cried the knowing. "It's the railway that is to be the future transporter of the world." "What is a railway?" men asked, and the newspapers told them: "You put a thing they call a locomotive, propelled by steam, on an iron track, and it will"—few believed it—"draw a coach thirty miles an hour! It has been done and is being done in England." And tales began to spread across the country of "Puffing Billy" and the "Rocket"—the two most famous of early English locomotives.

Erastus Gary could have told you how fast, once launched, the railroad idea moved. Moreover, he undoubtedly told his Illinois neighbors how these roads were built and worked, for when he went West in 1831 he must have seen the first one actually operated in the country.

When he reached Illinois in 1831 he found discussion of a central railroad, that is, one running from the north to the south of the State—the Illinois Central—already on foot. In 1836, when the flushed and excited Illinois legislature started on a grandiose scheme of internal improvements, granting charters for railroads, canals and river improvement in all directions, one of the roads chartered was the Galena and Chicago Union Railroad. Note that Galena stands first, being the more important town at that moment. The actual stock of the road was to be $100,000, and it was to be operated by "steam or animal power," as proved best.

The preliminary survey for this road did not take it as near Erastus Gary's Warrenville farm as he had reckoned, when he arrived in 1831, that the first road westward from Chicago would go; and it was then that he bought the land to the northeast, of which I have already spoken. This first railroad undertaking was destined to collapse, however, as did all the fine schemes for transportation adopted in 1836. The panic of the years following took all heart out of Illinois for a time, and it was not until ten years later, in 1846, that the Galena and Chicago was revived. In that year a great convention was called in Rockford to stir up things. Farmers were asked for subscriptions. Meetings were held all up and down the route, and in the fall of 1847 the contract for the first seven miles west from Chicago was let—the thing was going through.

It was then that Erastus Gary decided that the land he had bought at the time of the first excitement should be put under cultivation. Turning over the Warrenville farm with its full equipment to his brother Jude, he tackled the new undertaking in 1848, when he was forty-two years old. In making this move he was not going among strangers, indeed he was but changing one family group for another, Jesse and Warren Wheaton having settled near the tract he had been holding in 1833, when they first came into Illinois. They were the influential men of the settlement—so influential, indeed, that the three men had been able to persuade the railroad to come a mile and a half nearer to their land than the original survey had proposed.

The next year, 1849, Erastus Gary was ready to move his little family from the log house he had built when he first came to Illinois to a new frame house, close to the present town of Wheaton, and within sight of the incoming railroad. This little family was made up of Susan

Gary and two boys, the older, Noah, five years of age, the younger, Elbert Henry Gary, two and a half. It is with the younger that this story is concerned, and it is to his childhood and boyhood in the new house near the building railroad that we now turn.

CHAPTER II

THE BOY ELBERT

EARLY childhood for most of us is a region of haze, or half haze. It is passed under a sheltered routine where discoveries come so gradually and naturally that they blend into a misty whole. It is only when something out of the ordinary happens that memory is sufficiently aroused to lay hold and keep hold. A new home is one of the unforgettable experiences of a child. And with reason. There is the surprise of learning that there are other scenes than the one he knows. And moving brings adventures—personal adventures which stamp themselves on the mind. The earliest memories of the man whose life we are following in this narrative come from such an experience.

The new house was a large one for the time—the largest in the settlement. Erastus Gary in building had in mind no doubt the pleasant Connecticut homes of Pomfret and Woodstock—for he followed their usual plan of a central hall and staircase with comfortable rooms on either side. "The big white house on the hill" it came to be called, for it stood on an elevation overlooking the valley through which the railroad was coming, as well as the settlement the railroad was to father. By agreement this place was named Wheaton from Erastus Gary's two relatives who had settled in the neighborhood when they first came to Illinois. The railway station was located where the three farms of the Wheatons and Garys cornered.

The way of the pioneer in building was usually to make ready a living room where the family could camp while the carpenters went on completing their task—a discouraging thing for a housewife, but the greatest fun in the world for children, for here you had the excitement of watching frames go up, roofs and floors laid, partitions put in, and doors and windows set. You had the joy of curly shavings, the fun of lumber piles. Little Elbert and his brother Noah found continuous excitement in this building of a new home over their heads. It brought Elbert his first unforgettable experience.

Of course the children climbed the ladders when there was nobody near to forbid, and one day Noah, now five, went up to the second story, still unfloored, and succeeded in getting safely to the loose boards laid at intervals across the rafters. His little brother was not slow in following. He reached the top, not an easy thing. Judge Gary when he tells you the story to-day will almost certainly jump up from his chair and make a gesture of pulling up the dress that he wore to show how difficult it was for him to get to the top of that ladder! He still feels the mystery of what happened when he got there. His little arms and legs were too short to scale the distance to the board where Noah was perched and down he went, fifteen or sixteen feet, into the cellar. And then—oblivion! With him as with all of us this first experience of passing suddenly from awareness to nothingness—the strangeness of remembering everything up to a certain point and then nothing more, is still green in memory.

Not only did the Gary children have the excitement of watching the building of a new home, they had the still greater excitement of the building of the railroad. It brought groups of strange men—Irish mainly, with a brogue on their tongue new to their ears. It brought a transient settlement of shanties—mighty diggings—laying of tracks. This strange confusion and activity, the men and women of the camps, the revelries that sometimes went on there—all made its impress on the little boy.

And there was the coming of the first train! The Galena and Chicago had acquired from an eastern road a secondhand engine and five or six equally secondhand freight cars. The train might look funny to Judge Gary to-day, but when it came rushing by for the first time it was a wonderful and fearsome sight. He must have felt almost a proprietary interest in it, too, for the tracks ran through a cut on Gary land. The highway by which the family came and went crossed close to the mouth of this cut—a dangerous spot—where accidents might and did happen because of the failure of the company to keep its promise to Erastus Gary to bridge the railroad—a promise made when he gave them without charge a right of way across his land. It was the beginning of a grievance against railroads in the man's mind—a grievance others in the settlement shared and which the road took no pains to allay—rather defied and fed. The little boy was getting his first lesson in the ways of corporations—some corporations!

The new house was not finished, the first train had not passed, before the orthodox system of training a child, accepted by Erastus and Susan Gary, was being applied to young Elbert. The Garys held to the New England belief that as soon as a child had control of hands and feet it must be taught to use them in tasks necessary to the daily life of the family. These tasks were supposed to be fitted to a child's strength and age and, laid down, there was no escaping them. By the time this boy was four he was picking up chips to start the fire, filling the wood box, running errands. There was outside work, too; following his father in the field at planting time, dropping corn; straddling a horse, helping his brother round up and bring in the cows at night; spending long hours through the day watching them lest they wander, for in the first years on the new farm there were few fences, and cattle had to be almost continually guarded. By the time Elbert Gary was seven he had learned to milk and to do the easier night and morning chores. Year by year new tasks were taken on so that by the time he was fourteen or even before, he could do and did the work of a man on the farm.

What the boy, turned over to school, gets to-day in downright knowledge of life and discipline to meet its experiences looks thin enough compared with what this boy was learning in his forced grapple with the daily tasks of the Gary farm. Unconsciously and naturally he acquired control of muscles and nerves—self-reliance in unusual situations—skill of hand—a sense of his relation to the group—the understanding that if you shirked your part, performed it badly, the whole family suffered, the day's work was dislocated—respect for labor, the knowledge that upon it depended the health and increase of stock, the size of crops, the family's food and clothing, his own and his brother's future education.

Not that school was neglected. As soon as a child could walk he was old enough to "begin school," according to the early New England pedagogue. When he was three years old Elbert was being carried or led to the

"District School," a half mile from "the big white house on the hill," to which all the new settlement sent its children—a primitive one-room school, with benches, a blackboard—little else.

"Going to school" had its excitements. You went early, carrying your dinner pail. On the road you met your mates and nine times out of ten you stopped to open the dinner pail, compare notes, perhaps trade pie for cake, a doughnut for an apple. School was "called" at nine, then two hours of work, then recess, with all sorts of merry games—tag, drop the handkerchief, crack the whip, old cat, Andy over. When the bell brought you back to lessons there was a rush and scramble for a drink out of the tin cup or long-handled dipper fastened to the water pail.

This water pail provided one of the few diversions of the day, for a teacher rarely refused when you raised your hand if your request was to get a drink. The pail was soon emptied and then two boys, to their great joy, were sent to fill it. Noon was a social hour over the dinner pails—quiet inside and games outside. And going home after the day's work was a happy romp.

What you learned depended upon the teacher. Luckily for the generation growing up around Wheaton, the men whom the school trustees were able to obtain—they were generally men in that school—were devoted to their business. One in particular seems to have stamped himself on the community—Horace Barnes, who for many years taught the winter term, laboring with a growing constituency. Before he left he was handling in one room at least seventy-five pupils, ranging from three to eighteen; and he trained this unassorted collection so that few of them ever forgot him—always loved him. At ninety-two years of age he wrote joyous letters on the beauty of life as he was finding it, to more than one who had been his pupil in the fifties—Judge Gary among them.

There were definite things which even the child of three was expected to begin to learn: his letters, to count—first to ten, then to twenty—the number of days in the month, the name of the oldest man, the wisest man, the meekest man, the most patient man, the whole long list of "Instructive Questions and Answers" of the *New England Primer*—the names of the apostles and the prophets—the names of the presidents of the United States and the capitals of the states. All these things Elbert learned at home. There were rhymes to help him fix these facts so meaningless to him—rhymes sung to him frequently, no doubt, as he was rocked back and forth by father or mother when tired or grieved. Thus, there was one for the capitals of the states, beginning:

Maine, Augusta on the Kennebec river.
New Hampshire, Concord on the Merrimac river.

There was one for remembering the days of the months:

Thirty days hath September
April, June and November;
February twenty-eight alone,
All the rest have thirty-one,
Excepting Leap year—then the time
That February has twenty-nine.

At school, too, there was much memorizing, for every Friday afternoon there were exercises where you were expected to speak a piece or take part in a dialogue, and at the end of the term, if you had shone brilliantly, to appear at an exhibition, to which people came from far and near, packing the schoolroom to overflowing. Young Elbert was hardly out of dresses before he began to make his appearance on Friday afternoons and at school exhibitions. His first performance was the first of a whole generation of Americans, declaiming, with gestures which varied according to the teacher's ideas of appropriateness, the classical lines:

> You'd scarce expect one of my age
> To speak in public on the stage,
> And if I chance to fall below
> Demosthenes or Cicero
> Don't view me with a critic's eye
> But pass my imperfections by.
> Large streams from little fountains flow;
> Tall oaks from little acorns grow;
> And though I now am small and young,
> Of judgment weak, and feeble tongue,
> Yet all great learned men, like me,
> Once learned to read their A, B, C.

* * * * * *

> Oh where's the town, go far and near,
> That does not find a rival here,
> Or where's the boy but three feet high
> Who's made improvement more than I?
> These thoughts inspire my youthful mind
> To be the greatest of mankind;
> Great, not like Cæsar, stained with blood;
> But, like Washington, great in good.

As the child grew older "numbers" received an increasing amount of attention. At one period in this Wheaton district school rapid calculation became the chief test of scholarship. A teacher had taken the school who held the practice of particular value in mental training, so daily he put on the blackboard examples in partial payments. Two pupils at a time were sent to the board to see which could "get the right answer" first. Elbert came to be both accurate and rapid, beating even his brother—"the best mathematician in the community." "Indeed," Judge Gary tells you, "we never had a teacher as good in mathematics as Noah, but I think I could beat him in rapid calculation."

Luckily for Wheaton, Lorin Barnes, a graduate of Yale and brother of its favorite schoolmaster, Horace Barnes, who took his brother's place for two terms, had a thorough knowledge of music. He was not only able to keep his pupils happily interested in their studies but to arouse in them a love of singing. "It was always the best part of the school to me," Judge Gary will tell you to-day; and he will tell you, too, that by the time he was seven years old he could read music fairly well. This was thanks to Erastus Gary who began early familiarizing his little folks with notes and staffs, with flats and sharps, helping them out with rhymes such as this one:

> *When on one staff*
> *You see the treble clef*
> *The lines of that staff*
> *Are E—G—B—D—F.*

At sixteen he was singing bass in church, later he was a member of a quartet which did considerable work in the community. People who attend the Metropolitan

Opera House and have watched Judge Gary sitting quietly in the rear of his box through a long opera may have wondered whether opera to him was a social or business affair, or whether he really understood the music. There are few men who follow the opera in New York that understand it better. He can read the score with the best of amateurs and is so familiar with leading operas that he partly follows them textually without a score.

The boy's progress in school was even more carefully watched by the father and mother than by the teacher. "My father watched my lessons with the same vigilance that he gave to his crops and live stock," Judge Gary tells you to-day. Every night he was examined in his studies, every day put into contest with some one of his age, told how Noah had known all these things before he was as old as he—how his cousins in Warrenville could count faster or farther.

This attention to what the child was learning did not lapse as he grew older. Mr. and Mrs. Gary continued to take the liveliest interest in whatever their children were studying. They had both been teachers—they still were learners. "What did you learn to-day?" was a daily question. Quizzes in dates, spelling and names, examples in mental arithmetic, recitations, singing, went on constantly. A favorite exercise was correcting false syntax. This indeed was a daily habit of the Garys. Let somebody say, "That's a good thing for you and I," and father, mother and children would jump at the error.

The Gary children were brought up to read newspapers, magazines, books. Their father, like all liberal minded men of his time, took the *New York Tribune,* and read it page by page. A little later he added to it the

ELBERT GARY AT ABOUT TEN YEARS OF AGE

THE FIRST "GARY SCHOOL," POMFRET, CONNECTICUT. HERE JUDGE GARY'S GRAND-
FATHER, WILLIAM GARY, TAUGHT FOR MANY YEARS

Chicago Tribune, giving it equal attention. Susan Gary had her magazines: *Godey's, Peterson's, The Ladies Repository.* Into all of these the children dipped and found what was for them, but they liked books better. Charles Dickens' *Child History of England,* Dumas' *Three Musketeers,* and, best of all, volume after volume by Charles Dickens. The first novel that Judge Gary remembers having read was *Barnaby Rudge,* and after that he never missed one of the flood that in these years was poured forth. They listened to many French stories, too, for a cousin who "read French," was a member of the family for some time and delighted in her little audience.

This training in work and study was based on religion. The shiftless and ignorant were not fit to serve God, and to learn to love and obey God was the chief object of life. It was the Bible in which you found the rules of life, hence you must know the Bible. There were times and places set for its reading and interpretation, and you must no more neglect them than you did the chores or school. Thus there were family prayers every morning before breakfast, though not before the stock had been fed, the cows milked. Then the household gathered, the Scriptures were read, and the father or mother offered a prayer. As each child learned to read he was expected to take his turn with the verses. For a number of years German Bibles were used in the Gary household, the readers translating as they went, the listeners correcting them if a mistake had been made. This was the older Gary's practical way of teaching the children the German language, something he felt would be particularly useful because of the number of German workmen always employed on the farm, many of whom could speak no

English. This early reading took young Gary back and forth through the Bible several times, printing on his alert and impressionable mind a knowledge of the book such as practically no child gets to-day.

You were expected to go to Church, to Sunday school, to camp meetings, as regularly as to attend family prayers. The Garys were Methodists. To their mind a child could not be too young to be taken to church. In fact, there was no other way for the pioneer mother. Sunday thus became a special day in the week for the child. No unnecessary work was to be done, you were expected to listen to the preaching for you were catechised when you came home. There was a quiet afternoon, singing of hymns and reading aloud from serious books—*Pilgrim's Progress, Clarke's Commentaries*, articles from *The Christian Advocate*, with drills in pious jingles:

> *In Adam's fall*
> *We sinnéd all.*

> *The Deluge drowned*
> *The earth around.*

> *As runs the glass*
> *Our life doth pass.*

> *Young Obiedias*
> *David, Josias,*
> *All were pious.*

> *Zaccheus he*
> *Did climb a tree*
> *Our Lord to see.*

The best of Sunday, however, to this particular little boy, was that he was "dressed up." From his earliest years this was one of the pleasures of his life. He liked his Sunday clothes, he liked to be clean. His mother used to say that he was the only one of her children that allowed her to "scrub his ears without a fuss!" His pleasure in his Sunday clothes was such that he always took them off before milking time in the evening—something that his brother Noah did not usually do, with the result that Elbert was always the better dressed! It was the beginning of a care if not an extravagance in dress that followed him through his manhood—followed him, in fact, up to the breaking out of the Great War, when he literally stopped buying clothes, turning that part of his budget into his war fund. I think Judge Gary takes as much pride in not having bought any clothes between 1916 and 1924, in showing you boots and a coat bought in 1912, as he ever took in those early days in having a cleaner looking suit than his brother Noah!

It is too much to expect that the severe code into which the boy was initiated would be accepted always without disobedience, neglect, or revolt, but very little of it has come down in family tradition. The child seems to have agreed that if he broke the code it was just that he be punished—but the punishment must be just. That is, he must have been at fault, and a grievance that he nourished for many years against his father came from a punishment which "hurt" and which he believed was undeserved. It was a difference of interpretation.

He and his brother Noah had been set to watch the cows, but had failed to keep them away from a neighbor's broken fence. They had destroyed corn for which Erastus Gary promptly paid. He also promptly flogged his sons for allowing the mishap. Elbert pleaded that he did not know that the fence was down, that he should have been told. As long as the elder Gary lived his son regularly taxed him with this injustice, but never could get more than a wise smile. "Evidently," the judge will tell you, "Father believed that I was there to watch those cattle and I should have known whether the fences were in good condition."

This resentment at a punishment which he considered undeserved took a more positive form when it was a teacher, not a father who administered it. By all accounts he was a mischievous boy in school—mischievous with a genius for escaping punishment. "He got all the fun and I got all the lickings," his closest school crony said ruefully in later years. This may be partly explained by his habit of deciding for himself whether or not a "licking" was just. "I never allowed a teacher to punish me if I didn't think I deserved it." I have heard him say, and there are tales to prove this true. Once when a teacher attempted to give him a whipping for something he had not done he took the ferule from her and broke it into pieces. If his father ever heard of this exploit he made no sign. If it came to his ears he probably first satisfied himself that the boy had been unjustly charged and was right in his revolt—that would have been like Erastus Gary.

The delicate task of snuffing out bad habits and breaking up associations with "bad boys" at the start was never shirked by these conscientious Garys. It was to be expected that a child would pick up things, the evil of which he could not know, therefore the responsible parent had his eye always open for them. Little Elbert heard the farm hands using words that probably seemed to him to express their emotions unusually well. He picked up one—"Damn it!"—and tried it on his father. The father impressed the sin of it by a whipping, but the whipping did not finish the work. The little boy went out behind the barn and shouted the forbidden oath to the skies until he literally exhausted its appeal. From that time on he seems to have had no temptation to copy the bad language which he may have heard others use. With his father's help he had worked it out of his system.

The severity of these prompt punishments was regulated by the mother. "That's enough, Erastus," she would say, and Erastus would drop the switch. Later she became the consoler and the interpreter. At night, after she had heard his prayer—a prayer graduated to his age, the earliest, the simple and lovely lines:

> Now I lay me down to sleep,
> I pray the Lord my soul to keep;
> If I should die before I wake
> I pray the Lord my soul to take—

after she had heard his prayer and tucked him in, they talked it over. "It hurts your father more than it does you," the boy was sure to be told—and with men like Erastus Gary this was in the main true. In these talks the mother poured out her anxiety lest he get into bad company, learn bad habits—told him of her prayers that he grow up to be a useful Christian man.

A beautiful memory—a powerful guard through life! Work, study, obedience—with punishment if you shirked or broke the rules; up at five in the morning with a day of twelve to fourteen hours when the farmer's "busy season" was on—a strenuous program surely, but the farmer's boy in such a family as that of the Garys had plenty of sport sandwiched into the year.

What boys are taught by masters to-day in confined places—artificial pools, riding academies, skating rinks —these boys taught themselves in the good out-of-doors. The only sports for which they had trained instruction were boxing and wrestling. This came from a Canadian farm hand—an expert athlete—a young man of twenty-three or four, who lived in the Gary family for a year or so, going to school with the boys and incidentally teaching them the sporting arts he had mastered.

They played baseball—the early variety. Young Elbert at ten was captain of a team, catching behind the bat. He became a marble champion and an expert self-taught swimmer. "I lay on the water and found I could swim," and knowing that, he learned the rest—diving, treading water, swimming—"frog fashion" and "dog fashion."

As soon as the boy could walk he straddled a horse. Erastus Gary raised horses for the market and, as there were often forty or fifty in the lots, handling them was an important part of the farm work. Little Elbert was on horseback helping drive up the cows when he was four or five years old, and he was not much older before he and his brother and cousins were racing horses, standing up by choice, bare backs and bare feet! They began to drive before they were six and one of the excitements of their early days—exciting and not always safe—was racing teams. To race four horses attached to a big bobsled over the half-broken, snow-covered roads of DuPage County, took a skill and a daring equal to that in most of the highly developed sports of to-day, and these boys were doing that in their early teens.

From the time he was six or seven the boy used a gun. He had watched his father morning after morning load his shotgun and from the back door shoot for breakfast a couple of the prairie hens that always roosted on the grain stacks near by. It was Erastus Gary's thrifty habit not to fire until he had two birds in range and invariably he brought down two with one load. Elbert was only six or seven years old when he decided that he, too, would like to hunt. He made the ancient muzzle-loader ready, as he had seen his father do, and started across the field. He had the luck to run across a half dozen snipe. Following his father's procedure, he worked his way up close and then, with one knee on the ground, took aim and actually brought down a bird. It was a great day for him and the beginning of more and more hunting as he grew older, not only of birds and rabbits but occasionally a lynx or a fox.

The winter brought more leisure for fun, as well as more opportunities. Besides coasting and sleigh riding there was skating, and a wonderful range they had, for the low, undrained prairies or sloughs—they called them "slews"—frozen, made a continuous skating pond for miles around. The Gary boys could easily go on their skates from near their home in Wheaton to their cousins' home in Warrenville, five miles away across country; they could visit neighbors north and south, and occasionally in winters of deep snow or when a frost had followed a January thaw, they skated over the fences on the crust —a never-to-be-forgotten excitement!

The boy thrived on this life of work and sport. He grew husky, hard, red-cheeked. One of his sisters—for two sisters came after the family settled in Wheaton—gives a captivating picture of him: "a boy full of energy and pranks, yet truthful; dark haired and plenty of it; dark blue eyes, changing with his moods and usually thought black. A boy always ready to meet an emergency, first in games at school, loyal to his friends, particularly his elder brother. I remember he was once a little round-shouldered and thereafter he always read lying on his stomach, his head thrown back."

More important than this picture is the appraisal of his intellect and character which crops out in the recollections gathered from members of his family, his schoolmates, his teachers. Most valuable of all are the rare words which Erastus Gary let fall about his son and which have been remembered and quoted by others. This silent, observing, just man was not easily fooled about anybody and least of all about his own children. His rigid ideas of a father's responsibility drove him to see them as they were, forbade his glossing over any fault or weakness he detected in them, compelled him to hold them to their best, to praise them sparingly. Thus his estimate of this beloved boy—for he was that to the man —is trustworthy. Elbert had a "good head," he conceded; that is, he could put two and two together—and he did, sometimes to the amazement of his elders. An early judgment of his father was that Elbert did not like to be beaten. It was a trait that grew as the years went on, and whether it was spelling or baseball, singing or wrestling, he liked the first place. But most satisfying to the man was a conclusion to which he early came and which his family heard him express more than once— "Elbert is pretty honest, pretty honest."

Another characteristic that pleased his father was his

thoughtfulness, coolness, resourcefulness. "He is the 'longest headed' boy that I ever saw," he used to tell his mother. It was something of a wonder to his companions as well as to his elders that he never flew into a passion. His elder brother Noah was impetuous, hot-tempered, quick to resent. Elbert was the opposite. "The only way we ever knew he was angry," one of his friends says, "was that the top of his head turned red!"

That is, Mr. and Mrs. Erastus Gary had very good material to which to apply their code of training, and the boy thrived under it. The life of this farmer's boy might have been hard, but it certainly developed him, gave him, as he says, "strength, vigor, courage, confidence in himself." Moreover, life presented itself under this régime as something regular, fixed; it had no uncertainties. It was settled that he labor, that he study, that he go to church, that he enjoy certain sports. His elders had no uncertainties. They knew what they wanted, freely expressed it, struggled for it, and he had been accustomed to seeing them able to overthrow interferences, hold on to what they had built up. This was true in the matter of acquiring property—in the matter of the church, the family—and it was true in that field which he heard called politics. He knew his father as a Democrat—without political ambitions, but holding as strongly to his political opinions as he did to his religious opinions, as good a Democrat as he was a Methodist.

The first great unsettling in this well established world came when Elbert was eight years old. The whole of northern Illinois was in a tumult—a tumult caused by something that a man who had been a political idol of the Democrats had done—Stephen A. Douglas, the beloved United States Senator from Illinois. He had

sponsored a bill in the United States Senate that outraged Erastus Gary's deepest convictions—the Kansas-
Nebraska bill, threatening to allow slavery in territory
which had been set aside for freedom.

Erastus Gary had been born in Connecticut. As a boy
he had been accustomed to seeing on the front page of the
Hartford Courant advertisements headed "Runaway"
—asking for the return of men and women, blacks seeking
freedom. He had been reared to hate it. One of his
satisfactions in settling in Illinois was that it was a land
pledged to freedom by both state and federal action. It
was his judgment that no more territory in these United
States should ever be opened to slavery, and in 1850,
when the struggle over the future freedom of the land
acquired by the Mexican war was on in Congress, the
Democrats of his district had passed at a convention held
only seven miles away at the county seat, Naperville,
resolutions destined to play a part eight years later in
the great Illinois Debate on slavery extension. They
were out-and-out enough to suit the most radical of the
day:

Resolved, That this Convention is in favor of the Wilmot
Proviso both in *Principle and Practice* and that we know of
no good reason why any *person* should oppose the largest latitude in *Free Soil, Free Territory* and *Free Speech,* and;

Resolved, That in the opinion of this Convention the time
has arrived when *all men should be free,* whites as well as others.

Erastus Gary believed these things in 1850—he believed them quite as strongly in 1854 when Douglas introduced his Kansas-Nebraska bill; and he entirely sympathized with the demonstration in Chicago against Douglas
when he came on from Washington to explain his position
to his alarmed and revolting constituency.

When he reached the town, Douglas had found the flags hung at half-mast and for an hour before his evening speech he heard the bells tolling in sorrow for his apostasy. He found, too, when he tried to explain his bill that the majority of his audience—Whigs and Democrats—would not listen—it could not be explained.

Boys in those days were much with their elders. They labored with them, sat with them in gatherings of every sort, wormed their way into groups that collected on the streets, in the courts, by the fireside. They followed with attention the grave discussions that went on now. Young Gary saw his father break with his old party. It was the first great change he had seen in life. His father was not what he had once been, a Democrat—he was a new thing —a Republican. He was facing the fact that the accepted things were not necessarily eternal. Parties passed away, new ones came—a leader falls, a new one rises. There was a new one beginning to be talked of in the Gary household—Abraham Lincoln.

This new leader, of whom men knew so little, challenged the old one. The boy was old enough—twelve years—to follow with some understanding the debates of 1858, and he must have watched his father reading them word for word as published in the *Chicago Tribune;* heard him talking about them; heard the conclusion—"Lincoln is right. We must keep this thing back or it will spread all over the country. What we have to decide is whether the United States shall be all slave or all free."

Lincoln was defeated, but he discovered that the defeat did not end it, that it was as Lincoln said, "a durable struggle." He was old enough to remember the events of Lincoln's election, and how it brought to pass the final stage of the great dispute—the stage where brains no longer counted and men turned to war.

He was all for the fight. One of the earliest books he had read—the one he had heard most talked of at home, at school, in church—the one that had stirred him deepest, had been *Uncle Tom's Cabin*. Of course such things must not be allowed to happen in Illinois, and what Lincoln meant was that unless they held fast now they might happen in Illinois. Slavery should not pass. The state was free—it should stay free if they must fight for it.

By April, 1861, when the Civil War broke out, Elbert Gary, now fourteen years old, was a student in what was then known as the Illinois Institute, a Wesleyan Methodist college that his father had helped found in Wheaton. It was his father's intention and his ambition that he should "go through, have a college education." And being the kind of boy he was, with the pride of finishing what he had started, it seemed certain that that was just what he would do. But nothing suffers more than colleges with the coming of war. Colleges are filled with youths, many of them old enough to fight. The colleges of the United States practically disbanded when the Civil War broke out. If you did not go to war you had not the will to study. Elbert Gary could not go on. Scores of boys he knew joined the army, among them his brother Noah. He tried to follow, offering to enlist several times in DuPage and surrounding counties but he was always refused as too young. Finally, in 1864, he ran away with a regiment.

He was sworn into service and, while waiting for his company to be moved to the mustering-in place, was given a position as regimental postmaster and his training was begun—roll calls, drills, parades. Then suddenly in May,

1864, two months after he had left home, a letter came from his mother. His brother Noah had been desperately wounded in a charge upon the defenses of Resaca, Georgia. His father had been asked to come at once if he would see his son alive. He had gone and she, the mother, was alone. She needed him. He was a mirror. He must come back. The colonel of the regiment thought so, too, and promptly granted a leave. It was the end of soldiering for Elbert Gary.

Things were never again to go on as they had done in the Gary family, for when finally the father was able to bring his wounded son back North for months of care in a hospital, he determined to make a change which he had looked forward to for his later years—that is, rent the farm and move into town. This he did almost at once.

As for Elbert, he could not take up life where he had left it at the beginning of the war. A school was offered him and for a term he taught. But it was only a makeshift, he had no idea of teaching as a profession. It was before this first term of school was over that he found an objective—a real one this time, something which promised a field for his active mind and his no less active ambition.

It came logically enough. A brother of his mother, Colonel Henry Vallette, a lawyer, and a good one—one of the best in the county, with an honorable war record as the leader of an Illinois regiment—was now back in his office at Naperville, the county seat, with his partner —a man as prominent in affairs as himself, Circuit Judge Cody. Both Colonel Vallette and Judge Cody were friends of Erastus Gary. They knew this boy Elbert and they evidently had said to themselves, "He has the making of a lawyer," and in 1865 they suggested his coming to them to read law. The boy jumped at the suggestion. And naturally enough. For twenty years or more his father had been one of the most trusted magistrates in DuPage County. Cases of all sorts limited in amount were submitted to him in the court he held in the sitting room of "the big white house on the hill." He tried them sometimes with a jury, sometimes without. Well-known lawyers not only from the county but from adjoining counties had been in the habit of appearing before him. That is, Justice Gary's court was one of recognized importance. Everywhere, too, it was highly held because of the respect for the just mind of the man. As time had gone on Elbert had become more and more interested in what went on in these trials, and his father, understanding probably what a wonderful school in the nature of human beings, their behavior and their relations, such a court as his must be, encouraged the presence of the boy. The experience had given him an appetite for the law which he had not realized until the chance to study with a firm so distinguished as that of Vallette and Cody was given. His father thought well of the idea. "Some day," he said, "Elbert may have a little property and a knowledge of the law may help him to keep it."

It was characteristic of the boy that, having determined to study law, he acted at once, would not allow himself to be diverted. The trustees of the school in which he had been teaching, pleased with his work, came to him to beg that he go on for just one more term, offering him a substantial increase in salary; but he was clear in his mind. This was the thing he was going to do, and so in the spring of 1865, in his nineteenth year, young Elbert Gary entered the law office of Vallette and Cody in Naperville, Illinois.

CHAPTER III

STUDENT—LAWYER—JUDGE

THE Illinois law student in the middle period of the nineteenth century enjoyed an intimacy with his elders in the office where he read, quite unlike anything that we find to-day, save possibly in some old-fashioned town whose traditions and customs have escaped the invasion of modernity. The wisdom of the firm was at the student's command—a condensed wisdom born of experience. Perhaps the most valuable feature of it was impressing upon the boy that, if he was to be a lawyer, he must make himself one, that it could not be done for him. I take it that much of the counsel was similar to that Abraham Lincoln gave to a young man who had asked to read law with him:

"If you are resolutely determined to make a lawyer of yourself the thing is more than half done already. It is but a small matter whether you read with anybody or not. I did not read with any one. Get the books and read and study them till you understand them in their principal features; and that is the main thing. It is of no consequence to be in a large town while you are reading. I read at New Salem, which never had more than three hundred people living in it. The books and your capacity for understanding them are just the same in all places. . . .

"Always bear in mind that your resolution to succeed is more important than any other one thing."

I presume that young Elbert Gary, who at eighteen years of age began to study law in the office of Vallette and Cody in Naperville, Illinois, received about the same counsels. He needed them less than many a young man would have done. As a matter of fact, they were already a part of his youthful philosophy for success in the world.

There was no other boy in the Gary connection, brother or cousin, who took hold of work more closely than he did; he not only accepted it fully, but joyously—liked it, thrived on it. That is, this young law student whom Vallette and Cody had admitted to their Naperville office was of a temper and intelligence to go far and to bring the firm credit.

Vallette and Cody, like many other lawyers of that day, had their office in a little one-story Colonial building, set up in the corner of a yard fronting on the Courthouse Square. You find these stout little structures in almost every town of the South and Middle West. They took the litter of book and papers, the confusion of many callers and long conferences, out of the house where in the days of the first settlements the work was carried on, frequently even the work of courts. In Wheaton young Elbert had for years seen the family sitting room used as a court room by his father, Justice Gary.

It fell to the law student to take care of the office. That is, like a trade apprentice he was expected to perform various tasks outside of his studies, such as sweeping out, dusting, bringing in wood, keeping the fires, arranging books and papers—all the very primitive housekeeping of a pioneer law office. As Elbert Gary usually had a companion student, the tasks were shared.

From the beginning of his connection with Vallette and Cody, the young man was very much on his own in his

JUDGE HIRAM H. CODY   COL. HENRY VALLETTE

JUDGE CODY AND COLONEL VALLETTE BEFORE THEIR LAW OFFICE IN NAPERVILLE,
ILLINOIS, WHERE ELBERT GARY BEGAN READING LAW IN 1865

studies. He and his companion examined each other on the books which they had read—much more severely than they were ever examined by their elders. They went out of their way, voluntarily, to perfect themselves in certain things which they felt would be advantageous in practicing their profession, such as rhetoric, grammar, oratory. Nothing, indeed, which had a bearing was neglected.

A matter to which Gary gave infinite care was penmanship. All legal documents in those days had to be written out in longhand, and a clear, readable hand was an asset. The boy saw it and worked to secure it. He was particularly keen in mastering the forms of legal procedure, going regularly to court when it was held in Naperville, at odd times assisting the circuit clerk, the county clerk, the treasurer, the sheriff, in their routine work. To be sure, he received small fees for his services, but that was not his aim. It was to acquaint himself as thoroughly as possible with the machinery of legal business. These efforts were almost entirely self-determined and self-directed. One gets a pleasant picture of a healthy, cheerful, hard-working farmer boy, intent on being a lawyer—a lawyer as good as the best of them, and putting his whole force into the purpose.

Chicago and the surrounding territory was not so crowded in those days that the men of a profession did not know fairly well what was going on among their associates, even down to the fact that in this or that firm there was a particularly promising law student. The only law school in the vicinity, the Union College of Law of Chicago, afterwards transferred to the Northwestern University at Evanston, kept an alert eye on students scattered in law offices in the nearby county seats, and the head of this school, Judge Henry Booth, an acquaintance of the Garys and the Vallettes, suggested to Erastus Gary that it would be wise to let his promising son finish his studies at the law school. Young Gary snapped at this opportunity. His father loaned him the money, and in the fall of 1866 he entered the institution, the youngest student there. The thoroughness with which he had been directing his own studies, the practical knowledge of legal procedure which he had acquired in busying himself about the courts gave him at once a leading place in the school.

One of the favorite institutions of the Union College of Law was the Moot Court, where fictitious trials were staged to give students an opportunity to apply their knowledge and practice procedure. Everybody connected with the institution, as well as some outsiders, took a lively interest in the Moot Court, and it was frequently presided over by members of the faculty or even by visiting lawyers. Gary was soon chosen clerk of this court. He kept its records, helped in making cases ready, helped on pleadings. Frequently he appeared on one side or the other of a case. He took this work with great seriousness, as indeed the school did, and was soon ranked high by its leaders. "Is any question presented ever decided against Elbert Gary in this court?" the lawyer opposed to him asked one day after a series of rulings in Gary's favor.

"No, sir, not as long as he is right," the presiding judge retorted.

In June of 1868, Gary graduated at the head of his class, and a few days later was appointed a deputy clerk of the Superior Court on the recommendation of Dean Booth. His salary was twelve dollars a week, with a promise of increase in strict proportion to the increase in his value. It was a chance to acquaint himself still more definitely with the ways of courts, their rules and forms.

The young lawyer took hold of the work with the same zest that he had shown ever since he began his studies. He found things to do outside the duties assigned him, particularly in improving the technique and methods of the business. A man was to be hanged. The clerk of the court must furnish the sheriff documentary authority under seal. He never had done such a thing. What was the proper form for directing a man to be hanged? He did not know. Young Gary hurried to the books and brought back from his investigations a form for a mandate which the lawyers interested at once accepted, and his superior gratefully used.

As time went on there were frequent chances for similar work. Wherever he found a form inadequate or lacking, he promptly prepared one. He suggested improvements in those which were already in use, until he had made ready a series which were adopted and printed as the official forms of that court.

It fell to him to write the law record of the court proceedings, and here his skill in penmanship came in. Volume after volume was prepared. He aimed at perfection in all of them, and, in the case of the last one, achieved it—a volume without an error, an erasure, an interlineation. Its writing was clear as copperplate. It was the show piece of the court. What a shame that it, with its companions, should have gone up in the Chicago fire!

Gary was not merely a paragon of exactness, a stickler for correct forms. All of the old lawyers and judges who to-day remember him as a clerk recall his lively interest in the cases and the help that he constantly gave. They remember, too, the meticulous honesty of his ad- ministration. "He never would allow us to touch a sheet of court stationery," his sister, who occasionally visited him, says. "He told us it was not honest." Judge Jesse Holdom of Chicago recalls his success in making the lawyers pay their "*boarding* fees" of fifty cents a month. That is, he was a young man interested in everything that concerned his office, and very insistent that things be done right. He seems even to have been able to look after its manners. Judge Holdom recalls an occasion when one of the clerks became for some reason highly offensive in the court, and Gary, who by this time had risen to be chief clerk, took it upon himself to thrash him.

It took him only seven months to arrive at the position of chief clerk, his salary being increased from twelve to eighteen and finally to forty-five dollars a week. John H. Batten, afterwards Judge Batten, who took the twelve-dollar place, says that he wondered what Gary could do with so much money as eighteen dollars a week!

With his advancement to the post of chief clerk and a salary of forty-five dollars a week, Gary felt sure enough of his future to marry. He had fallen in love with a young woman of Aurora, a neighboring town, Miss Julia Graves, the daughter of Captain Amos C. Graves of the Union Army. The young couple settled in Wheaton, which had become the county seat of DuPage County, in a home of their own, and for the next thirty years he commuted back and forth between that town and Chicago.

Soon after his marriage Gary determined to resign as chief clerk and to set up for himself in the law. By this time his uncle, Colonel Henry F. Vallette, with whom he read law in Naperville, had come to Chicago and gone into the firm of Van Armen and Vallette. In the spring of 1871 they offered to take him into partnership with a certain percentage, or to give him a salary of one hundred dollars per month, with an office and the use of their library, allowing him to take on any business which he could get for himself. It was entirely characteristic of this self-reliant young person that he should have accepted the second proposition. From the start he found himself with considerable business. His three years as clerk of the Superior Court had given him a wide acquaintance in the profession. Many of the ablest of the bar had come to look upon him as an authority in pleading procedure and form. They were friendly to him, too, liked him, and were glad to turn business his way. Life was a full, promising, joyful affair, with no disturbance or setback in sight, and then suddenly one came.

Going into Chicago from Wheaton on Monday morning, October 8, 1871, Gary's train, due at nine o'clock, was held up at Canal Street, and there he learned for the first time that Chicago was burning. For twelve hours, at least, an uncontrolled fire had been raging. He went to reconnoiter, found the court house gone, his office gone, all the familiar places in their neighborhood gone. It was not until he reached Lake Street that he found the fire. All day long he followed it, mile after mile, sometimes so near that the heat scorched his face.

Within two days the fire had burned itself out. What vast desolation it left behind! Two hundred lives, at least, ended—one hundred thousand people homeless—every building on over two thousand acres destroyed—a total loss never exactly estimated, but running up into something like $200,000,000—a vast sum for those days.

But when Elbert Gary returned to Chicago Tuesday morning, he found a courage at work, greater even than the disaster, for on every side men were starting business on still smoking ruins!

Although the Chicago fire destroyed permanently the firm of Van Armen and Vallette, Van Armen preferring to retire, Gary and his uncle, Colonel Vallette, decided to go on, each for himself. They found two vacant rooms at 59 West Madison Street—the second story of a frame building; each of them took one, and soon their shingles were hanging out over the sign of a restaurant running below them. Here in this office Elbert Gary began his independent career as a lawyer—began it well, for in that first year he made more money than he had ever made before in his life—twenty-eight hundred dollars.

But he was making, in this time, something more valuable than money. It was a reputation as a young lawyer who knew his business. People noted that he won cases. They noted particularly his skill in cross-examinations, that he could force the truth from a witness and be scrupulously fair and courteous in doing it. It was his skill in cross-examination that won him one of his first important cases. In the year he had acted as the assistant of Van Armen and Vallette it had fallen to him to cross-examine a man worth impressing—General Benjamin J. Sweet, a lawyer by profession, formerly living in DuPage County. General Sweet had had one arm permanently crippled in the Civil War, and held, at this time, the position of Commissioner of Internal Revenue in Washington. Young Gary's ability and adroitness in cross-examination had driven Sweet into a corner so effectually that he had been compelled to admit facts which he had been reluctant to disclose. The party af-

ELBERT GARY IN 1871, THE YEAR THAT THE CHICAGO FIRE BROKE
UP HIS LEGAL CONNECTIONS AND LED HIM TO OPEN
AN OFFICE OF HIS OWN.

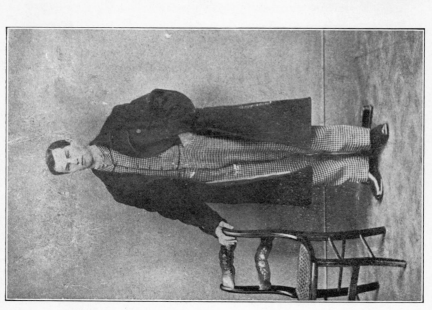

THIS PICTURE OF ELBERT GARY AT EIGHTEEN YEARS
OF AGE WAS TAKEN IN NAPERVILLE, ILLINOIS,
JUST AFTER HE BEGAN TO READ LAW.

fected was a friend, and the disclosures lost the friend his case; but the way the thing had been done delighted General Sweet.

Only a few months after Gary had set up for himself, he received one morning a telegram from the General, asking him to come to Washington at once. It was a great hour for the young lawyer. Without waiting to go to Wheaton for his bag and toothbrush, he took the first train East. It was his first sight of the capitol, but he lost no time in sight-seeing, presenting himself at once at the commissioner's office. A greater compliment could hardly have been paid to a young man than the one General Sweet now paid Elbert Gary.

Briefly, the General told him that through the dishonesty of a partner he was in danger of losing everything he had in the world, amounting to some $25,000, invested in Colorado ranches and live stock. He had formed such a high idea of Gary's ability in the cross-examination he had undergone at his hands the year before, that he wanted him to act as his counsel. Of course the young man accepted the case. Gathering up all the papers and information General Sweet had, he left at once for Chicago and, a few hours later, was on his way to Colorado. The case ran on for a year or more, and in the end Gary not only secured Sweet's full claim, but placed the entire property in his hands.

A year afterward the General died and Gary found that by the will he had been appointed executor. He managed the property for two or three years before it was finally settled, and did it without ever asking or receiving a commission as executor.

Perhaps no case ever gave Elbert Gary more satisfaction than this of Benjamin Sweet. It came to him as an unusual tribute of confidence in his qualities from one whom he regarded as a "big man." It was a great chance. It must have made him feel, too, that he was on the right track, and have strengthened a conviction natural to him, intensified by his training and his observation, that a man can be a lawyer and still be a gentleman.

The Sweet case gave young Gary special satisfaction, but the case which gained for him a pronounced reputation in his home county, DuPage, and vicinity, was that of *Hough* versus *The Illinois Linen Company*. In this case the plaintiff, a prominent Chicago business man and president of the company, had sued for a share in certain profits, outside of his salary. As the Chicago courts were badly congested, the venue had been changed to DuPage County, where Judge Cody, with whom Gary had read law, was then sitting as circuit judge. Hough had already engaged two well-known lawyers, but wanted further counsel, and on Judge Cody's advice chose Gary.

Night after night, after days spent in listening to the unusual mass of testimony, which included much complicated accounting, Gary went home to study and digest what he had heard. While his colleagues in the case, as well as his opponents, were amusing themselves, he was making himself so familiar with the evidence that whenever a question of fact came up, a disagreement over a point, he could immediately refer to the record written up day by day by the court stenographer. His client was so impressed by his mastery of facts that he asked him to make the closing argument. His leading opponent, Judge Leffingwell, a lawyer of ability and prominence, in summing up talked for six and a half hours, but Gary outdid him, talking ten and a half hours! After the first two or three hours, the opposing counsel, evidently overwhelmed by his familiarity with the testimony, and his verification of statements by the records when objections were made, left the room; and in the end the jury rendered a verdict for the full amount claimed.

The judgment of his friends who had watched the case was that "Elbert won because he studied nights while the opposing lawyers played poker." There was to be more than one victory in his subsequent career to which the same explanation could be applied!

In telling this story Judge Gary is certain to add a characteristic remark. "If you ever say anything about this case, you must be fair. You will have to mention that the Supreme Court set aside the verdict, though on a point different from that for which we fought, and that was that Hough, as president of the company, had no right to a share in the profits that he claimed outside of his salary."

Business was now flowing into the young man's office from all directions—business of all kinds. Within two or three years he found it necessary to have assistance, and took in as partner his brother Noah, who, after recovering from terrible wounds received in the Battle of Resaca, Georgia, in the fall of 1864, had read law. The firm became Elbert H. and Noah E. Gary, and a little later, Gary, Cody and Gary—Judge Cody, his old preceptor, whose term as elected judge of the Circuit Court had expired, having asked to come into the firm. This was a fine connection, for Cody was an able judge and lawyer, greatly respected by every one.

At times the firm really was crowded with business, for they made it a practice to accept all kinds of cases that they considered "legitimate." They had clear ideas, however, of what was and was not legitimate, and were not afraid to express them. Judge Gary tells a story of his brother Noah which illustrates very well one phase of their professional ethics. A man had called to engage the firm in a suit that he proposed bringing. When he had told his story, Noah said, "If that is the case, that beats you."

"Well," the man replied, "I will change my testimony."

"I was watching my brother," said the Judge, "and I saw him spring up excitedly and heard him cry angrily, 'Get out of this office. A man who would perjure himself cannot find a lawyer here.' Like most lawyers, we were offered more than one retainer that we could not touch; there are things that a lawyer cannot do."

The rapidly growing practice of the young firm brought Judge Gary into constant contact with the best lawyers, not only of Chicago, but of the adjoining counties—a remarkable set of men, including several that had been associated with Abraham Lincoln: Leonard Sweet, General Stiles, Melville W. Fuller, John Van Armen, Isaac Arnold, and many others. One of his associates comments on the fact that from the start Gary never shrank from meeting any of these men, and he adds, "He rarely came off second best."

The Judge is proud to-day of this competition—"first-class competition" he calls it. "There were any number of very able lawyers in Chicago, Aurora, Elgin, Joliet, all around that country," he will tell you, "that I would rather have try a case for me before a jury than any lawyer I can get in New York City to-day."

He won suits which brought him more business, and he won clients who never left him. There was William Deering of the Deering Harvester Company. Gary had been employed by one of his representatives to prosecute a suit to be heard in the court of Belleville, near St. Louis. When he arrived at Belleville, he found his client had not a single witness to contradict important testimony that was being presented by the defendant. In listening to the chief witness, however, Gary became convinced that he was dishonest and that his only hope was to break down his testimony in cross-examination. In beginning his cross-examination he took care not to let the witness know what he was after, but the opposing lawyer soon saw his tactics and objected, arguing the questions in such a way that the witness would understand the point. Finally Gary said to the Court:

"I know, and the counsel of the other side knows, that the purpose of objecting is to keep this witness advised of the effect so that he may shape his testimony accordingly."

"Mr. Gary is absolutely right," the judge said. "You can make your objections if you wish, but I shall overrule them without discussion, unless I deem it necessary to hear you."

This cross-examination went on for two days. After many contradictions in the answers, Gary's last question was, "Do you know whether you have told the truth or not?" and the witness said "No!"

"I was much worried," Judge Gary says, in talking of the case. "It was dangerous business, for we had no witness of our own to contradict the defendant. I closed my argument by saying, 'Gentlemen of the Jury, if the chief witness the defendant, doesn't know whether he is telling the truth or not, can you give him the verdict?'

"While I was talking, Mr. Deering who had arrived from Chicago, came into the court room, and after I had sat down he came over to me and said, 'Mr. Gary, I want to tell you that whatever the jury does I am perfectly satisfied.' The verdict was for the plaintiff. This was in the early days of an association of some twenty-five years.''

And this was only one of many cases that could be cited of clients that had once come to him because of a first favorable impression, and remained because they found that he took care of their interests; such good care that, as time went on, several large concerns made it a practice to turn over all their difficulties to him, to settle as he saw fit, out of court if possible. Indeed, in a few years he had attained a reputation for settling cases without suits, although for about ten years he was in court nearly every working day. He seems to have had Lincoln's idea—''discourage litigation.'' One of his favorite stories to irate clients, who insisted on bringing suit when the Judge thought the matter might be adjusted, was of a DuPage farmer who in the early days had a bull that thought it could lick anything in the country. When the railway came the bull looked upon the locomotive with hatred and derision, and made up its mind that it would try an issue with it. One morning the farmer heard an awful tooting, and looking out, saw that the bull had jumped the fence and was rushing, head down, towards the approaching locomotive. A moment later there were only spots of hide and hair on the track. ''I always liked your pluck, old bull,'' the farmer said sorrowfully, ''but dang your discretion.''

Much of his success unquestionably was due, as the above incidents show, to his skill in cross-examination. In the years in which as a student and clerk he had so closely watched and estimated the conduct of lawyers, he had not only learned the value of cool, adroit, careful examination of witness but had become thoroughly convinced of the value of courtesy. "Cross-examination is a high art," he says, "and courtesy is at its base. A lawyer should be a gentleman in justice to himself, but if that doesn't interest him, he should be a gentleman because he has the jury against him if he is not." He has numberless tales in his great legal repertoire to illustrate how being a gentleman pays in legal practice.

But courtesy was backed by a superior knowledge and judgment of men, a thorough knowledge of the law, and a power of clean, strong argument. His father, Erastus Gary, was a wise and shrewd appraiser of human nature, and his sons had learned from him. Then those years in which he had watched men filing in and out of courts had whetted his naturally keen sense of the honesty, decency, and rightness of people. He knew men so well that he could practically always tell when a witness was lying, and could find a way of making the judge and jury sense it; or better still, of bringing him around to the point where he would tell the truth.

A spectacular instance of the latter kind occurred in an insurance case in Chicago. A warehouse owned by Jewish merchants had been burned with all its contents, and an elaborate claim had been made against an insurance company for which Gary was general counsel. There was no proof of what was in the warehouse other than the statement of the owners, and Gary in questioning them became convinced that they were lying. Now, it happened that during the progress of the case he was told by the general adjuster, that if a Hebrew takes the oath of his religion, he will not swear to a lie. This gave him a hint that he followed. He subpoenaed the secretary of the firm, a young Jewish woman, and proposed that the peculiar oath of her faith be administered.   Judge Gresham, afterwards Secretary of State, under Grover Cleveland, was on the bench.   He did not understand the reason for the suggestion, but suspected Gary had a sound one, so, against the loud objections of the plaintiffs, consented.   It is a solemn ceremony, this Jewish oath, requiring lighted candles and a beautiful ritual.   The girl went through it reluctantly, but put on the stand told the truth, which was that the inventory was not made from an examination of goods but largely out of the imagination of her employers; the verdict was for the insurance company.

Gary knew men, but he always took care to know the facts in his. cases.   The general verdict of his associates, clients, judges, fellow lawyers, is that he was indefatigable in informing himself.   Those who faced him for the first time, knowing nothing of his record, were apt to underestimate him, he was so unassuming and courteous.   More than one opposing lawyer waked up to find that, as one of Gary's colleagues says, "he had tried the case in every detail in his office long before it had been called."

This preparation went even to investigating on the spot, to see whether a thing could have been as it was claimed.   Take the personal injury cases in industrial establishments and on railroads, many of which came to him both from corporations and injured individuals. If possible he made sure of what had happened by personal verification. In one case a man claimed large damages for permanent injury to his arms from the blow of a lever on what he claimed was a defective machine. Gary visited the factory, and after making sure by inquiry that the machine in question was in the same condition as at the time of the injury, he had it set in motion, and in the presence of a number of disinterested witnesses, went through a series of operations to see whether it was possible for the lever to do what the injured man claimed, that is, crush his arm. First, he let the lever strike a blow at a small piece of timber loosely held, then bits of scantling rigidly placed, then he tried the same experiment with other materials and shapes. Finally, he let his own arm take the blow and when he found he was not hurt, he concluded that there must have been fraud involved. And this he was afterwards able to prove. The plaintiff lost his case.

But he could not have gone so fast or so far as he was going if he had not had a real passion for the law, a continuous interest in its intricacies, an indefatigable energy in adding to his own legal equipment. Not infrequently he stayed by cases in which there was small hope of substantial fees—this after he was commanding handsome ones—because of his interest in the legal problems involved. He still holds it as a matter of pride that one "little case," to which he stuck faithfully, became a leading cause in Illinois.

"It is some satisfaction," he told H. S. McCartney, still a well-known lawyer of Chicago, a few years ago when the two men were recalling early legal experiences —"It is some satisfaction to have afforded a useful decision to our legal profession."

It must be some satisfaction, too, to realize how often he was right in forecasting the trend of the law towards corporations and changing industrial conditions. James Shaw of the Aurora, Illinois, Public Library, who was a court stenographer in those days and heard Gary conduct more than one case, says in a private letter to the author:

He (Gary) came to the bar on the eve of revolutionary changes in the law—changes that have been so gradual that historians have taken little notice of them. Nevertheless a tremendous advance has been made in the law itself, and in its interpretation by the courts. This advance is in conformity with the changes wrought in the social structure by the great inventions and discoveries of the last two or three generations. A great era of railroad building began just about the time that Elbert Gary appeared on the stage of action. That was followed by the telephone. The construction and operation of these appliances found the law silent as to their rights, duties and obligations. The factory system arose, or rather it became enormously extended. Concerns employed hundreds, and even thousands of men and women. How should the rights of these human beings be protected? At first the law dealt harshly with workers who met with accident. There was the principle known as the "fellow-servant" doctrine, which held that a workman injured by the neglect or ignorance of another workman could not hold the employer liable. There was also the doctrine of "assumed risk," which held that an employee injured by a machine that he knew to be defective, could not call upon his employer for compensation for the injury.

These peculiar doctrines, and others of a similar nature, materialized as lawyer-made or court-made laws. With the development of the labor union, and its influence. in procuring the enactment of laws more humanitarian, these doctrines have gone the way of other harsh laws. The conditions for working people have become humanized.

Judge Charles D. Clark, of Chicago, who entered the Gary firm in 1886 as a law clerk, says of his attitude towards the undeveloped law:

There are two kinds of lawyers: First, fellows who must find precedents to indicate to them the decision they should make or the action to be taken: and second, lawyers from principle.

E. H. Gary was of the latter kind. Any new legal proposition would be thought out minutely and logically. He would then say to his juniors, "I think the law in this matter ought to be so-and-so; see what you can find to back me up." He would often anticipate in the entire absence of precedent, what the decision in the courts would have to be, and would direct his course accordingly. Inasmuch as corporation law in those days was very scarce he had to adopt this attitude. He could see in advance the handwriting on the wall farther than anyone else.

Obviously the cases referred to above are only typical. It is not practical in a sketch of this nature to attempt to cover thoroughly Judge Gary's professional career. It is enough for our purpose to know that his practice included a great variety of cases, involving large interests, complicated questions, and stubborn contests; also that his ability and energy were rewarded by increasingly handsome earnings.

It is significant of the man's attitude towards his legal achievements that he frankly says to-day: "I was too successful, too busy. I came to a point where I could select my cases. I did not continue to study as I should like to have done, was not profound.

"Judge Joseph E. Gary, of the Chicago bench, who I suppose was a very distant relative, warned me of this. He was one of the most honest lawyers I ever knew, and there was nothing ostentatious in his honesty, it was natural. It was this Judge Gary that tried the anarchist cases. He was often confused with me at the time of the trial. My wife went one day to a meeting held by the women of Wheaton to pray for the judge in the case, and she found they were praying for me.

"Judge Joseph Gary made a specialty of law. At one time when I was trying a case before Judge Barnum, he held against me on a technical point. I disputed it, and the Judge got very angry and rebuked me. Going out, I met Judge Gary and told him the case. He said, without hesitancy, 'Barnum is wrong. You ought to have known that. The case Barnum relies upon was later overruled by the same court.'

" 'Judge,' I said, 'I am too busy to look up all these things.'

" 'That's it, you are *too* busy.' That was true. I had no time to be a perfect lawyer. In earlier days I worked harder."

If this young man who so rapidly strode ahead at the Chicago bar, and made his way by such logical and honest practices, appears a bit too faultless in retrospect, the recollections of certain of his contemporaries add an occasional grain of salt to the story and hint at traits of character apt to be obscured in a narrative of this kind. While no one who remembers him fails to comment on the way he kept his head under all circumstances—cool, collected, impossible to ruffle, they all insist that he was quite capable of using his fists if necessary. There is a tradition, running through all the reminiscences of Gary as a young lawyer, of a time when a bumptious opposing counsel, who threatened to knock him down, found himself suddenly lying flat on the other side of the rail. That is, physical vigor went with his mental vigor, and came into play when he considered it necessary.

Nor did his absorption in business in these years destroy his family and social life. He loved the town of Wheaton where he lived, and found endless opportunities to serve it. As a matter of fact he was leading in Wheaton in those busy early years an attractive, important, all-around life. He and Mrs. Gary were carrying on the Gary traditions. Social life in Illinois towns in those days, as almost everywhere else, centered in the church. The Methodist church to which the Garys belonged was the strongest and most active in Wheaton. It was the church in which Gary had been trained to work, and as he came into an active professional life he never neglected its interests. The Gary Young Ladies' Bible Class was, through all these years, up, indeed, to the time when Judge Gary left Illinois, a kind of church Junior League, an institution to which every girl connected with the church aspired.

From boyhood he had been a member of the church choir, and though he no longer sang regularly he "filled in" when the choirmaster was short of a baritone. He served on the official board, he was a "wheel-horse for work," one of his colleagues has said, but we have it in a letter from one who was his pastor for a long period, that, active and generous as he was, he never abused this position, never showed any desire to become a church boss.

Along with this serious service went a great deal of joyous social activity. He *liked* church suppers, socials, picnics—liked the games—even the clothespin game!— the singing, the frolicking. Indeed he was a man who knew how to play "when it did not interfere with work," he is careful to tell you to-day! One of the healthiest features of his life during these years was his insistence on getting a certain amount of outdoor exercise and sport. He rode horseback, and his old coachman, still alive in Wheaton at this writing, loves to tell how for several years he had Prince, which he describes as "some horse"— "nervous, vicious, and a goer"—ready at six o'clock for the early ride that Judge Gary regularly took before breakfast. He kept this up for years, until one morning Prince came back without his rider. Frightened, he had jumped over a deep ditch, fallen, and thrown his rider. After four or five weeks in bed, the Judge gave up his morning horseback ride, but he always continued to drive fast horses. "A horse never could go fast enough to suit Judge Gary," the coachman says.

As for sports, his old associates in Wheaton evidently remember him as very keen on them all. "He was one of the best side-hold wrestlers in this county," says one of his townsmen who grew up with him and had tested him out both in sports and hunting. "He was decidedly handy with his fists as well, as some people learned. One of the best billiard players in town, an authority on croquet, a member of our crack baseball team, fond of hunting and an excellent shot. We made many trips of from two days to two weeks in Iowa and Minnesota, shooting prairie chickens and ducks, and we often went fishing." This long-time intimate of the Judge gives a remarkable testimony to the cleanliness of his habits as boy and man. "He did not smoke or chew tobacco, never used profane or vulgar language. I have never heard him tell a story or utter a word that he could not have told in a parlor full of ladies, and it was always understood that he didn't care to hear any stories that were off color, or any profane or vulgar talk."

It is difficult to understand just how Judge Gary could have found time, with his law, his church, his family and his sports, to give to the affairs of the town of Wheaton the attention which he did. As a matter of fact, he was a part of it almost from the first. He was still in his early twenties when he was elected president of the town council—a position he held for three successive terms.

When Wheaton was made a city he became its first mayor, and until he left Illinois in 1898 he had much to do with the organization and management of its affairs. The only incident of importance in the history of the town in which he seems not to have taken an active part belongs to the early days. It is known in local history as the "Wheaton Raid." By considerable pressure and possibly some wire pulling, the voters, under an act of the state legislature, had been persuaded to transfer the county seat from Naperville to Wheaton, and Naperville, outraged in its pride and its interest, refused to give up the county records. One night Wheaton men went after them and after an exciting fight brought them back. If you ask Judge Gary to-day if he was one of the raiders, he will tell you, with a burst of irritated regret, "No, I wasn't and I have been mad ever since."

But if he missed the raid he was the center of the fiercest legal battle Wheaton ever fought—a fight to keep itself dry. But let the Judge tell the story:

"It happened when I was president of Wheaton. It was decided to make Wheaton a temperance town. It was a college town—a town of homes. We didn't want saloons there and we had driven them out, but there was one of the saloon-keepers that was fighting. He defended suit and engaged good lawyers. They wanted me to take the case for the town, but I was very busy, so Noah took it. One night as I got off the train, I found half Wheaton at the station. They told me that those lawyers were twisting things in such a way that the town would surely lose if I didn't take hold, that I must stay and conduct the fight. Of course there wasn't anything else for me to do.

"We had an exciting time. The house was packed

every day—on one side the drys, on the other all the
saloon interests of DuPage County, as well as some from
Chicago. The defendant's lawyers grew more and more
abusive. Finally one of them, when Noah questioned the
truth of something he had said, jumped towards him
shouting, 'You are a liar!'

"Noah was excitable and bounded to his feet, as the
man came toward him. But Noah was not disposed to
fight—he had been shot all to pieces in the war and never
after was quite as strong as I. So I jumped in between
them, and as the man rushed at me, I struck him once,
just once. The whole court room poured down around
us, thinking there was going to be a fight, and I can see
now a leading citizen of Wheaton, a pious, dignified-
looking man, a spectator in the back of the room, bounding over the seats and, it seemed to me, over the heads
of the people, crying out as he landed at my side, 'I don't
believe in fighting, but if there's going to be a fight,
I'm in it.'

"But there wasn't any fight. The lawyer cooled off,
and we went on with the case, and won it. It was
appealed to the Supreme Court, and we won it there—
Rickert versus *The People*. It was regarded as a leading case in the state, lawyers everywhere that were fighting the saloon using my argument."

This town activity of his was partly self-protective,
for before he was thirty years of age he was one of the
largest property owners in Wheaton and its neighborhood. His father's counsel to buy land, run in debt if
necessary for its purchase, had been adopted by young
Gary, though, as a matter of fact, he had been so thrifty
that he never needed to hamper himself seriously with
debts. He bought land in and near Wheaton until, at

the time that he left, in 1898, he owned some 2,500 acres outside and inside the corporate limits. Moreover, when he was about twenty-five years old he had helped members of a National Bank of Chicago to establish a private county bank in Wheaton. The bank did very well for some eighteen months, when its parent failed. A run on the Wheaton branch began immediately and Gary saw that unless confidence could be reëstablished the results might be very serious. It was he and his father and brother and uncle and cousins that came to the rescue and offered to lend their names to the firm. Such was their standing in their community that the old depositors began immediately to come back and many new ones were added. The bank became, and still is, prosperous, and he remained its president until he left Illinois.

This experience, although costly to young Gary, was also valuable in the future when his legal business brought him frequently into touch with banks. Such was the value of his counsel that in later life he was invited to the board of directors of many banks in Chicago, and afterwards, in New York, served as chairman of one, and member of the executive committee of another. Out of this experience he holds that the two most important things for a banker to bear in mind are: First, that it is better to let the funds of the bank remain idle than to loan them on doubtful security or to a dishonest applicant; and, second, to learn how to refuse an accommodation in such a way as to keep the respect and friendship of the applicant. He insists that this can be done if a banker is willing to give a man frankly his reasons, at the same time showing that he is sorry that he cannot do what is asked.

Of course a young lawyer, forging ahead in his profession and in his fortunes, particularly a man in whom a whole county believed as thoroughly as DuPage County believed in Elbert Gary, was bound to be regarded as political timber. Indeed, in Illinois at that period, politics were considered an almost inevitable adjunct of the law, but Elbert Gary never seems to have had any inclination toward politics. He loved his profession too well to give it a rival. At the same time he found in his healthy Wheaton life and interests too much satisfaction to wish to share it with politics. So, whenever the game was open to him, he refused. However, in 1882 the lawyers of DuPage County prevailed upon him to run as county judge. It was what might be called a part-time job, since the two annual sessions of the court rarely ran over two or three weeks, so that it did not seriously interfere with his practice. He was elected by a large majority and served two terms of four years each as judge of DuPage County, but refused reëlection for a third.

The qualifications he had shown as a lawyer marked him as a judge. Particularly did he insist that the proceedings before him be conducted with courtesy and decorum. The thing in which he was particularly interested was breaking up the too-common practice of browbeating witnesses. He declares that he never hesitated if necessary to run the risk of making the lawyer before him angry by saying, "You are not treating that witness fairly, you cannot do those things in this court." It was part of the man's nature—you must be fair. He meant to be fair himself, and wherever he had authority he meant that others should be fair. Courteous as he was as a judge, he could, if necessary, be sarcastic. One of his contemporaries still tells of his saying to an officious young man who, every time a ruling was required, would march up and stand close by the Judge:

"If you have a photograph you might stand it here on my desk this afternoon, just to show you are present."

His work as judge was not confined to DuPage County; frequently he was called upon to serve on the bench in Chicago, because of the absence or illness of a judge or to help clear up the docket, and steadily he seems to have gained in the estimation of the legal fraternity.

Judge Jesse Holdom, a member of the Chicago bar, who remembers Gary from the time he was a clerk and forced him and others to pay their "boarding fees" promptly, declares of him as a judge, "There were no rough spots in him, not one."

A tribute paid to him as a lawyer and judge, years later, by U. S. Senator A. J. Hopkins of Illinois, in a public address in Wheaton, expresses the general opinion of his fellows in his profession, and gives, too, a fellow-lawyer's opinion as to how he reached the place he held. Senator Hopkins and Judge Gary had started in the law about the same time, around 1871.

"During the period of more than a quarter of a century that we both followed our profession as lawyers," said Senator Hopkins, "I saw much of him, both as an associate in the trial of cases, and as an attorney and advocate opposed to me in the trial of cases. His first efforts in his profession foreshadowed the eminence which he subsequently attained. He was cool, collected, self-confident, and aggressive in the trial of a case. I never saw him disconcerted or apparently surprised by any change in the trial of a case. He seemingly had anticipated any emergency that might arise, and was prepared to protect his client's interest under any and all conditions. . . . His self-confidence was not tinctured with egotism that makes such a quality sometimes offensive; but it was of that character that leads a client to place implicit confidence in the judgment and ability of his attorney.

"His rise in his profession was neither spectacular nor phenomenal. It was steady and progressive. Every year added to his experience and ability; and long before he abandoned the profession of the law for the business career in which he is now recognized as one of the great captains of industry, he had attained a position in the first rank of his profession in the state of Illinois.

". . . . Had he remained in his profession he would before this, in my judgment, have been one of the distinguished members of the Supreme Court of this state, or would have held an honorable position on the Federal Bench."

Senator Hopkins' judgment of the judicial honors that were within Gary's reach would have been realized before the Judge left Illinois, if he had not refused the positions on the bench that he was urged to take. After his refusal of a third term from DuPage County, a movement was set on foot by the lawyers of the district to make him a circuit judge of the state and he was nominated unanimously, but he would not undertake the job. He was suggested for the Supreme Court of the state, but refused to be the candidate, because of his sympathy for the judge who then held the position and was a candidate for reëlection. There was much talk of him once as a federal judge, but he was too engrossed in important affairs to pay attention to it.

By 1892 Judge Gary had been in general practice for twenty years, engaged in law and chancery cases of large importance. He had made money; his position was secure. He had represented many corporations during this period and had opposed others. He had been president of the Chicago Bar Association. He had more business than he could attend to, when something happened which was to affect his whole future career. He became interested in steel.

CHAPTER IV

GARY GOES INTO IRON AND STEEL

A FIRST undertaking in an Illinois settlement of the 'thirties and 'forties as early as the first general store, was a blacksmith shop. In these shops and the foundries which soon sprang up beside them were made shoes for horses, simple and rough iron work for wagons and plows, and frequently the tongs, pokers and andirons for the household as well. It was with difficulty that the smithies kept pace with the demands of the western settlers.

These settlers were progressive buyers. That is, they were open to new tools, asking nothing better than to spend money for that which enabled them to do their work more quickly. It was this attitude of mind that, in 1847, brought Cyrus McCormick from Virginia where he had developed his reaper and where the Virginian wheat farmers had proved too conservative to give him the market he sought. It was different in the West. There the farmers bought his machines faster than he could ship them, and he saw that the natural thing was for him to go to the center of this great trade.

It was so with other things. One of the earliest recollections of young Elbert Gary was of lightning rods. In his home town of Wheaton there were two factories making them. Then there were plows, the merits of which he saw tested again and again in the exciting contests at the fall fairs which were one of the great events of his boyhood. A show place in Naperville, the county seat seven miles from his home, was a steel plow factory that by the time he was ten years old was boasting in its advertising literature that it had "never been beaten at any state or county fair." As a matter of fact it was one of the oldest plow factories in the West, if not the oldest. It made the enormous number of fifteen plows a day, at an average price of fifteen dollars each!

While energetic and resourceful farmers like Erastus Gary were taking advantage of all sorts of new inventions, they were frequently forecasting, by their ingenious devices, inventions which were to be of incalculable importance in future agricultural and industrial developments. There was the important matter of fencing the prairies. Rails and board fences were not satisfactory, wind and fire sweeping them down regularly. Another of Judge Gary's earliest recollections is of his father inclosing their Wheaton fields first with rails, and afterwards in wire fencing; and a little later, when he was about twelve years old, of being set with his brother Noah at making roughly finished barbs and staples for the wires.

Erastus Gary's device was simple enough. He drilled a hole in an old anvil and, cutting strips of wire diagonally with a cold chisel, directed the boys to stick one end in the hole and with a hammer bend the strip. This was then fitted around the fence wire with a pair of pincers— the result was a fairly successful barbed wire fence.

But Erastus Gary was not the only Illinois farmer whose wits and fingers were busy on the problem of protecting fencing. Thirty or forty miles from Wheaton, near the town of DeKalb, lived one Joseph Glidden, who, with the help of his wife and a grindstone, had made something so practical that he had it patented. This was in 1873, a few years after Erastus Gary and his boys had begun to inclose their fields in their homemade product.

Glidden bought his wire from a local hardware dealer, one I. L. Ellwood. Ellwood proposed that they set up a factory. They were soon turning out such quantities of fencing that the manufacturers from whom they bought their wire, the foremost and oldest in the country, Washburn and Moen of Worcester, Massachusetts, became curious and sent a man to investigate. As soon as he put his eyes on the Glidden and Ellwood barbed wire, he saw that here was a product with a future. The upshot was that he bought out Glidden, and arranged with Ellwood to manufacture at Worcester, Ellwood taking the western market and he the eastern and southern.

But trouble awaited them. One of Glidden's neighbors, a carpenter, a German by the name of Jacob Haish, had also experimented with barbed wire and, only a little later than Glidden, had secured a patent, and in the second story of his carpenter shop had begun to manufacture. The Washburns had always been aggressive defenders of their patents, and they immediately began circularizing the trade with a threat to sue any dealer who bought a barbed wire which did not bear their license tag. Jacob Haish was not one to be easily frightened, and he followed up the Washburn threat with an elaborate, illustrated circular, declaring that his fence wire was "sold on its merits and not through the influence of threatened lawsuits." It was the beginning of a war which was to prove long and cruel.

But it was not only disputes over patents that worried Ellwood and Washburn. They were pestered with pirates of particular audacity and ingenuity, men who, seeing the fortunes that lay in barbed wire and emboldened by the disputes over the patents, set up factories of their own. One of the earliest and altogether the ablest of these poachers was a young man of twenty-three or four by the name of John W. Gates.

Ellwood had employed Gates as a salesman, and he had proved himself a genius at the business. He had a natural passion for selling things—anything—accompanied by equal energy and audacity. Recognizing that Texas was a fertile field for barbed wire, if the ranchmen and cowboys could be persuaded that it would hold their wild horses and cattle, he dropped into the state and, when the merit of his "line" was questioned, built a barbed wire corral and sent invitations far and wide to bring in the wildest animals and let them test the new invention. It was a wonderful exhibition that followed. I have heard it declared that no rodeo ever equaled it. The ranchmen were convinced, and Gates was loaded with orders.

As the story goes, Gates felt that this was too much business to pass on, so, going to St. Louis, he persuaded a couple of gentlemen who had capital to go quietly into the manufacture of barbed wire. Before Ellwood knew it, and indeed while he was telegraphing over the country for his lost salesman, the Gates plant began operations.

An injunction was served on him in Missouri, but he and his partners picked up their machinery and slipped across the Mississippi River into southern Illinois, and went on turning out the pirated product. Every move that Ellwood made Gates checkmated, until finally, in despair, his pursuer concluded that it was better to license than to fight him. And thus it was that about 1885 John W. Gates became a legitimate wire manufacturer. But he was not satisfied with his St. Louis plant, and rapidly secured an interest in four others—three of them in Pennsylvania, and one in the West.

Now, these scattered concerns had to live under more or less cruel trade conditions. Pirates sprang up who scoffed at patents as Gates had done. The price of the rods from which the wire was drawn fluctuated extravagantly. The railroad frequently favored their competitors who, in spite of trade agreements on prices, freely undercut when they thought it to their advantage. John W. Gates was well fitted by temperament and experience to hold his own under such conditions, but he realized that survival in barbed wire was only to the strong, and he began talking to his partners in the five scattered factories about combining. By 1892 he was ready for the amalgamation. A lawyer was needed, and Gates went at once to Judge Gary, who at the time, because of the extent of his practice, had refused to take a third term on the bench.

Gates went to Gary not only because he had always known him—he was born only twenty miles from Wheaton—but because of a profound confidence in the man's legal ability and fairness. It was a confidence born of experience, for Gary had been the opposing lawyer in a case against Gates and had been successful —a fact that had so won his respect that he had afterwards frequently consulted the Judge in legal difficulties. Besides, by this time Gary had become not only a successful practitioner, he was widely known as thoroughly versed in corporate law. As a matter of fact he was often employed by railroad companies, as well as by a number of industrial organizations, and had become the general counsel for some of them.

It was a simple matter to put together the five concerns as an Illinois corporation. It was done in exactly the same way, Judge Gary tells me, in which six years later he was to frame the Federal Steel Corporation. That is, the owners of the plants, having agreed on the amount of stock to be issued—$4,000,000—settled by negotiation what each should have, and exchanged their old shares for the new. The complete block of stock in the concern, which they called the Consolidated Steel and Wire Company, was held by the owners of the old concerns.

The framing of this first important combine caused great uneasiness in the country's wide-flung wire circles where Gates was liked by some and suspected by others. The Illinois public questioned it—it was another Trust. The new combination arrived, too, at an unhappy moment. The panic of 1893 was close on its heels. There were threats of reduced tariffs from the new Democratic administration. There were serious labor troubles. Men like Gates and certain of his associates in the combination found business depression hard on their nerves. The new board was more or less discordant, and its counsel, Judge Gary, soon found peace-making one of his duties. They appreciated it, frank men that they were. They began to discover, too, that he gave them something more than counsel on legal matters, that he gave them sound business advice, and it was advice which resulted from reflection on the actual condition of business, the details of which, they discovered, he knew in many cases as well as, or better than, they themselves did. It was

not long before he was invited to the board of directors
and began to buy stock; for, from the first, Gary had
believed that the Consolidated was an entirely sound
business proposition; that is, that it was worth the
$4,000,000 at which it was capitalized, or more.

John W. Gates now had a strong enough wire and nail
unit to enable him to compete with the best of those in
the business, but he was not satisfied. As he traveled
back and forth from east to west and dropped in to rival
plants to talk over matters with the owners, he frequently
broached the subject of a larger combination; and when
he came back discussed the matter with Gary, who
was himself gradually coming to the conclusion not only
that there would be economies and better service in such
an undertaking, but that it was possibly the only means
by which the manufacturers could be brought to observe
their own marketing arrangements. The pools which
they were constantly attempting almost invariably ended
in bitter rows and accusations born of their suspicion
of one another. The suspicion was generally well placed.
One of the frankest of the group of wire manufacturers
of that period, John Stevenson of the New Castle Wire
Works, said once, in testifying as to the difficulties in
trade that they had at that time, "Every man's hand
was against his neighbor; we were all Ishmaelites, every
one of us." And he went on to tell of a meeting of manufacturers in which a price of $1.50 had been fixed for
nails in the keg, and one of the leaders in the group,
hurrying out to the telegraph office, entered an order
for 10,000 kegs at $1.40! By accident this message fell
into Mr. Stevenson's hands at the telegraph office just
after the meeting had adjourned for lunch, and he had
the pleasure of laying it before his colleagues when they

reconvened. It was that kind of thing, so Mr. Stevenson claimed, that caused 80 per cent of the mortality in the wire and nail business, and not consolidation, as was publicly charged.

One of the chief things that the best men in the business at this time felt the need of was protection from one another.

It was not until late in the summer of 1897 that matters came to a focus. Gary had been in Europe—his first trip. Indeed, the first long vacation he had ever taken. He had kept himself fit as few men do through many years of continuous hard work by his joyous and temperate social life and by his unbroken interest in outdoor pursuits—horseback riding, fishing trips, and every now and then a few days' hunting in Iowa and Minnesota. But early in this year, an eastern lawyer who had been associated with him in a case in Chicago had, as the Judge says, talked him into the notion of going abroad. And that notion once in his mind, nothing could change him.

With Mrs. Gary and one of his daughters, he had started in June for a three months' trip, every detail of which seems to be as clear in his mind now, after more than twenty-five years, as when he returned.

He proved to be the same kind of traveler that he was lawyer, sportsman, Sunday-school teacher. He had a tremendous interest in everything—the beautiful English country—Chester, the first walled town he had ever seen, with its story of Charles II watching from the tower while Cromwell defeated his army—his failure to get to Mr. Gladstone, though he had bought his way with gold pieces straight up to the private secretary, and undoubtedly would have succeeded with him, if it had not been for Mrs. Gladstone, a rigid enforcer of doctor's orders. "It would not have hurt him a bit," the Judge grumbles to-day. The greatest piece of vandalism of his life, as he considers it, was sitting in Gladstone's pew in the Hawarden church and tearing out from his hymn book the flyleaf on which the great man had written, "Shall we go out before the last hymn?"

He recalls still the solemnity of London, if you first see it, as he did, about twelve o'clock on a Saturday night! In spite of guides and counselors, he knew what he wanted to see in the great city. First, Bunyan's grave, then Charles Wesley's church and grave, then Dickens' "Old Curiosity Shop"—memories of things that had impressed him in his youth. Later, the British Museum, the courts, the National Gallery, the Tower, Westminster Abbey, St. Paul's, the Bank of England, Oxford, Cambridge.

He was as tireless in his sight-seeing as in the law. He loved "watching the folks" and would rise every morning at five o'clock to visit the markets and see the people going to work. At night, after a hard day in churches and galleries, he was out to watch the night life of the towns and cities. But the real excitement of his journey was his pilgrimage in search of the twelve greatest pictures of the world. Mrs. Gary knew what they were, and he wanted to see them, every one of them; and they did it, from "Mona Lisa" and the "Immaculate Conception" in Paris, through Italy, Austria and Germany, to the "Descent from the Cross" in Antwerp. It was his first experience with great pictures, and aroused in him a love of painting which he has steadily cultivated through the years.

A man comes back from his first trip to Europe, if it

has been put through as thoroughly and as joyously as Judge Gary put through this trip of his, heartened, enlarged, refreshed. He had got his hand on something which was to mean much to him in the revolutionary task that awaited his return, for when he reached Chicago there was Gates. He wanted Gary to begin work immediately on the long-talked-of combination in wire and nails.

But could such a combination be financed? Would Morgan assist? For in 1897, as in 1925, the first thought of men wanting money for a big enterprise was Morgan. Judge Gary was not unknown to the famous banker. Some months before this, when in New York on business, he had been called in by one of Mr. Morgan's counsel to give his opinion on a railroad matter involving Illinois law and practice. "I don't think you can do that legally, Mr. Morgan," Judge Gary had said when the case had been stated.

"Well," said Mr. Morgan—and his "well" was always a challenging, often a terrifying expletive—"I don't know as I want a lawyer to tell me what I cannot do. I hire him to tell me how to do what I want to do."

"Tell me your purpose," the Judge replied, "and I will see what can be done."

Mr. Morgan, who always knew exactly what he was after, though he sometimes found difficulty in telling others, explained his purpose.

"There is a legal way to reach that result," Judge Gary said, and he explained what it was. The banker was immensely pleased. It undoubtedly made an impression on him which he never forgot, for he had a remarkable memory, particularly in matters which concerned men.

But it was not before Mr. Morgan, it was before the first ranking partner in the concern, Charles H. Coster, that Gates and Gary laid their plan for a steel and wire combination. They found him hospitable, and finally Mr. Morgan agreed that, if the wire manufacturers could be brought together, he would back a consolidation, to be known as the American Steel and Wire Company, its capital to be $80,000,000—one half preferred and one half common. A syndicate of $20,000,000 was to be floated, though Mr. Morgan told Judge Gary, when this was first under discussion, that such a flotation would cause a panic in Wall Street! Fifteen million dollars of the common stock was to be divided between the promoters of the undertaking, these promoters being Gates, Gary, and six other gentlemen who had presented themselves at the Waldorf-Astoria at the beginning of the negotiations and had shown that they, too, had been considering a wire combine. They made so good a showing that Gates finally consented to join forces with them, the understanding being that the $15,000,000 in common stock was to be divided fifty-fifty between the two factions.

Now began weeks of the hardest and closest kind of work for Judge Gary, for it was to him that the bargaining largely fell. As group after group of wire manufacturers was rounded up he went over with them the reports of the expert accountants and engineers that had been examining their plants, in order to reach a fair basis on which an exchange of stock could be made. There were few of these manufacturers who did not believe—honestly enough for the most part—that their plants were worth more than the expert appraisals claimed, and it was a part of Judge Gary's business to

with sincere regards
J Pierpont Morgan
June 26th 1899.

J. PIERPONT MORGAN

convince these doubters. He did it with remarkable success, and gradually the men with whom he was dealing, both manufacturers and financiers, began to see that here was a man not only of an amazing capacity for work, but of an amazing patience in negotiations. In speaking in a former chapter of Gary as a young lawyer, I quoted the remark of one of his DeKalb County observers, that, while the lawyers of the defense spent their evenings playing poker, Gary worked over the testimony. That was what happened now. John W. Gates was not the only poker player among the wire makers. As a rule they went out from their meetings to their games. The Judge, it was noted, stayed by his figures.

Another thing developed that made an impression. He had a passion for square dealing. You had to show him that the thing you were trying to put over was fair before you could get his approval. It was not too much to say that, every day that these wire negotiations went on, the respect for Judge Gary's ability and fairness increased.

The general public paid little attention to what was on foot at the headquarters of Gates and Gary at the Waldorf-Astoria, but the iron and steel trade watched the negotiations with anxiety and doubt. Even the leader of the trade journals, *The Iron Age,* seems to have had little precise information of what was being done, though it knew the general purport of these gatherings of wire and steel interests. "The undertaking is by far the greatest and most far reaching recorded in the history of the iron trade," said this journal in November. "Its ramifications extend far beyond the wire trade people. . . . As a buyer of steel, such an enormous aggregation of mills and works would have an overshadowing influence. If the negotiations now in progress, with what is pronounced to be fair prospect of success, should end in consolidation, then the whole iron trade of the country would have to face greatly changed conditions."

By the first of February, 1898, this "fair prospect of success" of which *The Iron Age* spoke seemed to have become a sure thing, and then suddenly, on the morning of the 15th, came news that staggered the country—the *Maine* had been blown up in the harbor of Havana.

The negotiators at the Waldorf shook their heads. What did it mean to them? The tense days that followed made their anxiety greater. By the end of ten days, the wise Mr. Morgan had concluded that this was no time to launch a new venture in Wall Street, and so in a note sent to the gathered wire men he told them that he did not feel justified in going further at that time. The reason he gave, however, was not what had happened in Havana Harbor. He was disappointed, Mr. Morgan said, that one of the concerns that was wanted for the combination had made a poorer showing in the previous year than he had expected. If it did better later he hinted that he might reconsider.

Judge Gary caught at the straw. Possibly the matter could be suspended for a few months and, after the trouble was over, taken up again; but the negotiators were done with it for the time—"tired" of it, they said. If Mr. Morgan would not go ahead, they would not. When John W. Gates came out from the meeting he said to the interested parties, anxiously waiting at the door, "The jig's up. There's nothing to do but go home."

It was the next day, as several of the western contingent were traveling toward Chicago, that Ellwood of the DeKalb plant, who was keen for the combination, said to Judge Gary, "Why should not the Consolidated take in my plant?" The head of the Salem, Ohio, wire manufacturers was there. "I would like to put mine in," he said. Gates was consulted. By the time the group reached Chicago, they had practically agreed to attempt to unite the western manufacturers on the same basis that had been worked out for the national consolidation. The undertaking was turned over to Gary for consummation and in less than four weeks from the time he had left the disappointing final meeting at the Waldorf-Astoria he had the new company incorporated—The American Steel and Wire Company of Illinois, it was called. It was a $24,000,000 concern—$12,000,000 of which was in preferred stock and $12,000,000 in common. It could not be said to be an overcapitalized company for, according to *The Iron Age,* the combined plants had earned on an average, in each of the three preceding years, $1,666,000.

Judge Gary came out of these long negotiations without a cent of the profit he had expected. His reward in the first combine was to have been in stock; in the smaller one, which was then launched, it was honorary; he was made general counsel and director. But what he had lost in money he had more than doubled in reputation—reputation of the solidest kind among men difficult to convince. He was a patient, intelligent bargainer, they told one another, and, still rarer, he was "fair"—fair on principle.

E. J. Buffington, the present president of the Illinois Steel Company, tells a story which illustrates what was happening in many quarters of the trade at the moment. Mr. Buffington was part owner and the director of a plant at Anderson, Indiana, which the western men wanted to include in their combine, but he and Gates could not settle upon a price. Finally Gary was called in.

"I found at once," Mr. Buffington says, "that I had an entirely different type of man to negotiate with. He had great bargaining ability, but also a desire to see both sides. He was inclined to believe at the start that I was putting too high a price on my plant, but his fairness in the matter led me to greater frankness than I had been accustomed to exercise in my business dealings. I soon found that I was putting all my cards on the table with him. I had engaged a lawyer to protect me in the negotiations, but after I had been over the matter thoroughly with Gary he agreed with me that it would be a wise move for him to go. Between us, Gary and I worked out terms of a settlement which both believed to be right. It was the beginning of my faith in the justice of this man." It was simply the passing on into business circles of a saying which persists to-day, and which had long been current in the legal circles of Chicago—"Gary is fair."

The American Steel and Wire Company of Illinois had hardly been organized before Judge Gary was unexpectedly launched into a new steel undertaking, one more basic and formidable than wire and nails. The new call came logically enough. Among his clients in Chicago for three or four years now had been the biggest steel concern of the West, the Illinois Steel Company. Its origin is worth considering, since it was to be the nucleus of what has become the greatest business in the world.

The Illinois Steel Company was rooted, like barbed wire, in the imperative demands of the newborn Illinois. With the first start of the railroad westward from Chicago, past Erastus Gary's Wheaton farm in 1847, there had come a call for rails, which, as the roads multiplied, the eastern manufacturers had found it difficult to satisfy. It was this demand that, in 1857, led one Captain Eber B. Ward of Michigan to put up a mill in North Chicago for re-rolling old rails. It had a capacity of one hundred rails a day, and the demand grew so rapidly that seven years later he doubled it.

Now, up to this time Ward had been obliged to bring ore and coal for his plant from Pennsylvania and Ohio, but in 1864 a tremendous thing for the Middle West iron manufacturers happened—transportation opened enabling them to bring ore from the Lake Superior mines. A little later it was found that Illinois yielded a coal which, mixed with Pennslyvania and West Virginia coals, could be used with this ore. The result was an immediate and immense expansion of the industry, not only in Illinois, but in Wisconsin and Michigan.

But it was not iron rails alone. Ward had seen the meaning of the Bessemer process and was the first man in the United States to undertake to apply it commercially. It was early in 1864 that he set up a converter in Wyandotte, Michigan, and here made steel ingots which later he turned into steel rails at his Chicago rolling mill—the first steel rails to be rolled in the United States.

It was not many months before farseeing men in the iron business realized that steel rails were bound to replace what they had been making for the railroads. Then began, all over the country, the movement to convert existing iron mills into Bessemer plants. It was expensive business. Few of the manufacturers could get the money it required. Captain Ward's North Chicago rolling mill was one that could command capital, and it accordingly began to gather in its less fortunate competitors in the Middle West; by 1889 it was able to capitalize itself for $25,000,000 and to call itself by a new name, the Illinois Steel Company. By this time there was only one city in the United States making more iron and steel than Chicago, and that city was Pittsburgh.

Now, for several years before, as well as after, this combination, John W. Gates had bought iron and steel rods for his wire from this concern. He had earned the reputation with them of always getting the best of the bargain. I have heard old-timers say that the Illinois Steel Company finally felt that it was safer to have him in the concern than out, and early in the 'nineties made him a director and, in 1894, president. At that moment the company was having a hard time. Its last dividend had been paid in 1892. In 1893, the panic year, it had suffered—indeed there had been serious talk of putting it in the hands of a receiver. Everybody knew its plight, because it was one of the few concerns in the country which published annually a partial report of its year's dealings.

In the difficulties of the company it was to be expected that sooner or later Gary would be called in for consultation, and when this had happened his advice was such that he thoroughly impressed the board of directors— and they were men worth impressing—Marshall Field and H. H. Porter of Chicago, Nathaniel Thayer of Boston, A. J. Forbes Leith of London and New York (afterward Lord Leith of Fyvie)—all men who had responded to the call for money and still more money, to meet the necessity of making steel instead of iron rails. At the suggestion of H. H. Porter, Gary was made General Counsel. It was the beginning of a close association with the directing board. Indeed it soon came about that they would refuse to hold a meeting if Gary was not present!

This was the Judge's relation to the Illinois Steel Company when, soon after he had finished the organization of the American Steel and Wire Company of Illinois of which we have been talking, he received a letter from Nathaniel Thayer of Boston, asking his opinion as to the purchase of the Elgin, Joliet and Eastern railroad, running from Chicago to the company's Joliet works.

Now by this time, 1898, Judge Gary had come to the conclusion that what the Illinois Steel Company needed was not more railroads but more ore lands, better manufacturing facilities. These acquisitions would bring about what he called "a rounded proposition," by which he meant a self-contained business owning its raw materials, controlling its transportation, with furnaces and mills to make finished as well as semifinished products, at prices which for one thing would put it in better shape to meet the formidable and threatening competition of the greatest iron master in the country, Andrew Carnegie.

Mr. Carnegie's first entrance into the iron and steel world was in 1864—the year before Captain Ward made the first steel rails in the United States. But it was with iron that Carnegie began. It took him eleven years to grasp the commercial possibilities of steel. Then (1875) so goes the story, he saw a Bessemer converter in blast and hastened forth to organize the company which built the Edgar Thomson Steel Works at Braddock, Pennsylvania.

Carnegie had the incredible good fortune to secure, as manager of this plant, Captain Billy Jones, whose success in doubling, redoubling and doubling again the output of steel amazed the steel manufacturers of the world and founded the Carnegie fortune.

After that, things went fast with Andrew Carnegie. One after another he bought in the plants, built in the Pittsburgh district to compete with his monopoly in steel rails—Homestead and Duquesne. He bought and leased ore lands in the Lake Superior region, built and bought railroads, and, in 1889, took Henry Frick into partnership, tying up with his enterprise the greatest coke-producing region in the country.

Carnegie wanted to control each essential factor in his producing problem, and by the time the Illinois Steel Company was organized in 1889 he had practically achieved his ambition. A few years later he was able to consolidate in one huge concern the various iron and steel undertakings which he had been fostering—the Carnegie Steel Company, superfluous partners and associations weeded out—his pet notion of a "close corporation" realized.

Andrew Carnegie was always a cruel competitor, feared as much for his ingenious devices in getting advantages on railways and in markets as for his conscienceless price-cutting and his irresponsibility in pooling arrangements, which were then almost universal in the iron and steel trade. "Artificial arrangements," he called the pools, "strengthening the other fellow," he once told his board, "as much as they strengthened you." This was "bad business."

The Illinois Steel Company had suffered from the Carnegie rivalry. The bigger the two grew, the more severe the competition had been. Judge Gary, as counsel of the company, believed that the concern's future depended first and chiefly upon its control of abundant supplies of iron ore which could be transported as cheaply as Carnegie was transporting from his vast Lake Superior ore interests. At that time the Illinois Company was buying from the Minnesota Iron Company—the second largest development in the northern ore country. Instead of simply buying another railroad, why not buy the Minnesota Iron Company, a coke supply, plants to round out their proposition and make themselves impregnable; and, this done, go systematically after foreign trade, establishing depots in various European countries. This was something that no American iron and steel maker had as yet accomplished satisfactorily, but which Judge Gary's recent European experience had convinced him to be practical. It was with this suggestion that he answered Mr. Thayer's letter asking his judgment as to the wisdom of buying the Elgin, Joliet and Eastern. Mr. Thayer's reply was a request that he come at once to New York to a meeting of the Board.

But would the Minnesota Iron Company sell? And could they finance any such combination as this would mean? The advantage of interlocking directorates came to the front at once. One of the directors of the Minnesota Iron Company, H. H. Porter, was a director of the Illinois Steel Company. Another, Robert Bacon, was a Morgan partner. Still another was H. H. Rogers of the Standard Oil Company. Another, Governor Flower of New York, was the head of the biggest brokerage firm in the country. These men, with others on the various directorates, were brought together by the Illinois Steel Company's board, and in very short order a decision was made to amalgamate the interests in one concern, if J. Pierpont Morgan could be persuaded to undertake the financing. Mr. Morgan seems to have been favorable to the idea from the start, and a committee was promptly appointed, consisting of Governor Flower of New York, Senator Spooner of Wisconsin, Robert Bacon of the Morgan firm and Judge Gary, with full power to amalgamate the companies and purchase other companies if it was deemed advisable.

And so the Judge found himself again—and this time in midsummer—with the prodigious task of appraising the interests involved, coming to an understanding with the parties most interested in each concern, adjusting one thing to another, and making a showing which would justify Mr. Morgan in financing the amalgamation. It is not too much to say that the work, legal and business, was done almost, if not quite, by Gary, for Senator Spooner was on a vacation, and Governor Flower turned up only once. Bacon was too busy at the Morgan Bank to take much part. For three months the man put in the closest kind of work, and out of it came a concern which it was decided to call the Federal Steel Company, into which went the plants that have been mentioned, as well as some others of lesser importance.

The new company was capitalized at $200,000,000, about one half of which was issued in preferred and common stock. The book value of the companies that had been combined was about $56,000,000, but this was much below their actual value—$31,000,000 below, it was finally decided, an amount which Judge Gary contended at the time was too low.

The experience of the next few months proved him right, for in October of 1899, when questioned by a Congressional Industrial Commission, he was able to tell them of how enormously the various properties of the Federal had increased over their book values in twelve months. For instance, there were 1,132 acres of Connellsville coal, put down in the book at $500 an acre, and now selling for $1,000 an acre. There was an iron mine in the Illinois Steel Company that had cost about $75,000 for which the concern had just been offered $600,000 in cash. There were eight hundred and fifty acres of land within the city limits of Chicago that had cost but a nominal sum and whose value now ran into the hundreds of thousands. There was one mine in the Minnesota Iron Company which had been put down on the books as containing about 25,000,000 tons of ore and which now showed at least 75,000,000 tons of ore in sight. And these were only a few of a number of similar enormous increases in the value of the property that the Federal had combined.

The new concern had to have more money to perfect its plan, for in the combination there was only about $10,000,000 in liquid assets. It required several interviews with Mr. Morgan to convince him that this was necessary. Why had they not the money, was his pertinent question. Finally, after much argument, he consented to raise $14,000,000 new capital. There was much curiosity at the time as to how much J. P. Morgan and Company had received for their services. The question was asked in 1899 by the examiners of the Industrial Commission. "About $200,000," Judge Gary told them, and out of this sum they had to pay all the expenses, including a corporation fee to the State of New York of some $40,000—"comparatively a small sum," the Judge commented.

By September the work of organizing the Federal Steel Company had been completed, after three months of as hard toil as Judge Gary, hard worker as he always was, had ever put in. It was the first time in his professional life, so far as I have been able to find, that his friends became anxious about him. H. H. Porter, kind man that he was, insisted on picking him up and taking him away from the desk for a rest from the work over which he hung night and day, trying to bring order out of the complicated problems that had been put up to him.

But the last thing was done and Judge Gary was preparing to go back to Chicago when he was asked to come to Mr. Morgan's office. Several men interested in the new organization were present. J. Pierpont Morgan was not a man to beat about the bush, and without preliminaries he said:

"Judge Gary, you have put this thing together in very good shape. We are all very well pleased. Now you must be president."

It was the first intimation that the Judge had had that such a thing was in the minds of his clients. He told Mr. Morgan he could not think of it.

"Why not?" the great banker boomed.

"Why, Mr. Morgan," Gary replied, "I have a law practice worth $75,000 a year and I cannot leave it."

"We'll take care of that," insisted Mr. Morgan. "We must make it worth your while."

"But I must think it over."

"No," insisted the great banker, "we want to know right now."

"But who are the directors to be?"

"You can select the directors, name the executive committee, choose your officers and fix your salary," Morgan replied.

"Quite characteristic of him," Judge Gary will tell you.

JUDGE GARY AT THE TIME HE BECAME PRESIDENT OF THE FEDERAL
STEEL COMPANY

Judge Gary begged for a week. They gave him twenty-four hours. And twenty-four hours later, largely through the persuasion of Marshall Field of Chicago, who had known him intimately for many years, he made a contract for three years' service, refusing the longer period which was urged. Through others he could hold his law practice for three years, he felt.

And so, in September, 1898, Judge Gary went back to Chicago to close up his business as a lawyer. There was regret and grumbling from clients who, like William Deering of the Deering Harvester Company, had long depended upon him. "I am very sorry to lose your services as attorney," Mr. Deering wrote Judge Gary. "I believe you have had the major part of our common law business from the time you first opened an office. I wish to express to you the sense of obligation and satisfaction with which I review our long connection."

If leaving his law practice was a hard wrench, leaving his home in Wheaton was still harder. The town with its activities was dear to him. There would be no more church suppers or Sunday-school picnics. There would be no more fishing and hunting excursions. There would be times when he would regret it. One of his former hunting mates tells of finding him on one of his visits to Wheaton, years after the change was made, with his old hunting coat, game bag and gun on his knee. "I will never use them again," he said sadly.

But he meant to keep a connection, realize an early dream! In his boyhood, an aunt who lived in Haverstraw, New York, had been an occasional visitor to the family, and she told the children wonderful things of the beauty of the Hudson river. Her nephew Elbert decided that, when he grew up, he was going to have a home on this wonderful river. Since he now must leave Wheaton he would have that home. He had "Gray Gables," Samuel Tilden's country home, in mind; and, as he also wanted a town house, he considered the Tilden house on Gramercy Park. His sophisticated associates and other friends were quick to dispel that dream. The people of the world into which he had come had town houses on Fifth Avenue and summer estates at Newport and on Long Island!

It was in October of 1898 that Judge Gary returned to New York to take up his duties as president of what was then the biggest steel concern, but one, in the United States. Over night he had become a public character. It was "President Gary" that the Chicago newspapers interviewed and whose movements they immediately began to follow by long telegraph stories. *The Iron Age* carried a biographical sketch, the appraisement of various legal fellows, and more or less restrained editorials on the new figure in steel.

In New York it was the same. He was a figure, the more watched because he was new and from another city, another profession; marked, too, because Morgan had chosen him and had put him at the head of the most impressive directorate that had ever been formed in an iron and steel venture—a directorate including some of the best-known and ablest business men in the United States: Marshall Field, D. O. Mills, H. H. Porter, Robert Bacon, Nathaniel Thayer, H. H. Rogers, Governor Flower. One name that might naturally be looked for on this board, that of the president of the Illinois Steel Company, John W. Gates, was missing. H. H. Porter had refused to go into any consolidation in which Gates had an official position, and Mr. Morgan bluntly announced that he would not approve of him in the directorate, because he did not think property was safe in his hands. But, if they thought they were eliminating John W. Gates from the steel business, they were wrong. They were to hear from him again and again. Mr. Morgan, in fact, was to pay dearly more than once for his refusal to deal with this frank and daring plunger.

Had Morgan made a mistake in putting a lawyer at the head of a combination which the whole industry regarded with more or less alarm because of its size, its compactness, and its avowed purpose of developing the foreign field? There were many who thought so. "What did a lawyer know about business?" business men asked. "What could Chicago teach New York?" New York lawyers asked.

When Judge Gary put Wheaton and Chicago behind him, he was doing what his father had done at twenty-eight; his great-great-great-great-grandfather at thirty-six; he was pioneering, taking on a new and uncertain adventure, for there was a possibility of failure, as well as success, in the field he was entering. The possibility was the greater because in this new field a code of ethics was in force which violated in many particulars the code which he had been taught in his youth, and which the experiences of life as a lawyer had convinced him to be the only sound and practical one in human affairs, whatever their nature. The real question at stake in 1898, when Elbert Gary left Chicago and the law for New York and Steel, was what was to become of his code.

CHAPTER V

THE BILLION-DOLLAR CORPORATION

IT was in October of 1898 that Judge Gary, having put Chicago and the law behind him, appeared in New York City as the president of the Federal Steel Company—the most highly capitalized concern the country had ever seen. The first question the leaders in the iron and steel trade wanted answered was, "What did this western lawyer know about business?" It behooved them to find out. Even Andrew Carnegie wanted to know what he had to expect in the way of competition or coöperation from the husky-looking young rival. It was he who took the first step towards friendly acquaintance by inviting Judge Gary with Henry Frick and H. H. Porter to lunch at his New York home. If Judge Gary is in a reminiscent mood when he tells you of this, his first meeting with Mr. Carnegie, he will probably drop in the remark that they had canvasback duck!

However, it was not to discuss canvasback duck that Andrew Carnegie had invited the gentlemen to lunch. He began his probing of Judge Gary's business ability and attitude by suggesting a pooling arrangement in rails with the Federal; the two concerns should not be cutting each other's throats, he said.

"I am willing, Mr. Carnegie," said Judge Gary, "*if we can do it on an equal basis.*" Carnegie threw up his hands. He had been so long the master in the steel and iron business that it was hard for him to consider that anybody could be on a par.

"You have had the major part in the business up to date," the Judge told him, "but I don't think you have it now. We have $100,000,000 in stock and we have $100,-000,000 that we can turn into cash; any contract that we make with you will have to be on a fifty-fifty basis."

The discussion which followed apparently convinced the great iron master that he had an equal in the trade at last, for he, along with his guests, signed then and there a paper which Judge Gary drew up. It provided, in substance, that they would recommend to the Federal and Carnegie steel companies that they divide the total standard rail tonnage which they were able to secure on a 50 per cent basis. The recommendation was adopted and the two companies lived up to it until events so changed the relationship that they no longer needed a pool.

One may fairly ask, Was this not an illegal arrangement? It was not so considered at the moment. The courts at this time had not finally pronounced on the legality of pools, and Judge Gary was basing his contention that they were necessary to life under existing competitive conditions on a written interpretation of the Sherman Act which had been given in 1891 by its author, Senator George F. Hoar, to an inquiry as to their status under that law.

The following quotations from that opinion, now nearly thirty-five years old, has a singularly contemporary ring:

It seems to me [wrote Senator Hoar] that a contract, although in partial restraint of trade, which is reasonable and reasonably limited in point of time, which has for its object merely the saving the parties from a destructive competition with each other, is not prohibited by the statute above referred to. . . .

No manufacture can be established in this country without the prospect of reasonable permanence. To engage in the manufacture contemplated by these parties requires an expensive plant, large outlay for machinery, material, and supplies, and the gathering together of a sufficient number of artisans skilled in this particular manufacture. It is for the interest of the public that such enterprises shall be undertaken. They will not be undertaken without a prospect of reasonable permanence in prices, and they will not be undertaken by new and small establishments in competition with old and powerful ones, if they are to be exposed to what is commonly called the cut-throat or "cutting under" process.

The opinion of courts, like the opinion of the rest of the community, may vary in different generations as to what is reasonable. But the question of reasonableness will be a question of law for the courts, to be determined upon all the facts and in the light of experience, the business habits, and the public opinion of the present time. . . .

I cannot see the distinction in principle between a contract of workingmen not to work for less than a stipulated sum as wages, and a contract of employers not to sell their product for less than a stipulated sum. Both these, being intended for their legitimate protection, and not accompanied with any stipulation for unlawful, oppressive or fraudulent methods, seem to me to be lawful within the policy of the law as it now exists, and not to be in restraint of trade, but in advancement thereof.

Andrew Carnegie had sounded out his big rival and had been able to make a coöperative arrangement with him, but that arrangement did not end his competitive problems. Indeed, his, as well as Judge Gary's, were enormously increased in the winter of 1898 and 1899 and the months following by a veritable avalanche of steel combinations. It might be said of the coming of all of these as Dan Reid said of the Tin Plate Trust in which he was so important a figure, when a witness in 1912 in the government's suit against the United States Steel Corporation: "It came like that!" (snapping his fingers).

The sudden appearance of the Tin Plate Company was due to the adroit work of the chief trust promoters of the period—the Moore Brothers. Judge Moore, the elder of these two men, was known as the founder of the Diamond Match Company, a concern launched in 1889—not alarming for its capitalization but very alarming from the proportion of the industry which it controlled—fully 85 per cent! From matches the Moores had gone into biscuits, forming the National Biscuit Company, and from there to iron and steel. It was not strange that, with their experience and the conditions in the tin plate industry, they should have been able quickly to emerge with practically all the mills in the country (265) in their combination.

But it was not Judge Moore's Tin Plate Company that worried the iron and steel trade as much as the one that followed immediately on its heels—the American Steel and Wire Company. It looks a little as if John W. Gates, being refused by J. Pierpont Morgan an official place in the Federal Steel Company, saw his chance to let them know he was still in their world, for in January he suddenly launched the American Steel and Wire Company of New Jersey.

It was not a difficult thing to do. He had in his hands the bargains and the plans of organization which Judge Gary had prepared in the fall and winter of 1897-98 for the combine which Mr. Morgan was looking on with favor but which blew up with the *Maine*. With this material, Gates quickly brought the trade together. All the $15,-

000,000 worth of common stock which, according to the original contract, was to be divided between the promoters of the undertaking—that is, between Gary, Gates and certain associates—probably went to Gates.

On top of Steel and Wire others came tumbling—the National Tube Company, the American Steel Hoop Company, the American Sheet Steel Company, the National Steel Company, the American Bridge Company.

It is not to be supposed that these consolidations which followed so rapidly were simply sudden runnings to cover of scared interests, or that they were forced by some superior sinister individual determined that a particular business should belong to him. For many years now, the almost daily changes in the making of steel and its products, the enormous amount of fresh capital incessantly in demand, the lawless methods of competition, the indifference to contracts, as well as a growing feeling that demand could only be met with economy and regularity by larger units, had grown almost unconsciously on men in the trade. They were yielding to forces greater than any man or group of men could cope with.

No better presentation of the metallurgical and financial reasons for these consolidations has ever been made, and none more authoritative, than that by Percival Roberts, Jr., on his examination in 1912 in the suit against the United States Steel Corporation. Mr. Roberts was one of the few men in the United States who at that time looked on steel making as an art. He had been trained in the Pencoyd Iron Works near Philadelphia, established by his father in 1852, and had learned there the importance of adapting iron and steel operations to every new invention—every changing process. He had risen to the presidency of the original company and by 1900 had become convinced that it was no longer possible for it to live as an independent unit.

Mr. Roberts based this judgment on the rapid and revolutionary changes which, in the preceding years, had been going on in metallurgical art. When his father had established his iron works in the fifties, a small plant could operate successfully, so simple was the process, and the country was dotted with them; but when men learned to make steel in commercial quantities, the little old wrought-iron plant became at once useless. It either had to make itself over or to go out of business. Making itself over was so elaborate and expensive a matter that obviously very few of the original furnaces and forges could be expected to develop into steel-making plants. Frequently, however, a group of these units combined their resources and equipped themselves for making steel; individually they were not large enough to operate, but combined they could do so.

Moreover, as Mr. Roberts explained, in the days of wrought iron one man had the ore, another the blast furnace and another produced puddled iron. There was no continuity of process practiced or required; but as soon as they began to make steel, a continuous operation was necessary. That is, from the time the ore was charged into the furnace until the finished product came out, the temperature of the metal was never allowed to drop to the cooling point. The success of the process depended upon its continuity, and as continual improvements were made in this process the advantage of larger and larger units became obvious.

Such changes were made in the Bessemer process as time went on that not infrequently an expensive plant became obsolete overnight. The steel maker who succeeded was the one who did not hesitate to destroy what he had just finished. If he did not do this he soon found himself out of the race. Then came the "Open Hearth" process, revolutionizing still further the industry. When electricity was adopted as a motive power in the steel plants, works had to be practically rebuilt, and this again meant more money.

It was a succession of changes and improvements, all calling for vast expenditure, and the only way the money for these expenditures could be obtained was by combining forces.

Another disadvantage under which independent units like the Pencoyd Iron Works labored was inability to control their supplies. A combination like the Federal owned its ore, its transportation—the smaller concern did not; and, because supplies were not always dependable, the individual unit frequently found itself unable to satisfy the most important factor in practically 90 per cent of all its contracts—the time of delivery. Failing to deliver on time, you stood little chance of a second contract from the party you had disappointed.

Still another handicap which embarrassed and sometimes ruined the independent concern was inability to secure sufficient working capital to finance the contracts which in these days were growing rapidly in size. One has but to trace the story of the use of iron and steel beams, girders, etc., in walls, bridges, structures of all kinds, to understand the seriousness of the position in which a small concern bidding for a contract frequently found itself. In 1890 only a few tons of iron and steel went into what was then a big building, a big bridge, but with every year the quantity increased. By 1900 it had grown to thousands of tons and by 1910 to tens of thousands. An independent steel plant usually depended on the plant which made its steel billets for financing, its paper being renewed every four months. The cost of all this financing was excessive, for sometimes the final settlement was not made until two or three years after the order was placed.

These difficulties increased. There was no way of escaping them except through the command of almost unlimited capital. The combination offered the capital, and there were very few men in any branch of the iron and steel industry in 1900 that hesitated at taking one or other of the alternatives—combine or sell.

But while the steel and iron manufacturers were more or less the puppets of things for which they were not responsible, the conduct of many under this pressure was like that of most human beings in such circumstances— fear, greed, speculation, irresponsibility, hope of a big advantage which would save them from future struggle and effort—all of these human propensities worked at their highest capacity, although with them worked also farsightedness and knowledge, courage and steadiness and a passion for the upbuilding of the country, often greater than desire for personal profit.

The public watched these hurried and, as they seemed then, ungovernable combinations with the suspicion and anxiety that ignorance of causes naturally produces. Their feelings were not shared by the combiners. With them all was confidence. Not for years had there been such profits in the industry. At the close of the Federal's first year of business, Judge Gary had been able to pay dividends on both preferred and common and to show a three-million-dollar surplus. In making his report his outlook for the future was most optimistic. Their books were overloaded with orders, he said. They had "nothing to sell."

This prosperity extended through all the trade. In February of 1900, the American Steel and Wire Company paid a 7 per cent dividend, and Mr. Carnegie was said to have made in 1899 at least $20,000,000 and to have declared that in 1900 he would make $40,000,000.

It was not combination that was doing this. Prosperity had returned after seven lean years. War—the Spanish-American War with its demands for wire and steel; the Boer War, turning English workmen to making cannon instead of plows, or drawing them out of the factories and putting them on the battlefield. America received orders from England and South Africa, as well as from disturbed European countries who fear, as always when war is on, that they may be drawn into the fracas.

Men who had been holding on in the past years of the steel industry, losing money yet expanding daringly with the changes of processes, felt that the doubling of prices which had come, the trebling of orders, was only what was due to them. One of the ablest and most experienced men in the business, Abram Hewitt, said at this time, when there was criticism of Mr. Carnegie's profits:

"From 1893 to 1899 there was no money in the steel business. Now we are back to a fair average price. At our works in Trenton we had a furnace lying idle for five years, with fifty thousand tons of pig iron stored near by. Our money was tied up in that ore. Then came the prosperous times, and we started the disused furnace and used up the ore. That's what we bought the ore for—to use it up at a profit. Why should there be any wonderment at Mr. Carnegie's profits at this time? The present prices for steel are nearer normal than any we have had for many years.''

But in spite of his prosperity Mr. Carnegie was restless. The changes that had come rushing into the business where he had been so long the most powerful figure seem to have increased rather than weakened a desire that he had been nourishing for some time, and that was to get out from under. He was a very rich man. When he died he wanted to leave behind him a reputation not of being the greatest iron master in America, but the greatest philanthropist. Three years before this, in 1897, he had tried to sell to Standard Oil interests, and failed. After the Federal Steel Company was organized he seemed to feel that here was a possible purchaser.

The first important overture was made in the spring of 1899, when Mr. Frick, Mr. Carnegie's chief partner, came to Judge Gary to discuss amalgamation, and the two went over the properties, putting a tentative value on them. This paper, with the values that Frick and Gary assigned in the spring of 1899, is still in existence. There was much discussion between the interested parties, but when it was finally discovered that Mr. Frick would not agree that the whole Carnegie organization, himself included, would remain with the Company and coöperate in carrying on business, the Federal negotiators dropped the proposition. They did not consider the Carnegie properties, they told Mr. Frick, anything like as valuable without as with the organization, nor would they agree to consider them without, and so for a time the matter was dropped.

In May of this same year (1899), the newspapers announced that Judge W. H. Moore, who had put together the Tin Plate Trust, was with Mr. Frick at the Holland

House and that they had an option on the Carnegie properties in their pockets. It was rumored that they were pushing a bigger combination than the world had yet heard of. John W. Gates who hovered around the negotiators talked about a billion-dollar combination. But nothing came of the Frick-Moore attempt; nothing save that the promoters forfeited to Mr. Carnegie the million dollars they had paid for the option.

Mr. Carnegie was not idle. If he could not sell, at least the new combinations should be made to feel his power. His letters of instruction to his buyers and associates in these years were full of virile competive counsel. For instance, this written to his board of managers just after the avalanche was loosened:

In the case of this Tin Plate Company as in the case of the American Wire Company, if our President steps forward at the right time and in the right way, informs these people that we do not propose to be injured, on the contrary, we expect to reap great gains from it; that we will observe an *"armed neutrality"* as long as it is made to our interest to do so, but that we require this arrangement—then specify what is advantageous for us, very advantageous, more advantageous than existed before the combination, and he will get it. If they decline to give us what we want, then there must be no bluff. We must accept the situation and prove that if it is fight they want, here we are "always ready." Here is a historic situation for the Managers to study—Richelieu's advice: "First, all means to conciliate; failing that, all means to crush." Shakespeare has it: "First in your right hand carry gentle peace"; but after Peace is gone the worst policy in the world is "gentle war."

We should look with favor upon every combination of every kind upon the part of our competitors; the bigger they grow the more vulnerable they become. It is with firms as with nations; "Scattered possessions" are not in it with a solid, compact, concentrated force.

When the National Tube Company was announced he wrote:

"I note pipe combine, which I hope is to go through. We want to play independent producer there, but should keep the matter very quiet."

While Mr. Carnegie was threatening his competitors in this robust fashion, he was, and had been for some time, carrying on with his principal partner, Henry Frick, probably the most exciting fight of the business annals of the period, peppered as they are with bitter personal struggles between powerful and ambitious money-makers.

Mr. Frick had been associated with Mr. Carnegie for some eleven years. He had brought into the combination the splendid Frick Coke and Coal Companies of Westmoreland County, Pennsylvania—his own creation. He had brought tremendous business ability, but gradually that ability, his own ambitions, the differences of temperament in the two men, had created an intolerable tension. The fight developed in intensity and culminated early in 1900 by Frick's bringing a suit against his partner. Judge Gary has an interesting story to tell of an experience of his with Mr. Carnegie while this trouble was at boiling point.

It was in the spring of 1900. He was going west on a night train on which he found Mr. Carnegie, and the two men fell to talking. "I have something to show you," Mr. Carnegie said to the Judge. "Frick has filed an abusive bill against me, and here is the reply which I want you to read."

"I did so at once," Judge Gary says, "and found that Mr. Carnegie had excoriated Frick in violent language. 'I would not file that reply, Mr. Carnegie,' I said, 'it's too abusive.'

" 'Well,' he said, 'he deserves it. His lawyers have abused me in their bill.'

" 'This paper won't do you any good in court; it will hurt you. The judge will think less of you than if you used dignified language. Your lawyers will tell you just what I am telling you.' Mr. Carnegie was plainly disappointed, for he believed he had done a fine thing, but he agreed to show the paper to his counsel. It was never filed in that form."

The results of this quarrel were that Mr. Frick severed his partnership with Mr. Carnegie, and a new company was organized in the spring of 1900—the Carnegie Steel Company, and at the head of this company was put his favorite—Charles M. Schwab. He had grown up in the steel plants—a fine product of Mr. Carnegie's system of making a man, by a vigorous application of the doctrine of the survival of the fittest—a product who not only had proved himself a great steel maker but an extraordinarily likable human being.

The reorganization of the Carnegie interests in the spring of 1900 did not check Mr. Carnegie's desire to sell. One of Mr. Schwab's duties, indeed, seems to have been to continue to sound out possible buyers—preferably the Morgan interests. Soon after the new company was formed he appeared in the Federal office. "You ought to take over the Carnegie properties," he told the Judge, "ought to buy them." After considerable discussion Gary agreed to talk to Mr. Morgan.

The two men went over the proposition carefully, the Judge urging the purchase. He had a strong case, for the Federal Steel Company was not developing into the symmetrical business which both he and Mr. Morgan had in mind when it was formed. In the first place it had not

CHARLES M. SCHWAB IN 1901

H. C. FRICK

been able to get the money which was needed for new developments. Mr. Morgan had been exceedingly cautious in the matter. "Why do you not have money?" he would ask; and it took hard arguing to convince him. Not having money Judge Gary had been unable to carry out his original plan of establishing iron and steel depots in Europe—a plan which had attracted much attention when it was announced in 1898, had, as a matter of fact, thrown the German trade interests into an excitement which was reflected back here in our newspapers.

"Now, if we can buy the Carnegie Company, we will immediately have the capacity we need to develop a systematic foreign trade," Judge Gary argued. But Mr. Morgan could not see it. "I would not think of it," he finally replied, "I don't believe I could raise the money."

All through the summer of 1900 the discussion of the possible sale of the Carnegie interest to somebody went on. But Mr. Morgan was still obdurate. He was still obdurate in December of 1900, when invited to a dinner —famous in the history of steel and iron—given by Edward Simmons, a New York banker, and Charles Stuart Smith, a New York financier, to Mr. Schwab— ostensibly in recognition of courtesies shown to them by Mr. Schwab, on the occasion of a visit of Pittsburgh.

Mr. Morgan, as the most important person at the dinner, was placed beside Mr. Schwab, and it was noted that through the dinner the energetic young man talked busily to the great banker. When the hour for speeches came, Mr. Simmons stated that he would call upon only one person to talk—the guest of honor.

"Mr. Schwab started out," Judge J. H. Reed, Mr. Carnegie's chief counsel, who was present, told the examiners in 1913 in the suit against the Steel Corporation, "by saying that he could not talk about anything but steel. I remember that," Judge Reed said, "because he always starts every speech that way."

The only trustworthy report of what Mr. Schwab said on this important occasion is the one that he himself gave in his testimony in this same suit.

"What did you talk about?" the examiner asked, and Mr. Schwab replied, "I talked about the advantages that might be derived from doing a manufacturing business on a larger scale than had been attempted.

"Instead of having one mill make ten, twenty or fifty products," Mr. Schwab told Mr. Morgan, we may say, for it was to him in reality that he was speaking, "the greatest economy would result from having one mill make one product, and make that product continuously." He talked of metallurgical, mechanical, transportation economics that could be effected by large scale production, and a better location of markets. He talked of the possibilities of expanding the export business.

That which especially stirred Mr. Morgan's imagination in Mr. Schwab's talk, however, was what he said about steel cars, of which, curiously enough, the banker knew little or nothing. There were a few companies in the United States, Mr. Schwab said, who were engaged in the manufacture of bridges and other fabricated materials, who were attempting to manufacture steel cars, but they could never be successful. The successful way was for some one works to devote itself exclusively to their manufacture.

When the dinner was over, Mr. Morgan did not go away immediately as was his custom, but he took Mr. Schwab into a corner to talk matters over. A few days later he had another long interview with him, the upshot of which was that he asked Mr. Schwab if an option could be secured on the Carnegie properties. Mr. Carnegie refused a written option, but he penciled his price on a slip of paper and sent it to the banker. The price and terms on that memorandum were those afterwards accepted and carried out.

Why should Mr. Morgan, after two years of resistance to Mr. Carnegie's overtures, have changed his mind? Mr. Schwab's contagious eloquence, his prophetic picture of the future of steel and iron, are not a sufficient explanation. It was the water that had run under the bridge.

Mr. Morgan had already a highly successful steel corporation in hand and he had found for its head a man in whom he had a thorough and growing confidence, but he was realizing what that man had been telling him for months now, that the Federal Steel Company, profitable as it was, was not the rounded proposition which they both had had in mind at the start. If he controlled the Carnegie interests he might develop what the Federal had not had the capacity to do.

But even stronger, possibly, was Mr. Morgan's anxiety over what might happen in the industry if Mr. Carnegie, determined as he was to sell, should allow his great property to get into hands which he considered unsafe— John W. Gates' hands, for instance.

In his two years' experience with steel he had been reminded more than once that this powerful and daring individual had not been sobered by the great responsibility he had assumed in putting together the wire interests of the country. That he still loved speculation more than stability had been demonstrated in April of this very year when suddenly, at a moment of real pros-

perity in iron and steel, he had precipitated a panic which
an indignant press and industry declared was worse than
anything that had ever been done by Fish and Gould.
Mr. Morgan had seen his own steel and iron undertakings
for the moment seriously disturbed by Gates' wanton
performance. He must not be allowed to get a hand on
the Carnegie interests.

And then there were still at large the bitter antag-
onisms and trade hates born of the fierce competition
that Mr. Carnegie had waged in past years and which he
was still threatening.

Indeed in the two years since the advent of the pro-
cession of great iron and steel combinations, he had continually pushed his partners toward war. Only a few
months before the dinner at which Mr. Schwab so stirred
Mr. Morgan's imagination, Mr. Carnegie had written his
partners:

If I were czar (of the Carnegie Company), I would make
no dividends upon common stock, save all surplus, and spend it
for a hoop and cotton-tie mill, for wire and nail mills, for tube
mills, for lines of boats upon the Lakes for our manufactured
articles, and to bring back scrap, etc. . . .
Put your trust in the policy of attending to your own business in your own way and running your mills full, regardless
of prices and very little trust in the efficacy of artificial arrangements with your competitors, which have the serious result of
strengthening them if they strengthen you. Such is my advice.

The first step towards realizing this program had already been taken, 5,000 acres of land on the shore of
Lake Erie having been purchased as the site of what
was announced to be the greatest pipe and tube plant in
the world. No wonder Mr. Morgan, who was financing
the National Tube Company, was concerned, or that Mr.

Schwab, who was trying to sell him the Carnegie Company, took care that he should know of the kind of rival his own tube plant would soon face—unless he bought! Whichever way he looked Mr. Morgan saw his steel interests forced into disastrous trade wars.

Now, J. Pierpont Morgan had a sincere, if domineering, sense of responsibility towards doing his part to keep business steady, and there can be no doubt that in considering Mr. Carnegie's offer he was influenced by what might happen in the business if he did not see that the great Carnegie property was in hands that he regarded as safe.

All this was certainly in his mind when, one Sunday morning, some three weeks after the Simmons' dinner and after Mr. Carnegie's penciled offer had been put into his hand, he sent his partner, Robert Bacon, to the Plaza, where Judge Gary was then living to ask him if he thought there was anything practical, from a business standpoint, in buying out Carnegie.

"Can it be done?" the Judge asked.

"Yes," replied Mr. Bacon, "Schwab has brought a proposition from Carnegie, and Mr. Morgan wants to know your opinion."

"Bring the proposition to me," replied Gary, "and I will look it over."

He spent all that afternoon and until one o'clock the next morning blocking out a plan under which, in his judgment, the purchase would be justified; and the next morning, at the bank, laid it before Mr. Morgan.

"How shall we start?" the banker asked.

"With Federal Steel."

"Will they agree to it?"

"We can get them together and find out."

Porter, Rogers, Mills, Ream, Nathaniel Thayer were all in New York, and Judge Gary saw them that morning. Marshall Field was in Chicago and he talked with him on the telephone. Their general answer was, "Whatever you say goes."

It was late in the afternoon before the matter was settled, and, as he was leaving, Mr. Morgan said to Judge Gary:

"Now, there's one thing I want understood: *if I go into this you are to go with me, not only as my lawyer but as my friend—that is, you are to stand by me.*"

The plan which the Judge had laid before Mr. Morgan and which he was now directed to go ahead and carry out was, in principle, what he had had in mind when the Federal Steel Company was organized—a rounded-out proposition that would enable them to make, at the lowest cost, all the principal forms of finished steel for sale in all parts of the world. Judge Gary insisted at the time, and has repeatedly insisted at various governmental investigations and suits, as have others connected with the organization, notably Robert Bacon, that there was no thought in the minds of any one concerned in the proposed organization to secure a monopoly or to restrain trade. "Our intention and our effort," he has repeatedly said, "was to sustain trade and to foster competition."

The way he proposed to do this was to add to the Federal Steel Company not only the Carnegie, but a half dozen of the new combinations engaged in finishing products, such as the National Tube Company, Mr. Gates' American Steel and Wire Company, the Tin Plate, Steel Hoop, and Sheet Steel companies. This would give them, he believed, all that they needed. But would they go in?

For the next four weeks the Morgan offices were

the scene of as nearly exciting activities as was possible
in that dignified and controlled quarter. Judge Gary
set up his headquarters there, giving only his afternoons
to the running of the Federal. The Morgan lawyers and
partners were there, Mr. Carnegie's counsel, the officers
and directors of the various corporations which had
been approached—men came and went from morning
until night, and the newspapers were soon agog with
curiosity.

The public became anxious. Early in February it became necessary for Judge Gary—who "directed it all,"
as Robert Bacon, at that time the Morgan partner chiefly
interested in steel, said in the government suit in 1913—
it became necessary for Judge Gary to make to the public press some kind of an announcement as to what was
contemplated. Here is what he said:

Messrs. J. P. Morgan and Company are undoubtedly considering plans for the acquisition of the properties of some of the
largest iron and steel companies of this country.

Presumably they will not make or authorize any official statement until after the plans are perfected.

It is probable there will be such ownership or control as to
secure *perfect and permanent harmony* in the larger lines of this
industry.

It is not intended, however, to obtain control of any line of
business or to create any monopoly or trust, or in any way
antagonize any principle or *policy of the law*.

The method to be adopted in acquiring properties will not
permit any minority stock interest to interfere if such stockholder were so disposed, which is not probable, as his pecuniary
interest will influence him otherwise. He will be fully protected in any event.

The success of the enterprise will result in great benefit to the
investor in securities, the consumers, and the workingmen or

employees. Little, if any, new cash will be required, and therefore the present financial condition will not be disturbed.

This statement is made solely on my own responsibility.

About three weeks later, March 2, came the promised official statement. It was the famous circular of J. P. Morgan and Company, announcing the organization of the United States Steel Corporation, the formation of a syndicate of $200,000,000, of which they were to be the managers, which should exchange the preferred and common stock as well as the bonds of the new concern, for the stocks of the chosen companies. The terms of the transfer in each case were set down and all the provisions carefully detailed. The capital stock of the new company was announced as $850,000,000. An all-important point in this circular was the following paragraph:

The forms of the new Bonds and of the Indenture securing the same and of the certificates of the new Preferred and Common Shares, and the entire Plan of Organization and Management of the United States Steel Corporation, shall be determined by J. P. Morgan and Company.

In less than three weeks after this announcement, J. P. Morgan and Company sent out a second circular, announcing that the plan proposed in the first one had become operative by the acceptance on the part of the chosen companies of about 97 per cent on an average of both preferred and common stock.

While these negotiations were going on, the plans of the managers, large as they were, had grown larger. Judge Gary, particularly, was anxious about ores.

"We ought to have the Rockefeller ores."

"We have got all we can attend to," Morgan growled.

PERCIVAL ROBERTS, JR.

ROBERT BACON

Judge Gary told him what he thought.

"How are we going to get them," Mr. Morgan asked.

"You are to talk to Mr. Rockefeller."

"I would not think of it."

"Why?"

"I don't like him."

"Mr. Morgan," said the Judge, "when a business proposition of so great importance to the Steel Corporation is involved, would you let a personal prejudice interfere with its success?"

"I don't know," he replied.

The next morning, however, he came in excitedly, throwing up his arms in exultation and shouting to Judge Gary, "I have done it!"

"Done what?"

"I have seen Rockefeller."

"How did he treat you?"

"All right."

"Did you get the ore lands?"

"No. I just told him that we ought to have them, and asked him if he would not make a proposition. How much do you think we ought to pay?"

"I am not prepared to say. It would take me a week to figure out what I would consider a reasonable price."

"Well, tell me offhand what you think we ought to pay."

The Judge worked for half an hour, and finally announced, "there's an *outside* figure—so many millions."

"To my surprise," Judge Gary says in telling the story, "Mr. Frick brought in a figure from Mr. Rockefeller a few days later—$5,000,000 more than my outside figure. 'That is a prohibitive proposition,' I said.

" 'Judge Gary,' exclaimed Mr. Morgan, 'in a business

proposition as great as this would you let a matter of $5,000,000 stands in the way of success?'

" 'But I told you, Mr. Morgan, that mine was the outside.'

" 'Well, put it this way: Would you let these properties go?'

" 'No.'

" 'Well, write out an acceptance.' "

And so it happened that when on April 2 another circular came out, addressed to the stockholders, the Lake Superior Consolidated Ore Mines were included in the amalgamation, also the American Bridge Company. And here, again, there was no difficulty in making the exchange. There was one further important announcement in the second circular and that was that the capital stock which in March had been placed at $850,000,000 was raised to $1,100,000,000—Mr. Gates' "billion-dollar corporation" had been realized.

Three months after Mr. Morgan had looked at Mr. Carnegie's penciled price for his steel holdings, brought to him by Mr. Schwab, the steel combination was ready for business. How can so immediate a response from interests as powerful as those to which he had beckoned be explained?

There are several factors to the explanation. Most important, no doubt, was faith in Mr. Morgan's power to make money for everybody who joined—and that was what they wanted. The best of them believed not only in the man, but the process of integration. They believed it inevitable, beyond the power of men to resist.

There was, too, in the quick coming to call more or less fear of what might happen to them if they refused to listen. It was the general belief that Carnegie methods would prevail in the combination—it would be war for the outsider. Here briefly is the psychology of the rapid coalescence of iron and steel interests in 1901, under Pierpont Morgan's magic leadership.

In the course of the negotiations there had been, of course, some interesting incidents. One of the most entertaining—the most illustrative of the casual way in which a pivotal thing in a great enterprise may be treated by even a man like Pierpont Morgan—is an incident which Judge J. H. Reed, of Pittsburgh, then Mr. Carnegie's chief counsel, tells. It was some time after the negotiations with the various companies to be taken in were well under way that Mr. Morgan one day hurriedly summoned Judge Reed and one of his own lawyers. "Do you know what I have done?" he said. "I have sold myself short. I have agreed to take over, and I am taking over, the stock of all these companies, and I have not got a scratch of the pen from Mr. Carnegie which would hold him or his estate if he died."

They hurried up to Mr. Carnegie's house on the "L" and explained what they were after. "Of course Pierpont ought to have a letter," Mr. Carnegie said. (Judge Reed is very likely to remark that Mr. Morgan always winced when Carnegie called him "Pierpont.") "Of course he ought to have a letter." And summoning a stenographer he dictated a document satisfactory to the gentlemen, and, apparently, a great relief to Mr. Morgan when it was laid before him.

Altogether the most exciting episode in the negotiations—the only hitch that occasioned any trouble—came, as was to be expected, from the American Steel and Wire Company—or, more truthfully perhaps, from John W. Gates. Gates was determined, as was to be expected, to get a whacking price for his organization—a price that Mr. Morgan thought unreasonable. Unable to bring the wire men to his terms, he hurriedly summoned Judge Gary. "I'm through," Mr. Morgan told the Judge, "I cannot settle with them. I want you to take it up. They are all in the other room."

" 'Mr. Morgan sent me in to trade with you,' I said to them when I went in," Judge Gary says, in telling the story. " 'Luckily, I know the wire game as well as you do. You have been offered all your property is worth, and it is all you are going to get.' We wrangled for several hours, and gradually I was whittling away their points when, about four o'clock in the afternoon, Mr. Morgan— whose habit it was to go home at three—sent in word that he was going home. I sent word back, 'Don't go— wait another half hour.' At the end of the half hour, word came a second time that he was leaving for home. I sent back the same word. Along about five o'clock, when I found he was determined to leave, I went in. 'Mr. Morgan,' I said, 'I want you to come in and tell those men that the offer that you made will not be changed, that they can take it or leave it, but that, if they have not taken it in ten minutes, it will be withdrawn and the Steel Corporation will build its own wire plant.'

" 'All right,' Mr. Morgan said. In a moment he came in—big and fierce, his eyes like coals of fire. 'Gentlemen,' he said, pounding the desk, 'I am going to leave this build- ing in ten minutes. If by that time you have not accepted our offer, the matter will be closed. We will build our own wire plant.' And he turned and left the room.

"John W. Gates scratched the top of his head and turn- ing to Edenborn said, 'Well, William, I don't know whether the old man means that or not.'

" 'You can depend upon it he does,' I said.

" 'Then,' said Gates, 'I guess we will have to give up.'

"I sent for Mr. Morgan. 'The gentlemen have accepted your proposition,' I told him when he came in.

" 'Is that right?' Mr. Morgan snapped.

" 'Yes,' they all said.

"Never have I seen Mr. Morgan more elated. 'Now,' he said, 'let's go home.' We went up on the Elevated to Fiftieth Street, where his old electric car met him. He was like a boy going home from a football game."

When the bargains had all been made and the Corporation was ready to be launched, Mr. Morgan called in the big group of lawyers that had been concerned and said to them:

"Gentlemen, this is a very large undertaking. So far as the finances of the company are concerned, I have no reasonable doubt it will be successful. As to the legal features, I must rely upon the advice of lawyers, and I should like to inquire if it is the unanimous opinion that the organization is legal and not opposed to any of the existing laws."

With one exception, the lawyers expressed an opinion that the organization was legal and would be sustained by the courts in case of contest. Judge Gary was the exception:

"I believe, Mr. Morgan," he said, "that if there should be a direct attack by the Attorney-General against the new corporation at the beginning of its business career, the attack would probably be successful for the reason that so large a percentage of the iron and steel business is included in the new company; as the intentions of the organization have not been demonstrated, the Corporation is liable to be held to be a monopoly in opposition to the Sherman Law. But I also think that if the Corporation with its business is properly managed and it is allowed to continue in business until it has been proven that the intentions of the managers are good, that there is no disposition to exercise a monopoly or to restrain legitimate trade, that in that case, if there is a contest, the company will be held to be legal."

This little speech to Mr. Morgan is vastly more important than it may look to the general reader. It is the first announcement, so far as I know, of a classification of trusts which was to become famous in the next few years —good and bad trusts. It was also the first intimation that Judge Gary, president of the Federal Steel Company, who had been Mr. Morgan's confidential man in the preparing of the new organization, had ideas in his head about running such organizations which might not be in harmony with those of the body of his co-officials— possibly might not be in harmony with the ideas of Mr. Morgan himself, who had said to him, "You are not only to be my counsel, you are to be my friend in this enterprise."

But what it meant was all a matter of the future. The matter of the present was that on April 1, 1901, the organization was announced as beginning business and the announcement was met with such a cry of alarm as has never greeted any business enterprise in this country.

And it was not surprising. The "billion-dollar corporation" came on a country that, though it had learned to talk in millions, since the Civil War, had not yet become familiar with hundreds of millions, and could not say billions at all. It was a country that for twenty years had been seeing and feeling the abuses of monopoly. It could not believe that anything, so gigantic as this new concern seemed to be, could be handled without oppression. It was a country that for a dozen years now had been trying to learn how to control and regulate big aggregations and so far had failed. It feared size. That which to Mr. Morgan and Judge Gary and their associates seemed inevitable, reasonable, and capable of being handled for what they regarded as the general good, to the public was fearful, a sinister thing.

CHAPTER VI

WHO SHALL RULE?

BOLDNESS in assuming responsibility explains no little of the power J. Pierpont Morgan wielded in the financial world throughout his active life. What he undertook he directed. When he made up his mind in 1901 that the only method by which it was possible to create in this country a truly symmetrical steel business—big enough and rounded enough to lead the industry throughout the world—he neither concealed his purpose nor shirked the obligations of his sponsorship. The entire "Plan of Organization and Management" of the United States Steel Corporation was to be determined by J. Pierpont Morgan and Company, he announced.

Visualize, if you can, this United States Steel Corporation which on April 1, 1901, began business under Mr. Morgan's plan. At its head there was a board of twenty-four directors—picked by him. They came from banks—his own and his friend's, George F. Baker's—from the Law—the Stock Exchange—and from the boards of iron and steel companies which had been gathered into the Corporation. They included many a name famous in the business annals of the period—John D. Rockefeller, Henry Phipps, H. C. Frick, Marshall Field, Abram S. Hewitt, C. A. Griscom, W. E. Dodge, P. A. B. Widener.

The first task asked of the directors was to appoint

from their number executive and financial committees. Mr. Morgan had been so impressed by the success of the Standard Oil Company in handling its vast affairs through an executive committee which met regularly every day and which had, so to speak, the whole oil industry, not only of the United States but of the world, daily, even hourly, under its eye, he had decided that that was the way to run the Steel Corporation. Accordingly the by-laws drawn up by the board created such an executive committee, empowered to direct the Corporation. The chairman of this committee had all its powers when it was not in session, and the chairman whom Mr. Morgan chose for this powerful position was Judge Gary.

At the head of the finance committee was Mr. Morgan's favorite partner, Robert Bacon, a man beloved by everybody who knew him in the business world as well as in the world of diplomacy to which he was later transferred. Mr. Bacon was prepared for the position by his experience as one of the directors of the Federal Steel Company from its start, as well as the liaison officer between his chief and Judge Gary when the latter was directing the organization of the Steel Corporation. Thus Mr. Morgan had closest to him in his gigantic enterprise two men who had been associated in his steel ventures for more than two years—men whom he trusted and who trusted one another.

This arrangement gave Judge Gary a powerful backing as chairman of the committee which was to run the Corporation. Whether it was strong enough, however, remained to be seen, for this committee was no meek and truckling group. Six of its members, by order of the by-laws, were men who had had "personal experience in the conduct of one or the other branches of manufacture or mining or of transportation in which the company is interested''; and some of them at least had the practical man's doubt—if not contempt—of steel men trained in other schools—the law, for instance!

Most important officially among these practical men of the committee was Charles M. Schwab, former president of the Carnegie Steel Company—the man who had taken Mr. Morgan up into a high mountain at a famous dinner in the previous December and given him such a realistic view of the iron and steel world of the future that he had gone out and done what he had repeatedly refused to do in the preceding two years—bought out Mr. Carnegie!

Mr. Schwab had been made president of the Corporation. His function, according to the by-laws, was to carry out in the subsidiaries the directions of the executive committee.

But what was the aggregation which the board of directors and the committees and officers it had created were to run? It is more difficult to visualize. As a matter of fact, it was the greatest medley of properties and plants and of what was quite as important—though less obviously so to the country—of industrial experiences, traditions, methods, attitudes of mind, that had ever been brought together in any industrial undertaking. It was a corporation made up of corporations, each fully officered, nine of the eleven different companies in the combination being hardly out of their swaddling clothes, the oldest, the Federal Steel Company, less than three years old.

Into each of these several concerns had gone frequently scores of different plants; in the case of the Tin Plate Company it amounted to two hundred and sixty-five.

Certain of the combinations had been going through a consolidating process for a good many years. Thus, into the American Steel and Wire Company of New Jersey there had gone not only twenty-seven independent companies but the big Illinois aggregation which, as we have already seen, Judge Gary had put together in 1898 and which had in turn included the Consolidated Wire Company which he had formed in 1892.

If many of the plants combined were young, many were old. In the wire concern was the powerful Worcester Works, dating back to 1833. The nucleus of the Illinois Steel Company was a little iron works erected in Chicago in 1857—the plant where, in 1865, the first American steel rail was made. For miles along the banks of the rivers which unite at Pittsburgh to make the Ohio—the Youghiogheny, Allegheny, and Monongahela—were scattered great steel and iron mills, grown from little forges set up years and years before in the back yard of some enterprising blacksmith. Philadelphia was another such nucleus—plants born of "forges with engines, besides other Buildings and Erections" as the records of the day describe that into which the great-great-grandfather of Abraham Lincoln bought in 1722.

The United States Steel Corporation was a vast compilation—an encyclopedia, if you please, of industrial history.

But if the richest history in the industry went into the combination, so did the richest experience—experience in invention, in methods of manufacturing and marketing, experience in management, in handling labor, in meeting the demands of seemingly omnivorous consumers.

It was a great aggregation of trained men—men like Abram S. Hewitt, who had begun manufacturing spikes, bolts and rivets at Trenton, New Jersey, back in the 'forties and whose pamphlet on "Iron and Steel in the United States," presented at the Paris Exposition of 1867, is one of the industrial masterpieces of the time. Mr. Hewitt at Mr. Morgan's personal solicitation had gone on the board and later sold his works to the Corporation—the Nestor of the iron and steel family, they called him. There were men like Percival Roberts, Jr., trained in the Pencoyd Iron Works, established by his father in the 'fifties; men like Frank Baackes, whose father had helped start the first wire nail mill in the country—this was in Kentucky in the 'seventies; men like William Edenborn, who had learned wire-making in Germany, had built mills, joined each successive combination in the trade and had invented a succession of useful improvements in machinery and processes; men like F. C. Daniels, chief engineer of the American Steel and Wire Company—a man who when he died in 1913 had one hundred and fifty-one patents to his credit.

The aggregation was not richer in trained managers than in experienced workers. It took in the great body of Carnegie iron and steel workers who had begun their training under Captain Billy Jones and whose loyalty and enthusiasm over him no union had ever been able to shake. There were the skilled rollers of Vandergrift— the pupils of George McMurtry—owners of their own homes, members of their town council, wardens of their churches and members of their school board. And there were men who knew how to make tin plate, to draw wire, to turn out every variety of structural steel. One hundred and sixty-eight thousand of skilled and unskilled workers went into the United States Steel Corporation. The new combination was rich and strong, but it was

far from monopolizing the making of steel and its products—far from monopolizing all the talent and energy in
the business. Compare its production with that of its
competitors. Out of the 16,000,000 tons of pig iron made
in the United States in 1901, the Corporation produced
7,000,000. It made 8,500,000 tons of steel ingots to its
competitors' 4,500,000; 1,700,000 tons of rails to its competitors' 1,100,000; 6,000,000 kegs of nails to their 3,000,-
000; 62 per cent of structural shapes; 27 per cent of rods;
64 per cent of plates. Its proportion of the total rolled
products of the United States, amounting to some 13,000,-
000 tons, was 50.1 per cent—its competitors, 49.9 per
cent. That is, the popular notion that the United States
Steel Corporation at its formation was a practically complete monopoly is disproved by the figures.

And its competitors were not weak and cowardly, but
a hearty breed that alone could survive under the competition in which Mr. Carnegie rejoiced. Outside of the
aggregation, uninvited to join it—their overtures discouraged if made, as they were in some cases—there
existed such stalwart iron and steel concerns as Jones
and Laughlin of Pittsburgh, the Republic of Youngstown,
Ohio; the Lackawanna of Buffalo, the Cambria of Johns-
town, Pennsylvania; the Colorado of Pueblo, Colorado—
which, as I said above, turned out, with others, 49.9 per
cent of the rolled products of the United States.

What would happen to this 49.9 per cent was of course
an uncertainty, though there were multitudes of people
predicting that it would only be a matter of time when
they would fall into the maw of the young giant. It is
probable that not a few who had joined the aggregation
thought so too.

A more serious and puzzling question at the moment,

however, than what would happen to those outside was what would happen to those *inside*. These men who had combined were strong individuals: the plants they had created partook of their characteristics; no two of the plants were alike and none could be successful and happy unless its individualism was respected and a certain latitude in working out special problems and developing special talents was allowed.

How could the New York head know this, or realize its importance? I have heard more than one of the leaders of large and prosperous units, which went into the aggregation, tell of his sinking of heart when he considered that probably he must henceforth submit decisions to a distant and, to him, impersonal authority. It was impossible New York should understand, he said. Many a serious student looking on declared positively that no such aggregation could ever be united, that the most serious part of the problem would be welding the human elements.

It could not be welded, said the critics, and it could not be floated—it was bound to sink in its own water. You will find this prophesied in the writing of more than one of the ablest financial commentators of the time. How about this water? What is "water" in the financial vocabulary? Its supposed purpose is to increase capital quickly in order to cover expected larger earnings. It is a system of borrowing on the potentiality of a business. If we can get this money, the promoter tells the public, we can expand our business immediately, earning profits sufficient to make the stock or bonds you buy worth 100 or more per cent on a dollar and pay you dividends— turn the "water" to gold.

In 1901 the country had seen too much watering of

capital, done purely and simply for the purpose of specu-
lating with the stocks created, not to have a grave suspicion of the proposed financing of the United States
Steel Corporation. A capitalization of $1,100,000,000
and a bonded indebtedness over $300,000,000 were out-
rageously out of proportion to the real values—the tangible assets on which they were based—so said the public.

What were the "tangible assets" of the Steel Corporation in 1901? There has always been a contest on
that point. You still hear able and shrewd business men
declare heatedly that they were not a third of the billion-
dollar capitalization, and this was the opinion of more
than one student of finance at the time.

At various periods since the incorporation of the Steel
Corporation, government agencies have tried to estimate
the value of the tangible property in 1901. The Bureau
of Corporations in 1911 set it down as $682,053,385, but
in making this estimate it put in ores and coke and coal
fields at not far from the original cost. This left the
intangible assets of the Corporation at $721,328,839.
What were the "intangibles"?

In making its appraisements the Bureau of Corporations made no attempt to cover them. That is, it left out
the deciding factor in watered capital, and that is the
public demand for the production it is proposed to speed
up, the brains—business, financial and scientific—the experience in affairs and operations, the code of business
ethics, the definiteness and security of the conception of
the undertaking in the minds of those who are launching it.

A more important question about the Steel Corporation
in 1901 than the value of its tangible properties was the
purpose of its founders. Was it primarily to do busi-

ness? Or was it to unload on confiding investors great blocks of stock made up, as many critics contended, of pure water—not a pound of iron or steel in them? Was its purpose to build up a monopoly in iron and steel—stifling, one after another, the considerable number of good-sized competitors that were outside the combination? Or was it as Judge Gary, "speaking on my own responsibility," had declared when in his judgment the first rumors of the aggregation made some expression necessary: "It is not intended to obtain control of any line of business, or to create any monopoly or trust, or in any way antagonize any principle or policy of the law."

One cannot study the varying elements which Mr. Morgan had brought together in the board and in the committees which were to establish the purpose and the policies of the new concern without realizing that there was considerable ground for the suspicion of the public. There was a will both to speculation and to monopoly represented in the management. More than one of the gentlemen on that board had had the habit of joyfully participating in great stock market raids. As for monopoly, the concern which had created and operated the most nearly perfect monopoly we have seen in the United States—the Standard Oil Company—was represented by its strongest leaders, Messieurs John D. Rockefeller, senior and junior, and H. H. Rogers; and as for stifling competition, the greatest advocate of that robust policy which ever operated, the Carnegie Company, was represented by Schwab, Frick, and Gayley. The only one of the twenty-four gentlemen of the board of directors of the Steel Corporation, so far as I can find from a search of the public prints, who had openly and repeatedly declared that the purpose of the concern was in no way antagonistic to the public good was its chairman, Judge Gary. But Judge Gary, we must remember, was Mr. Morgan's chosen spokesman.

As we have seen above, the by-laws ordered the executive committee to run the Corporation, and the ranking officer of this committee—that is, the chief executive officer—was Judge Gary, while Mr. Schwab, president of the Corporation, was to see that the orders of the executive committee were carried out by the subsidiaries—an operating head, he might be called.

It was natural, I think, that Mr. Schwab from the first should have mistrusted the form of organization which Mr. Morgan had chosen. His experience had been confined to the Carnegie concern in which the president was an all-powerful figure. He believed that committee government was impracticable, said so—and acted so!

There were members of the executive committee who agreed with him, among them the majority of the practical men. Thus, at the very start of the attempt to bring unison into these hundreds of plants with their diversified experiences, prejudices, practices, talents, the governing body was divided on the essential point of, Who was to rule.

Mr. Schwab went confidently ahead, but it was not long before members of the committee became alarmed by the powers he had assumed. They considered themselves responsible, under the plan of organization, for the way the Corporation was run. That meant that Mr. Schwab must take orders from them, not give orders independently; and when on the first of July he brought in a plan of operation which practically eliminated, as far as he was concerned, the work of the executive committee, there was a very frank discussion. Judge Gary remarked that this seemed to him a very different plan from that Mr. Morgan had in mind, and in this Percival Roberts, Jr., backed him up. Mr. Roberts said he had been considerably troubled over the matter. The by-laws had made the committee responsible for duties which they were not performing. The question was, whether it was best to operate by a committee or directly by a chief executive officer as Mr. Schwab thought. If it was to be the latter, then the by-laws ought to be changed.

The discussion became so heated, veered so close to personalities, that Chairman Gary read them a lecture: It would be a bad thing, he said, for the committee to get into a discussion, such as they apparently were having, before the board of directors. They should avoid even the appearance of being personal in the conduct of affairs. There was trouble enough on hand (as indeed there was, as we shall see later, the day of the discussion being the day that the Amalgamated Association of Iron, Steel and Tin Workers precipitated the first strike with which the Corporation had to deal); they should take it to Mr. Morgan, he was responsible for the plan they were trying to execute, responsible for the concern. If the plan was to be changed it should be by his approval. The upshot of all this discussion was the proposal of a resolution which shows very well the state of affairs inside the Steel Corporation's governing body three months after it began to do business.

AND WHEREAS, The President has stated that in his judgment the business of the Company cannot be successfully conducted by complying with the requirements of the by-laws as above stated, and that therefore it is necessary for him to disregard the same, therefore

Resolved, That it is the sense of this Committee that unless the by-laws be amended by due and regular action as therein provided for, the President be and is hereby requested to furnish this Committee with full reports of the operations of the Company, and submit for their information and decision all matters requiring their supervision as set forth in the by-laws, or that a full statement of the differences of opinion now existing between the several members of the Executive Committee upon this subject be submitted to the Board of Directors for such action as they may deem advisable.

A dispute of this nature cannot be settled by resolution. It cannot be kept inside the disputing body, however desirable the good of an undertaking makes it. It is bound to spread, men are bound to take sides, and that is what now happened. The cleavage increased, imperiling what Judge Gary had from the start set forth as the most important business of the Corporation—set forth to Mr. Morgan before it went into action—and that was, demonstrating to the public that their intentions were good. If this was not done, he had warned Mr. Morgan, it was his judgment that the government would not allow so large an amalgamation to live.

From the very first, at meetings of the board of directors, of executive and financial committees, Judge Gary had seized opportunities to insist to his colleagues that this demonstration be their first thought. Now, how did he propose to demonstrate that their intentions were good? A tabulation of his points which, of course, came out gradually as events forced attention, shows them to be: by considering public opinion; by giving out frankly and honestly all the information asked, about the way the Corporation was conducting its business; by being particularly cordial to stockholders; by no longer damning the government any more than the public, but by trying to meet it half way, working with, not against; by instructing the operative body that all violations of the law, however advantageous and long continued, must be ended; by putting an end to the old methods of competition; by considering, not bludgeoning labor.

The lectures gradually took hold. Shortly there began to be heard inside business circles the term, "Gary policies," uttered often with something which bordered on a sneer. One director who dropped out of board meetings at the end of the first three months is said to have given as a reason that though he believed in Sunday school, he did not believe in turning a business into a Sunday school.

It was, of course, a novel, and to many of the gentlemen an amusing, if not irritating experience, to sit at a board where the chairman lectured them on primary ethics. What had ethics to do with business? It was obvious that, from the point of view of Judge Gary, they had everything to do with the future of the Steel Corporation. As a matter of fact, he was staking its life on whether or not it was possible to incorporate into its practices the teachings to which he was treating the gentlemen.

One of the first points on which Judge Gary came to a contest with his fellows was that of respect for public opinion. The classic attitude was the one so tersely expressed in Mr. Vanderbilt's famous alleged phrase, "The public be damned." It had been generally, and often advantageously, observed by those who were directing large affairs. Now, Judge Gary had very definite ideas about the value of public opinion. He did not believe that any human undertaking could establish itself on a

permanent basis without public confidence, and he realized that you could not long have public confidence unless
you took the pains to talk frankly to the public through
its established channels—the representatives of the press
who came knocking at your door, the representatives of
the government who called you before their investigating
committees. Your business was to satisfy the doubts and
enlighten the ignorance of the public. In the two years
and more that he had been at the head of the Federal
Steel Company, he had made that his practice. If one
will look through the press records of that time, the reports of the industrial investigation which went on in
1899, he will find frequent and apparently frank expressions of opinion by Judge Gary on all sorts of matters
concerning his own company, and steel and iron conditions in general. Indeed, in the investigation of 1899,
carried on by the Industrial Commission, he had emphasized in his examination his belief that the way to meet
the public criticism of large corporations was by full
publicity.

What he had said is worth paraphrasing:

The affairs of a great corporation should not be kept
secret.

The great benefit from such a Commission as this is
that it gives an opportunity to ascertain fully facts over
which the public mind is disturbed, to distribute information.

There are always two sides to great questions. Frequently it is the laboring man who is abused, frequently
the corporation, and frequently it is the public. Laws
governing corporations are sometimes too liberal, some-

times too harsh. What the public needs is knowledge of the facts.

People are not so dishonest that they will not do the fair thing if they have full information. People should be brought together. Laboring men and capital should be brought together. We should know all the facts, consider and decide these questions on evidence.

An example of his intention to hold to this policy came early in the life of the Corporation, when it began to be pointed out as an example of the extravagant management of the new concern, that Mr. Schwab was receiving a salary of $1,000,000. Mr. Schwab did not say no, and after two or three days Judge Gary took pains to tell the newspaper men that this was a mistake, that Mr. Schwab was receiving a salary of $100,000. The president of the Steel Corporation did not particularly enjoy this correction. He may have felt that the reputation of a million-dollar salary was not a bad thing in the gay, new world which he had entered on coming to New York. At any rate, if it was to be corrected, it was for him to do so. Now, the truth about the story, which was very widely spread, and which I have found people believing even to-day, seems to have been this:

When Mr. Carnegie reorganized the Carnegie Steel Company in 1900, eliminating Mr. Frick, he took pains to reward handsomely young President Schwab, who had been both loyal and useful to him in his long struggle with a partner who had become obnoxious, particularly in persuading the younger partners generally to do as he was doing. It was in harmony with his lifelong custom with favorites that Carnegie made a contract with Mr. Schwab to give him $5,000,000 for five years' work.

ANDREW CARNEGIE, THE "STEEL MASTER," ABOUT 1896

When the Carnegie Company went into the Steel Corporation, Mr. Schwab laid this contract before Judge Gary.

"What are you going to do about this, Judge?" he asked.

The answer was, "Nothing. Get rid of it—that is Mr. Carnegie's affair."

Mr. Carnegie did in some way take care of it, but the transaction crept out as a million-dollar salary paid by the Steel Corporation—a mistake that Judge Gary felt it was important for the reputation of the Corporation to correct at once. Perhaps the correction has never fully caught up with the rumor.

The question of publicity came up again in a new way at the end of 1901 when the first report was made to stockholders and aroused sharp discussion in the board.

It was an amazing report. The earnings in the nine months of operation had been nearly $85,000,000—after dividends were paid the Corporation had a surplus of nearly $44,000,000 on hand. It did not look like the immediate bankruptcy prophesied!

Moreover, the report drew a dazzling picture of the outlook for 1902—every facility would be taxed to supply the demand. Shipments of business actually booked were being called for faster than they could be supplied. Many products were sold nearly to the end of the year.

The most interesting point in this showing was that the profits had been made without an advance in price. The report emphasized this fact. Prices of iron and steel products could have been easily advanced, it claimed, so tremendous were the orders and so eager the consumers to have quick execution. There had been many offers of larger prices; but the Corporation had firmly held to the policy that existing ones were high enough to yield a fair return on capital and maintain the properties in satisfactory physical condition. In the long run everybody would be better served, not only the company and their consumers, but the general business of the country, if stability was maintained. It looked as if the Steel Corporation was beginning by an effort to flatten out the business cycle—prevent up and down peaks, if it could be done.

It was a fine report, so everybody agreed, but when, after its reading at the meeting of the board of directors, Judge Gary announced that he proposed at once to give it to the public, there was some demurring. Henry Rogers of the Standard Oil Company was a member of the board, and I have heard Judge Gary tell how, after the board had disbanded, he came into his private office. "Such a handsome figure of a man," the Judge is sure to say—and in that he certainly is right.

"Judge Gary," he said, "do you mean that you are going to give out that report to the newspapers?"

"I do," he replied.

"Now, Judge, I am an older man than you; I have been longer in business. Some day you will have a poor report, what will you do then?"

"Give it out, Mr. Rogers, give it out."

Mr. Rogers straightened himself up, looked the Judge in the eye, and shaking his finger at him said, "You won't do it." But that, of course, remained to be seen.

Several of the members of the board of directors were outraged because they had not had a chance at the report before it was given to the public. That was the practice in more than one corporation with which they were connected, and this inside or advance information was useful to them in buying or selling on the stock market. Some of them had added handsome slices to their fortunes by this kind of maneuvering. Now, Judge Gary had rigid ideas on the matter. His Methodist training, forbidding card playing and all forms of gambling, seems only to have been intensified by the observations and experience of his business life. Ever since he had come into the steel industry he had been associated with that Prince of Gamblers, John W. Gates, and here on the board of directors, although Gates was absent, there were several of his peers—H. H. Rogers, N. B. Ream, H. C. Frick, P. A. B. Widener. They loved gaming, for big or little stakes. So strong was this instinct in these gentlemen that it asserted itself even in the board room of the Corporation. A twenty-dollar gold piece was the reward for attending a directors' meeting. There were usually a few absentees, and to Judge Gary's amazement he found that those present claimed the fees of those who were not. At first they divided them pro rata. (The Judge confesses that though he did not like the practice he took his share at first, not wanting to make them feel that he thought himself better than the rest of them!) Finally, Mr. Rogers suggested that they match for them, and this was done for some time. Judge Gary finally came out resolutely with a declaration that the performance was not becoming to the members of a board of directors.

"I told them," he says, "that I was brought up not to believe in gambling and I thought the board of directors of the United States Steel Corporation should set a good example." They gave it up finally, but it took time. "I think H. H. Rogers was the only one who really listened to me and finally agreed to what I said. Frick finally came around to that point of view, but I don't think the rest ever did.''

It is easy to see that there was an element of the board of directors that considered their chairman a curiously pious fellow for such a position.

When it came to giving the board the Steel Corporation report before the stockholders and the public had it, Gary was obdurate. The Corporation, he told them flatly, was not to be managed for the stock market. To prevent this he had issued an order that the comptroller give the figures to nobody, not even to himself, until the day of the directors' meeting. They were not to be placed before the board until three o'clock—the time at which the market closed, and they were turned over to the public at the same time they were given to the directors. That is, he had devised a scheme by which a director had no better opportunity on the market than the public at large. The inveterate gamblers were at first very angry.

"As a matter of fact," insists Judge Gary, "I always thought this use of inside information by directors—very common at the time—was akin to robbery of their own stockholders, and I had no hesitation in making my disapproval of it so clear that everybody on the board would understand. They finally gave up trying to get information from me, though in one case one of our directors went to our treasurer or comptroller to get it. But I was able to stop that. It was wrong in principle and it set a bad example. How could we expect our officers and employees not to speculate if the members of the board did it?''

Another Gary policy that irritated particularly his fellow lawyers was his insistence that the stockholders who came to annual meetings, as they had the right to, should not only be allowed to speak, but should be invited to do so. An incident of the first meeting which found its way into the newspapers—largely because of its contrast with current practice—concerned the attempt of a visiting stockholder to speak to a motion. The man was on his feet when one of the lawyers present rose to a point of order.

"I cannot entertain it," the Judge said. There was an immediate protest from the legal representatives, but Judge Gary took occasion to read them one of his little lectures.

"This is our first meeting. We are establishing a precedent, and that precedent is that any stockholder who has anything to say shall be heard. I am not willing that this speaker be interrupted. Stockholders have a right to talk in a stockholders' meeting. We have announced that they shall be open and free, and I mean that they shall be."

One reason for his insistence at that moment probably was that stockholders' meetings had become a joke in New York. A current Wall Street story illustrates the attitude of corporation officers and lawyers toward them. P. A. B. Widener was presiding at a meeting—not of the Steel Corporation—when a stockholder rose to object to a resolution. "Hold on," called Widener, "we will pass the resolution, and then everybody that wants can talk."

"This," says the Judge, "was thought astute, a good joke, in the Street; but I did not consider it a joke at all."

It was natural of course that such encounters as this should have done not a little to intensify a feeling against Gary that had existed from the start in the legal profession of New York. It was inevitable that the distinuigished lawyers grouped around Mr. Morgan should have felt a certain jealousy of the place they saw Gary steadily winning with their patron. What was he but a western lawyer?—an interloper? And all this talk about right and fairness, what had it to do with the law? The law was a matter of intricate technicalities—a marvelous intellectual game. Why drag in moral homilies? That is, there was among the lawyers very much the same resentment of his disapproval of their practices as there was among certain of his business associates whose methods he had criticized.

Secretary Hoover, in a recent talk to the Associated Advertising Clubs of the World, told them that the milestone that marks the passage from a trade to a profession is the establishment of group ethics. He pointed out that in the law, medicine, engineering, it is not only training and skill which is required, it is the elevated code of relations with fellow men, the incorporation of responsibility to the community into the daily task, the insistence upon a high sense of service given, that marks their distinction. Twenty-five years ago Judge Gary was arousing both the irritation and the ridicule of powerful associates and running the risk of destroying his own opportunities in the business world by insisting that the first business of the Corporation of which he was chairman should be this establishment of "group ethics," of which Secretary Hoover talks.

But all of this seemed to intensify the division as to who was to rule. The handling of every matter which came before the executive committee was soon affected by what was rapidly becoming a political cleavage. The situation became so acute that Percival Roberts, Jr., who through all the difficulty had been insisting that the by-laws must be obeyed until they were officially changed, resigned. The newspapers of the day report him as saying that he had resigned "because he could not harmonize his views on the general policy of the Steel Corporation with those of Mr. Schwab." I have heard Mr. Roberts say in talking of these difficulties: "The crowd naturally had different ideas of running the Corporation. There was a banker's idea and a stockbroker's idea. There were able men at the head of the subsidiary companies, but they had different points of view. There were only a few that regarded it not as a combination but as a consolidation. Gary had to handle a basket of cats and dogs, and, if he had not been a man of infinite patience, the clash of these different points of view would have been too much for him, as it was for me."

It was rumored at one time in the newspapers that it was becoming too much for Judge Gary; that he was "to leave" or "be ousted." It was not known at the time, and is not generally known now, I think, that it did come to such a point in this first year's struggle over policies that he considered resigning. Judge Gary knew—nobody better—that in the final analysis the policies of the Corporation depended upon Mr. Morgan's support, and in these early months he came to feel that Mr. Morgan was not heartily supporting him, that he was leaning toward the Carnegie methods as represented by Mr. Schwab, president of the Corporation. It looked to him, too, as if the majority of the board was in favor of those policies. Now, it was but human that many of the men on the board of the Steel Corporation should have lined themselves up with the leader whom they believed the stronger—with Mr. Morgan. It was natural that some of the Morgan partners, under these circumstances, should have leaned in the same way, for at the start it was pretty generally believed by them that Mr. Schwab was Mr. Morgan's favorite. It was he who had said the word which had finally induced the banker to go into a combination to which he had been urged for two years without effect. It was Mr. Schwab who, in the first months of the Steel Corporation, occupied the center of the picture. A dashing figure he was, too, with his tradition of power and a million-dollar salary, his tremendous buoyant joy in his new position and what it was bringing him. It was Mr. Schwab's movements and words that were chronicled at this time, not Judge Gary's; and when, early in the first months of 1902, President Schwab took a vacation and it was cabled back to New York that he was breaking the bank at Monte Carlo, there was enormous public interest in his performance—though it was rumored that Mr. Morgan was disturbed, fearing the effect the publicity might have on steel stocks!

This could not go on, Judge Gary thought, and he finally went to the great banker.

"Mr. Morgan," he said, "I think that my day of usefulness in the Steel Corporation is over."

"Why? Why?" snapped Mr. Morgan. "What do you mean? You promised to stand by me, be my friend as well as my lawyer."

"Yes, I did, Mr. Morgan, but that implied that you would stand by me."

"And have I not done it?" Mr. Morgan asked. "I could not do a thing without you."

And then Judge Gary set down his notions. The directors had not caught his idea; he was meeting continual opposition. This was not a personal question. It was a matter of the life of the Corporation. If it was to live and succeed, it must be run in the way that he had laid down. He went over again his idea of playing fairly and frankly with the public, of considering in all dealings only the good of the Corporation and its stockholders, not the good of its directors and officers; of keeping firmly to the original purpose of acquiring nothing which was not essential in completing their rounded proposition. Mr. Morgan listened to the end.

"I didn't know that you felt this way, Judge Gary," he said. "Now, you remain where you are and, from this time on, when you want me to do anything or say anything, all you have to do is to tell me. You needn't explain. Just say, 'Do so and so,' and I will do it." And I have heard Judge Gary in telling this story comment, "And he never broke his promise."

The Judge went back to his work. It was not only Mr. Morgan that influenced him, but his sense of responsibility to the stockholders of the concern. He was thoroughly convinced that the United States Steel Corporation could not live except by bringing itself into accord with the policies that he had in mind. He must do his part toward preventing the loss to individuals and the demoralization of business which its failure would cause. He must have shrunk from the long process of education which he realized was essential to convert his associates and then to establish throughout the Corporation practices which would harmonize even partially with his notions.

If he could not get his ideas accepted by the men with whom he was in daily contact, there was little or no chance of bringing the vast and scattered groups which made up the subsidiaries to a different attitude toward business methods. If ever a man in our industrial life undertook a difficult task, it was Judge Gary, after withdrawing the suggestion that he had given Mr. Morgan that he was thinking of quitting.

The friction at the top must first be stopped. It came from rivalries between committees and heads of committees, between chairman and president. The minutes of the Corporation show plainly enough, it seems to me, the sincerity of the attempt that Judge Gary now made to help reorganize and readjust the management, for he was chairman of a special committee which greatly curtailed the importance of the executive committee of which he was chairman—as a matter of fact, put it on the road to extinction. This committee defined his own duties precisely as well as those of the president. Under the new arrangement it really became a matter of ability, character and attention to business which decided who was to rule.

The new plan went into effect at once, and a year later, in August of 1903, a second readjustment of the organization was made. This was done largely because Mr. Schwab resigned. He had been ill for many months. He also had become absorbed in affairs outside of the Corporation, like the United States Ship Building Trust. W. E. Corey, a Carnegie partner, took his place.

The executive committee now went out of existence, its functions having been largely assumed by the finance committee, of which by this time George W. Perkins was chairman. Judge Gary was now made chairman of the board of directors, a newly created position. As Mr. Perkins had been completely won over to the new chairman by the spirit of accommodation and disinterestedness which he had shown throughout the stormy times that they had been seeing, it looked as if there was a fair chance now of as much harmony at the top as is possible in human organizations. The prospect was the more hopeful by August of 1903 because, in the period which we have been following, the organization had weathered, among other things, a severe attack on the part of organized labor.

CHAPTER VII

LABOR

WHEN the United States Steel Corporation began, in 1901, to look over the companies which it was to control, at no point did it find greater contrasts in physical conditions, in practices, in attitudes of mind, in relationships, than in labor. If there were in its acquisition as unsanitary, disorderly, and utterly unfit mills and mines as ever existed, there were certainly some of the finest that the country had seen at that day; nothing better than the Worcester Wire Mills, nothing finer than the Pencoyd Iron Works or the McKeesport Tube.

If at many points there had been entire inattention to the living conditions of the workers, the Corporation had inherited the finest industrial town then existing in the country, one entirely owned and officered by workers, a town, curiously enough, little known—Vandergrift, forty miles northeast of Pittsburgh, built by George McMurtry in the 'nineties, as an adjunct to what was then probably one of the finest rolling mills in the world. If, in the majority of the plants, there was no attention paid to the health or the cultural advantages of the workers, this was not universal. Homestead had its imposing Carnegie Library, offering many opportunities for study beside books. The Illinois Steel Company had founded at its Joliet plant in 1889 what all contemporary students of conditions in industry declared to be a model institution. Any employee of the company was eligible to the Steel Works Club, as it was called. Its headquarters "The Athenæum," was leased by the men and contained a good gymnasium, a swimming pool, a library. The men ran classes, a savings bank, a mutual life insurance company, bought homes on the installment plan, and coöperated in the buying of flour, coal, potatoes and other necessaries.

The Steel Corporation not only started with this model club but with the man who had set it going, Walter Crane, who had gone from Joliet to the Carnegie Steel Company.

The temper and relations of workers and management were as varied as their conditions. There were plants like the Pencoyd where sons, fathers and grandfathers had worked and always in peace—self-reliant, independent men, interested only in making steel. There was every variety of unionism, from the out-and-out idealist, unselfishly intent on improving his group, to the out-and-out venal union politician, selfishly intent on keeping his group in turmoil. According to the best authority, the Amalgamated Association of Iron, Steel and Tin Workers, which led unionism in the industry in 1901, numbered only about 13,800 men out of about 434,000 iron, steel and tin workers in the country, 168,000 of whom were in the Corporation. Their hold in the plants of the Corporation which had been taken over was strongest in tin, practically the whole industry being then organized.

The most serious factor in this labor inheritance, however, was not numbers or conditions, it was an after-war state of mind in the Carnegie plants. The terrible Homestead strike of 1892 had left a suspicion and bitterness in the minds of men and management which made natural, free coöperation out of the question. There was a will to war on both sides. Management had been the victor, and as a body it was resolved that unionism never again should strike root in its plants. Mr. Carnegie had come to feel that one of the assets of his company was its nonunion basis. Mr. Frick, who had been at the active head of the Carnegie concerns at the time of the Homestead strike, and who had been shot and stabbed near to death by an anarchist sympathizer of the workers, was determinedly antiunion. The majority of the Carnegie executive officers and superintendents who now held important positions in the Corporation—Schwab, Gayley, Corey, were heartily with him. They had been leaders in the Homestead war.

While there still were hostile and aggressive groups among the men, probably two thirds of them were by temperament nonunion. Many of them were almost if not quite as suspicious of organized labor as of organized employers. They no more liked the idea that they could not get a job without joining a union than they did that they could not get it if they did join.

Now what was the Corporation to do with this labor situation? Was it possible to bring living conditions to the standard at Vandergrift, to build up institutions in which men could by coöperation provide for a rainy day, build homes, make sure of opportunities for recreation and self-improvement? Could they harmonize the divergent views of unionism so that one spirit would run through the body? That is, was it possible for the Corporation to have a labor policy, or should it be left to the subsidiaries, each to develop its own? The question was forced on the executive committee only three weeks after it came into existence by one of its most experienced members, William Edenborn, of the American Steel and Wire Company.

"The public ought to be informed at once," said Mr. Edenborn, "that the United States Steel Corporation is not an employer of labor; that each of its companies looks after labor in its own way—takes care of its troubles—settles its own strikes."

What did this mean? Chairman Gary and Percival Roberts, Jr., saw at once. It meant a degree of independence in the subsidiaries that might be fatal to the new undertaking, preventing the growth of a common spirit and of uniform policies in other things beside labor. To perpetuate the motley collection of practices they had inherited—to continue the antagonism and contradictions meant disintegration, not integration. They must have a uniform labor policy, but that meant time—time to examine what they had, to sift, compare, decide, educate. This was no question to settle as one might the purchase of ore lands, the building of a new furnace. They must take time, and the upshot of Mr. Edenborn's remarks was a decision to keep hands off the labor situation at the different plants until the Corporation was fully established—"temporize for the next six months or year," the minutes put it.

But they were not to have time. The scales which the Union Mills of the Corporation had signed with the Amalgamated were soon to be reconsidered; it was rumored the Association proposed not to deal with the individual plants, but with the "trust." The Corporation might decide to keep its hands off, but it could not remain deaf and blind to the fact that there was increasing danger of a challenge. Rumors and reports reached it from the newspapers, from its visiting subsidiary presidents and executives. The question it had decided to dismiss was soon—so the minutes show—receiving more consideration than any other. It was not merely whether or no the Corporation, as such, was to have a labor policy or was to allow each subsidiary to develop its own, it was their attitude toward labor—was it to be militant or coöperative? The discussion developed wide divergence of view, as an early incident shows. Judge Gary had asked a member of the committee, of large experience in handling men, for his opinion.

"I have always had one rule," said this gentleman. "If a workman sticks up his head, hit it." It was the Carnegie rule, born of war. "So long as I am here," said Judge Gary, "no workman's head shall be hit! You can get another chairman, but I shall never recognize that policy."

As the days went on, the discussion continued and uneasiness grew. Judge Gary, particularly, did not like what he heard of the plans of the Amalgamated. One may fairly ask why, if Judge Gary was uneasy, he did not insist on his publicly expressed policy, quoted in the last chapter, "Laboring men and capital should be brought together and we should know all the facts, and on that evidence all of us will properly consider and decide these questions." It was a policy that, as things were in the organization, had not a shadow of chance. President Schwab was speaking for operation in all its phases at that moment. He had assumed the direction of the subsidiary presidents. The last thing Mr. Schwab, with his Carnegie traditions, would have countenanced in 1901 was a call upon the Amalgamated for a conference. Moreover, the minutes show that Mr. Schwab was from the start most optimistic—no reason for anxiety, he in-

sisted. He and Judge Gary made a hurried survey of
their kingdom in May, and Mr. Schwab came back to tell
the worrying members of the committee that nothing he
had seen gave any reason to believe that the Amalgamated would force their hand.

If the Amalgamated holds to its reported position, the
anxious objected, there will be a strike.

"Only a remote possibility," laughed Mr. Schwab.

"If you are wrong," warned Gary, "it may be a big
strike."

Out of their uncertainties and their divergence of view,
they were steadily forced by events to find points on
which they could agree. By the middle of June they
adopted a resolution declaring in substance:

1. We are unalterably opposed to any extension of union
labor.

2. When the question comes up, we advise subsidiary companies to say that they are not going to recognize any extension
of unionism in mills where it does not now exist.

3. Great care should be taken to prevent trouble.

4. Promptly report trouble and confer with the Corporation.

It was the resolution of a divided and irresolute set
of gentlemen who found themselves adopting policies
which they were not sure they wanted to adopt; and as
Mr. Roberts claimed, before it was necessary to take
any position, since they were still uncertain as to the
Amalgamated's action, Mr. Roberts was the more emphatic because he had been insisting that the policy in
regard to unionism should be uniform throughout the
Corporation, this being of course the logic of his contention that the undertaking was a consolidation, not a
combination. If it was a good thing, said he, everybody
should recognize it; if bad, nobody. The latter was the

view of the Carnegie group. It was for casting out the unions, root and branch.

Judge Gary took a middle ground: "We found them here," he said, "we have contracts with them, we should let things stand as they are."

Their uncertainty was soon removed, for on July 1 the president of the Amalgamated, T. J. Schaeffer, declared that unless all the mills of the Sheet Steel Company and the Steel and Hoop Company, both of which were partially unionized and were prepared to grant something— not everything, signed the scales, he would call out on strike not only these companies, but the Tin Plate Company, regardless of the fact that it had already signed. The threat brought matters to a head in the Corporation. The board of directors became active now.

"We believe," they resolved, "it would be a fatal mistake to accede to the demands of the Amalgamated Association. It would compel us to recognize union labor in all of our works."

But if the Corporation was not willing to extend the union, it was not obstinate about consulting with its officers who were threatening to strike. Committees were appointed and there was much running to and fro. Anxious outsiders—members of the newly organized Civic Federation—put in their oar. There were meetings at Mr. Morgan's office, out of which nothing in particular came, though the fact remained that the financial head of the new Corporation had been sufficiently open-minded to make at least a coöperative gesture. Nor was the Corporation unyielding in regard to acts in the subsidiary companies which seemed to it unfair, for when a non-union plant at Wellesville, Ohio, finding that a lodge of twelve men had been established in the plant, discharged the men, the executive committee, looking on this as an unnecessarily hostile maneuver, ordered the men reinstated.

When Mr. Schaeffer found the Corporation would not accede to his demands, he called the strike for July 15. Thus, just three and a half months after the great aggregation began business, that happened which the minutes of the executive committee show its chairman especially dreaded. "It was the worst time of the worst year to have any trouble," he had told the committee. He had counseled concession—temporizing—anything, even if humiliating to pride, to settle. But the strike was on in spite of his best efforts.

His chief anxiety now was lest the men in the Illinois Steel Company should go out. This company, it will be remembered, was part of the Federal Steel Company, of which he had been the president up to the time that it went into the United States Steel Corporation. The men there had formed a plant organization which had affiliated with the Amalgamated. Judge Gary had been proud of the friendly relations between the workers and the management in the company. He dreaded to see them disturbed. The men had signed the scales—would they follow Schaeffer's order to strike? He became so anxious about it that he went to Chicago to consult with the particular vice president of the Illinois Steel Company who had labor relations in charge, and who was known to be on good terms with the officers of the plant association. If the men had any legitimate grievance, he told him, anything which would incline them to follow Schaeffer's order, he wanted to know it; and, if possible, adjust it.

But the men had taken the matter into their own hands by this time, and in August issued a circular to the public, explaining their reasons for not obeying the order of the president of the Amalgamated to strike:

The principles of union labor are as dear to us as to any men in the country who earn their living by honest toil [they announced], but we do not think we should be expected to violate every rule of business integrity and personal honor for a matter of sentiment, for this is a time when we must not let our sympathy get away with our better judgment.

It was not many weeks before it became apparent that the strike was to be far less disastrous than Judge Gary had feared. As a matter of fact, the Amalgamated strike of 1901 was not popular in labor circles. Leaders like John Mitchell of the Mine Workers and Samuel Gompers of the American Federation of Labor had advised against it, and when Schaeffer ordered out men who had already signed scales and certain groups refused to break their contracts, the strike was lost, though it did drag on until September, when the Amalgamated gave up.

Mr. Schaeffer came down to New York and in Mr. Morgan's office he and the Association's Secretary, and Mr. Morgan, Judge Gary and Mr. Schwab signed a compact, which a report to the board declared "most satisfactory."

It was on the basis [said this report] that all mills which had been nonunion heretofore should continue as such, and that all mills in which we had made even a preliminary start since the Strike was declared should be continued as nonunion in the future. This was agreed to. We might have exacted harsher terms with reference to the number of nonunion mills, but it was not thought wise by your Management to take the position of openly oppressing organized labor. We established other principles which we considered of much more importance; for example: that the Amalgamated Association would not endeavor to organize men in our nonunion mills, that if such men were organized, they would refuse to receive them into their Association or give them charters; this they agreed to.

The explanation of the settlement given by the Amalgamated press was in a very different tone:

The causes that led up to this unsatisfactory settlement were the overwhelming odds that the association had to battle against —the daily press, public opinion, the advice of prominent labor leaders and the withdrawal of credit by merchants. The injunction issued by the Federal courts, the degeneracy of the ex-members who happen to hold managing positions in the tin plate mills becoming strikebreakers and teachers of strikebreakers, going among their former associates in unionism, tempting and seducing them from the standard of unionism by bribery and promises of prominent and steady employment, the unlimited use of money by the United States Steel Corporation, and its evident willingness to spend millions to teach green labor to become experienced and skilled, its power to use all of the aforesaid agencies shows that the Amalgamated Association was left almost entirely to its own resources to battle with the greatest combination of capital the world has ever known, while the trust with its immense money power to begin with was aided by every agency the public could furnish it with. Thus it became evident that it was suicidal for the association to keep up a contest that would result in greater losses each week that it was prolonged.

The statement does not mention the point which did more than anything to turn public and men against the Amalgamated—breaking their contracts. That bit of dishonesty gave the Corporation a powerful weapon for the future. "You can't trust the Amalgamated. It signs and repudiates."

The strike of 1901 forced the settlement of two important points: The first, that the Corporation was to have a labor policy; the second, that the first article of that policy is to be the open shop—no dealings with organized labor save where it was established when the Corporation was formed. That plank has never been changed from that day to this. As a matter of fact, to-day it is probably stronger than ever in the Corporation, though one element involved in organized labor, some better means of communication between management and men, is recognized to-day as one of its unsettled problems. But more of that later.

If it had not been for the struggle for authority going on in the Corporation between chairman and president as well as between executive and finance committee, the second plank in its labor policy might very well have been its first, and certainly would have followed close on the heels of the first. As it was, a keen rivalry arose between the contending factors for the honor of originating this plank whose acceptance was a foregone conclusion. Robert Bacon, in his testimony in the steel suit, says that "one of the first things" considered by the new company was "a plan of coöperation and participation in the benefits and profits of the company" by labor—Judge Gary had long been interested in such a scheme and had talked it to Mr. Morgan, who, Bacon claims in this testimony, had the solution of no question so near to heart as that of creating more satisfactory conditions of labor. "This interest," declared Mr. Bacon, "had been evidenced in hundreds of ways in dealing with the questions that came up between the different corporations in which he was interested"—which certainly was not the popular notion of the Morgan attitude.

Abram S. Hewitt, upon whom Mr. Morgan had long relied for advice and who at his earnest request had gone on the Corporation board, had no doubt strongly influenced Mr. Morgan in these matters. Mr. Hewitt was

one of the thoughtful students of industry who saw that
what was needed under the changing industrial conditions
was the development of points of mutual interest, practices that would overthrow in demonstration the prevailing notion that the interests of labor and capital were
inherently antagonistic and could only be settled by force.
Ten years before this, in 1890, Mr. Hewitt had laid down
his views; he had continued to talk them and undoubtedly Mr. Morgan had often heard them.

"Most of the writers of the day," said Mr. Hewitt,
"have failed to comprehend the significance of the great
movement which pervades all civilized people. It is
toward concentration of management, accompanied by
diffusion of ownership. This is the keynote to the mighty
wave of association which is passing over the world, and
is particularly felt in this country, where the opportunities for development are greater than anywhere else.
The harmony of capital and labor will be brought about
by joint ownership in the instruments of production, and
what are called 'trusts' merely afford the machinery by
which such ownership can be distributed among the
workmen."

That was the philosophy which Mr. Morgan and Judge
Gary had accepted and which they particularly were
anxious to see realized in the new venture, but which was
being delayed by internal politics and jealousies. The
idea was generally enough accepted, however, for Mr.
Schwab to tell Mr. Schaeffer when the settlement between
the Amalgamated and the Corporation was signed on
September 15, 1901, that profit sharing with all employees
was under consideration.

And so it was, but months went on and it made no headway. The delay was particularly exasperating to the

outspoken Percival Roberts, Jr., who finally in February insisted that there be some decision. He pointed out that in some of the companies profit sharing among officers existed and not in others; that there was complaint— rightfully; that if the inequality continued there would be serious trouble. And, to force immediate attention, Mr. Roberts introduced a resolution whereby all employees shared, and which made the Corporation and not the constituent companies the distributor.

The debate that followed shows better than any others recorded in the minutes how far personal differences had gone, as well as what inroads on the authority of the executive committee the finance committee had made, for it brought out the fact that Mr. Schwab had already started that committee at work on a profit-sharing plan. Mr. Roberts protested that was a violation of the by-laws—the executive committee was the originating committee—"the finance committee feared if the matter got in here," commented Mr. Schwab, "that there would be a row!"

The "row" was so imminent that Chairman Gary read the committee one of his little lectures. "None of us ought to forget," he told them, "that this United States Steel proposition is something that a few years ago no man would have had the audacity to conceive, it has so many ramifications. It is to be doubted whether under ordinary circumstances ordinary individuals could have succeeded as we have succeeded. It is not possible we should not have difficulties in this committee, that there should not be difficulties between this committee and members of the finance committee. You remember I suggested to you at the start the line between these two committees was not fixed, that would have to be found out. Like ourselves they have the best interests of the United States Steel Corporation at heart. It is only a question of what is the right and proper thing under all circumstances. Let us get together, talk it over and come to some mutual understanding.''

The matter dragged until the summer of 1902, when George Perkins, who by this time was beginning to realize that the patience and spirit of accommodation which Judge Gary had been showing through the multitude of trials was an asset which he had under-estimated, brought whatever had been gathered so far to him for consultation. The two men spent much time over the scheme. It is to Judge Gary that Mr. Perkins gives chief credit for the result in a most generous tribute he once paid his colleague:

''Judge Gary,'' said Mr. Perkins, ''has a positive passion for doing good things, big things behind the screen of somebody else's personality; and credit that belongs to him—tremendous credit—lands elsewhere. Over and over he has made me protest against his in-sistence that I or another should accept applause for accomplishment directly belonging to himself; for in-stance, in employees' pensions and profit sharing.''

It was on December 31, 1902, that the circular announc-ing the perfected plan was made public—a New Year's gift!

What the plan proposed was to make it possible for every wage and salary earner in the Corporation, from those with $800 or less a year to those with $20,000 or more, to invest in the 7 per cent cumulative preferred stock of the corporation. As the par value of that stock was $550,000,000 and the most conservative estimate of the tangible value of the properties—good will not considered—was around $680,000,000, it was a safe investment, even at par. The corporation offered the stock at $82.50. Its market value was from $86.50 to $89.75 in January, of 1903, the month that the employers were mulling over the proposition.

The amount of the stock the employees could buy was graded. It amounted to 20 per cent of his income if he was receiving $800 or less, 12 per cent if from $2,500 to $5,000, and 5 per cent if $20,000 or more. He paid for his stock in monthly installments, running over three years. He received his 7 per cent interest from the first payment and was charged 5 per cent on deferred payments. If he kept his stock, remained with the company and showed proper interest in its welfare, he was to receive a premium of $5.00 a year for five years.

The announcement of the scheme —the first any corporation had tried with all grades of workers—attracted naturally a great deal of attention, much of it surprised like that of the *New York World:*

It reveals Mr. Morgan as something besides the most successful organizer of trusts and mergers. Behind this comprehensive scheme, carefully worked out as it is in all its details, there is evidently a mind moved by humanitarian impulses.

Some of it begrudging, like that of the *New York Evening Post:*

The scheme seems well adapted to its declared aim of attaching to the company its officers and employees and will probably be accepted by most of them, since they risk very little by so doing. It does not bear the character of benevolence or philanthropy in any sense, and makes no pretensions of that sort. It can be judged only by its results from the business point of view.

What interested the authors of the undertaking much more than public opinion, however, was the response from the workers.

The method of presenting the offer was simple enough. A circular, stating clearly what was proposed, was sent to the superintendents of the various plants with an order to post it on the bulletin board. The reception that this circular met with in the various plants and from the different classes of employees is interesting. C. L. Close, the present head of the Safety and Sanitation Bureau of the Corporation was at that time an assistant superintendent in the plant at Greenville, Pennsylvania. He studied the scheme closely, and, making up his mind that it was an excellent thing for everybody, promptly subscribed for all that the class in which he stood allowed. Other men in responsible positions did the same, but not a single one of the six hundred laborers, so far as Mr. Close could discover, took a share. He was disturbed by this. "It is because they don't understand it," he told his chief. "They take stock in all sorts of questionable enterprises, diamond mines and oil wells. Now here is something solid—sure. It ought to be explained to them." His superintendent warned him that he should do nothing more than explain, not try to influence, so he went out among the men in the plant, explaining. The result was that about one hundred of the six hundred men subscribed according to their means. Mr. Close will tell you that it often happens to-day when, in the discharge of his duties as head of the Safety Bureau, he goes into a plant where there is still at work some one of this original group, that the man will come to him and thank him for the interest he took in explaining the scheme to him. Often he will say that the investment made it possible for him later to buy a home which he now owns outright.

In this first year 26,399 men subscribed for stock.

It is interesting to know that through all the ups and downs of the steel stock—and they have been many— some of these men still held on to their original invest- ment. In the South Works of the Illinois Steel Com- pany there are nine workers who still own twenty-four shares that they bought in that year. They form the majority of a group of twelve stockholders whose in- come from stock subscriptions in the last twenty-one years was recently reckoned. It is running ahead of my story, but it shows how this plan has worked out. These twelve men, all of them in manufacturing processes, have bought in twenty-one years, 172 shares of preferred stock for $16,274. They have had a gross return on this stock of $30,223.21. They have also bought 354 shares of common—common was first offered in 1908—at a cost of $30,266. They have had a gross return on this in sixteen years of $25,377.38. The market value of these stocks which cost them about $46,500, was, at the close of 1924, about $63,500.

That is the way it has worked out for those who held it. But back in 1903 it was anything but sure, and when in the fall of that year the long period of prosperity which the steel industry had enjoyed came to a sudden halt, when wages and the quarterly dividend on common were cut and steel preferred, bought at $82.50, fell to $49.00, it looked serious enough.

There was much bitter criticsm of the Steel Corpora- tion for having led workers into something unstable and speculative. "It has been a matter of much amaze- ment to practical men," said John Moody in his "The

EMPLOYEES OF THE STEEL CORPORATION WHO WERE STILL HOLDING IN JANUARY, 1924
THE FIRST STOCK IN THE COMPANY OFFERED TO THEM IN 1903

EMPLOYEES' HOSPITAL, BIRMINGHAM, ALABAMA

(See page 313)

Truth about the Trusts," published in 1904, "that such an irrational and ill-considered scheme should have been accorded serious thought for a moment. Instead of being a *profit*-sharing plan it has already turned out in the short space of one year a *loss*-sharing plan, and the frightened employees, instead of being won to friendliness by being made partners, are apparently feeling that they have been unfairly dealt with and that the managers of the Corporation actually intended to unload on them."

While there were employees no doubt who felt as badly as Mr. Moody, it is a fact that in 1904—the year in which the earnings of the Steel Corporation fell to the lowest point in its twenty-four years of history, its employees dropped from 168,000 to 147,000, its average wage from $716 to $677, and its common stock received no dividends—9,912 employees subscribed for stock. Six of these were workingmen in the group of the Illinois Steel Company whose adventure under the plan has been described. There is no doubt that thoughtful workingmen throughout the Corporation had their confidence materially strengthened at this juncture by the serious effort that was made to take care of subscribers who had lost their positions through the slump in business It was not to be held against them, so a circular they received announced, that they were not able now to meet their payments, and when the plants opened again, if they came back, they could take up their subscriptions where they left them. They were to have their bonus regularly, too. It looked like an effort to play fair.

Then they were impressed by the fact that the Corporation was passing its common stock dividend. "At least,'' they said to one another, ''they are not helping themselves out of earnings when dropping wages and closing plants.'' But the men could not know the battle that Judge Gary had had with Mr. Morgan in order to bring this about.

Mr. Morgan had been very proud of the showing made so far by the Corporation. He had perhaps said more than was wise about its earning power and its ability to stand shocks. At least, when Judge Gary came to him at the end of 1903 to say that he believed the dividend on the common stock should be entirely passed until business had righted itself, he was obstinate in his refusal to consent. ''My business,'' says Judge Gary in telling of the episode, ''was to look after the future. I did not think it was safe to pay dividends at that time, and I took great pains to tell him why. But he did not agree with me. One morning in the course of this discussion, we began to talk about eleven o'clock and went on until it was time for him to leave, between three and four. He had not given in. 'Come back in the morning,' he said. I went back and we talked very nearly all that day. At last I felt it was hopeless. 'Mr. Morgan,' I said, 'I am going to be very frank. If it had not been for you this Corporation could not have been formed. It was your name and influence which brought in the competing companies. No other man could have done it. If anything happens to it, you more than any other man will be held responsible. For two days you have been trying to convince me that we should continue to pay dividends on the common stock, but you have had no influence on my judgment. For two days I have been trying to convince you that no dividends should be paid, and I have not influenced your judgment. I am going to leave you.

You must decide the question. I think I can bring the board of directors to ratify whatever you decide.'

"He got up and, putting his arm around my shoulder, said, 'My dear boy, I would not do that for anything in the world, you shall have your way.' "

And the dividend was passed—passed not only that quarter, but for eight successive quarters. And the fact that it was passed had no little to do with the fact that through this hard period a considerable number of employees not only held on to the stock they had taken in 1903, but bought of the offerings made in the two hardest years the organization ever saw.

They seem to agree with a steel roller who came to a stockholders' meeting of the Corporation a few years ago and exercised his privilege of speaking. Among other things he told how he felt about the stock subscription plan:

"I am not compelled to buy it: we take it as we want it. I am still buying every year, and I have every share that I have bought. I find it is a good investment; in fact, you cannot get an investment anywhere where you can pay two or three dollars a month on a share of stock and have the interest coming in to you right along from the moment you start."

The appearance of steel workers at the annual stockholders' meeting is not infrequent and usually they speak —if not on their own initiative—at Judge Gary's invitation. It is an evidence of the realization of at least one of the objects of this stock scheme, that is, a point of mutual interest and natural contact has been found.

Moreover, from the start in 1903 there have been proofs that the ownership of even one share created in some men, if not all, a sense of properietorship and a consequent sense of responsibility about property. Stock-holders resent waste of materials and watch not only their fellows but their executives. From 1903 until to-day there has been increasing evidence of this. Superin-tendents, presidents of companies, Judge Gary himself frequently receive letters calling attention to waste, care-lessness, improper use of materials.

Here is a letter from Judge Gary's desk:

As a stockholding employee of the U. S. Steel Corporation I consider it my duty to call your attention to some things which I think the Board of Directors should be informed of.

For instance wagon loads of lumber and other material have been hauled away from the works in this city and used in the building extension and repair of residences in different parts of the city.

Not only have the materials of the corporation been used in this way, but the teams of the corporation have been used to haul the goods away and the skilled labor of the corporation has been used to work such material into the buildings, and laborers from the mills have been used to excavate for the foundations for new residences.

Also rules made for the safety of employees have been habitually ignored by foremen thus making the corporation liable for damages in case of accident caused by such neglect.

Also stockholding employees have been discriminated against being laid off in time of scarcity of work, thus making it necessary for them to withdraw their subscriptions while less competent men have been retained at higher wages.

If you think this matter worthy of investigation, I am pre-pared to furnish proof of the above statements.

Another reaction that from the start has been noted and which is often commented upon by executives in the various companies of the Corporation is the pride in the certificate. Men frequently carry them with them and when a superior officer appears take a chance to pull

out a bill case from their hip pockets and show the
amount of their possessions. It is not only proof of their
thrift to their superior, but it is putting themselves in
his class—a partner in the undertaking. It is a natural
human instinct, this pride in a stock certificate, and it
would be a poor enough man who did not feel it. As for
the dividends, regular and extra, I have heard a Corporation president state that he had men who were as
proud of them as any banker of his bank!

While the stock subscription scheme took a first step
toward that "joint ownership" which Abram Hewitt
regarded as the outcome of the "trust" system and as the
ultimate solution of labor difficulties, it did not meet the
problem of rewarding the extra services, the improvement in methods, the unusual contributions of various
kinds which came from executives and workers continually in all industries, and which the Carnegie Company had always recognized by liberal bonuses. Indeed,
Mr. Carnegie had always sought opportunities to reward
employees. He did not want men he could not afford to
enrich.

When he sold in 1901 he had seen to it that his partners
shared in his millions and he had also insisted that the
men he had made millionaires should join him in setting
aside 2 per cent of their sudden wealth with which to
recognize two hundred men who in various departments
of the work were known to have given unusual service.
The two hundred chosen received from $5,000 to $40,000
each in United States Steel Corporation gold bonds. One
of the $40,000 class was a puddler of unusual skill.

"Hold on to this," said a chief to one young man
selected to share in the bonus. "It is not $5,000, it is
the badge which shows that you belong to the inner

circle.'' He tells me he still holds the bond and those who know him tell me he still belongs to the inner circle!

Executives in subsidiaries where there was no such division of spoils, no bonus system or a niggardly one, now clamored to the Corporation for consideration. It was one point where they all wanted uniformity. The delay caused much trouble. Early in 1902, Mr. Buffington, president of the Illinois Steel Company, reported to the Corporation that he was losing technical men because they had no bonus, and W. P. Palmer, president of the American Steel and Wire Company, reported dissatisfaction among his executives because of what they claimed was unfair discrimination. The upshot was that there was attached to the stock subscription scheme a profit-sharing plan, based strictly on value of service. It was for those who did more than routine work. It is still in operation. The money for it is raised in this way: When the year's profits exceed $100,000,000, but do not exceed $150,000,000, 2 per cent of such profits is set aside; when the net profits exceed $150,000,000, but do not exceed $200,000,000, the amount set aside is $2\frac{1}{4}$ per cent; when such profits exceed $200,000,000, the amount set aside is $2\frac{1}{2}$ per cent. No amount is set aside in any year when the net profits for the preceding year do not exceed $100,000,000.

Judge Gary, in a recent report on this scheme, which is operating to-day in the way it was originally planned, said:

Only 4 or 5 per cent of all the employees profit by it. Sometimes the percentage is less. The number of men to whom additional compensation has been given has rarely gone above 10,000 during any one year. These men, however, are the persons who are building the success of their respective plants. The majority of them are in executive positions, some major, some minor. A plant manager, a superintendent, a foreman who, by virtue of observation, study and ingenuity, discovers and applies a labor-saving process, a new operation, a better way of doing things, of speeding up production, of improving quality, is the man who largely adds to the profits of the corporation; and it is only fair and just that he should share in them. There would be little justice and less purpose in rewarding his fellow worker who has done nothing but the expected routine of his job. Certainly there would be little incentive for greater endeavor.

It is not executives alone, however, who profit by this plan. Position has nothing to do with it. It is service that counts. Our experience has been that the men who have come to the top have been the recipients of additional compensation. I am not presenting this as an argument for the theory that less skilled labor cannot take so great a part in the partnership as those of larger responsibility, but it might well be considered in this light. There have, however, been numerous instances where workers in the shops have received large rewards in the share of the company's profits. Such a case was that of a colored worker in one of our mines. The cashier and he were entrusted with the carrying of the company's pay roll and cash to one of the coal districts. On the way, the wagon was attacked by highwaymen and the cashier shot dead. The money was being transferred when the colored man in question pulled out his gun, shot the first robber who was instantly killed; then shot the second, who later died of his wounds, and finally shot the third, who was afterward caught in a wounded condition, and was subsequently hanged. That colored man had more than saved the company's money. He had staked his life. Nobody could have blamed him for running in an effort to save himself. But he didn't. It may have been foolhardy, but it was splendid. To-day he carries an engraved gold watch, of which he is prouder than of his birthright. He carries other things besides. He knows that he will never want for anything.

It will be noticed that it is by this so-called profit sharing that the Corporation takes care of the inventions and labor-saving devices of employees. This was one of the problems that was put to them at the start for settlement, by Mr. Schwab. An assistant superintendent at Braddock had invented a skimmer for use in a blast furnace, which was so useful that thirty-eight furnaces had adopted it. He wanted $9,500 for it. The matter came to Mr. Schwab, as president, and as he had no authority to authorize so large a payment, he put it up to the committee. What did the Corporation intend to do in such cases? asked Mr. Schwab. Many large iron and steel companies, he explained, when an employee got out a patent, or new process, paid the expenses of the patent for the privilege of using it in their mills, the patentee having the right to sell to others. In the Carnegie Company they usually made the employee a present and took over the patent. That was done in this case—that is, the man who had made the invention got the $9,500 and the Corporation got the skimmer. The profit-sharing plan now adopted was utilized to take care of these expenditures.

What the above amounts to is that before the Corporation was two years old, it had arranged to handle very essential labor problems—but others dogged its steps.

A valuable by-product of the long discussion over the stock-subscription scheme was that from it the Corporation learned of various enterprises for improving labor conditions, which the companies they had united had initiated or had in mind, and that they clearly saw, before their second plank was disposed of, other steps they must take and which they were ready to take, if they could agree on a way which would not oblige them to give up their pet notions about organization, the relation of officers to committee—of companies to Corporation.

There was the matter of the proper care of the injured, their compensation, the relief of their families. There was provision for sickness and old age. The American Steel and Wire Company had an Accident and Pension Department devised by Mr. Edenborn, the funds provided entirely by the Company. They naturally heard more or less of that from him.

Mr. Carnegie, soon after he sold his company to the Corporation, had set aside $4,000,000 for helping injured employees and their families in the Carnegie Steel Companies. Were these undertakings to be made general? That is, should the Corporation have a uniform policy regarding accidents and the relief of those who suffered from them, directly or indirectly? Should it provide for the sick and old? Judge Gary was deeply interested in the problems involved from the start. They were ones to which, as a lawyer both for corporations and for workmen, he had been forced to give attention. It was certain that as soon as the opportunity came, if it ever did, safety and relief would find a firm and intelligent friend in him; but for the moment it must wait. Another of his favorite policies was fighting for its life.

CHAPTER VIII

ROOSEVELT AND GARY

A GARY policy to which at the start the directors of the Steel Corporation paid little attention, was the avowed intent to work with, rather than to flout, the government. Corporation leaders at the time almost universally regarded the criticisms of public men as demagoguery and the efforts at regulation as ignorant interference.

There is no question that there is always an element of demagoguery in agitation and an even larger element of ignorance in efforts at regulation—there was then; but coupled with these was an earnest effort on the part of a large number of honest men to correct certain long continued abuses of power and to strip off a number of slowly acquired and harmful privileges.

Before the end of the first year of the Corporation's life, Judge Gary's avowed open-mindedness in this matter was brought to a test. It came in a difficult moment for him—the height of the struggle which had developed inside the Corporation: Was the executive committee to run the Corporation as the by-laws provided, or President Schwab with a cabinet chosen by himself as he insisted was the only practical plan? In this clash of opinions, ambitions had developed. The finance committee used it to further its inclination to take the place or at least to influence the determination of the executive committee; the subsidiaries to keep themselves as independent as possible of the Corporation—a situation which, as we saw in the last chapter, had complicated and delayed the answer to the first challenge which organized labor flung at the new undertaking.

Into Judge Gary's effort to bring peace to his "bag of cats and dogs" as Percival Roberts, Jr., characterized the group of 1901, Theodore Roosevelt injected in November a new problem for corporations—one that almost without exception they loudly and vituperatively resented. Roosevelt had become President in the previous September by the death of President McKinley. He had taken the first opportunity to redeclare for an old policy of his: Such governmental supervision of corporations that the public could know the quality of their acts, whether or not they were within the law, whether or not existing laws were sufficient for their control. Up and down the financial district went the reporters, asking for opinions, and they came to Judge Gary.

He was cautious enough in what he had to say, though he did not hesitate to declare that there could be no objection to publicity concerning the business of corporations: moreover, that there could be no question but unrighteous acts should be prevented or punished. After all, as he said, he did not know what was really in the President's mind, and until he did he was not willing to comment too sweepingly.

It is doubtful, too, if Judge Gary then realized how big a house cleaning was needed in Big Business. I have heard him say that when he came to New York he honestly believed that the public complaint, so loud against certain corporations, was not justified. He did not believe that certain illegalities and immoralities with which they were charged could be practiced; it was only when confronted by actual proofs brought out in one way or another that he became convinced.

But the practices Roosevelt had in mind were all of them practices to which from the start of the Steel Corporation Judge Gary objected. There was the matter of railroad rebates. If one will look over the minutes of the early meetings of the executive committee of the Steel Corporation he will be not a little startled by the frank advice of certain members to encourage the railroads in putting up freight rates on iron and steel as high as possible, but at the same time to insist that offsetting advantages be given the Corporation. The little fellow was to have the high freight, the big one was to have his rebate. He will find, too, Judge Gary saying positively that they could not afford to ask a railroad, directly or indirectly, to discriminate in their favor.

Every month brought to his knowledge proofs of some practice or other in the great aggregation that seemed to him unsound and unethical, and very early he began his preachments that they must be stopped, because they were wrong. "If you are not willing to stop them because they are wrong," he told his associates, "stop them because they don't pay." And his experience was, so he confesses, that the argument that they did not pay received more respectful attention from many than that they were wrong. It led him finally to add a further clause: "Remember that they are not good because they pay, they pay because they are good."

Roosevelt's continued hammering on regulation, which had taken the form of a Bureau of Corporations, with power to investigate and supervise, was naturally often discussed by the members of the Steel Board. Judge Gary was veering more and more to it; indeed he was

To
Judge E. H. Gary
with the hearty regard of
Theodore Roosevelt
Dec 30th 1904

THEODORE ROOSEVELT

pretty well convinced that it was wise and necessary, when in December of 1902, he received an invitation from the President, whom he had never met, to come down to Washington to talk things over. It was the first of a series of interviews running through the seven years that Roosevelt was in the White House.

Roosevelt's attention had been called by his friend George W. Perkins to Judge Gary's temperate comments on his policies, so different from the contemptuous and violent disapproval coming from most corporate quarters. Mr. Perkins, as we have seen, had been completely won over to Gary by the summer of 1902. The man's spirit of accommodation in the internal difficulties of the Corporation, his willingness to sacrifice himself if necessary to bring order and peace into the management had inspired a confidence and admiration Perkins had not felt at the start, and he had praised him enthusiastically to the President.

Gary took an instant liking to Roosevelt and from the fact that he was so frequently invited we can believe that the liking was returned. As a matter of fact, the two men found at the start that they talked the same language. They had much in common—the same sturdy ancestry, the same severe and consistent home discipline, the same parental drive towards overcoming handicaps. They had responded in similar fashion. Young Roosevelt's heroic effort to develop a frail body was matched by young Gary's equally determined effort to force intellectual opportunity from a new and meagerly equipped community. Both had won in the personal struggle. Overcoming handicaps, however different, establishes a basis for human understanding.

Both these men believed in self-reliance, self-help, self-restraint. It had brought them where they were, they had equal contempt for indolence, trickery, complaining, cowardice in the affairs of life. They both put things hard up to the individual. If he would win he must fight: if he fought he had a good chance to win.

Their notions of the business of government in a democracy were similar. They were willing to trust anything to public opinion, but they believed in taking good care to inform it, give the full facts, not leave it with the half knowledge on which the demagogue thrives. Both believed profoundly in the Christian code—believed it applied in business and politics as well as in private affairs. Each was firmly convinced of his own righteous intent.

There was a wide difference in the manner of their handling of men, their attacks on problems. Roosevelt was brusque, impulsive, self-confident, aggressive. Gary was cautious, courteous, suave. He listened better, reflected longer, had more patience with those who disagreed with him. Also he understood better the motives of men.

It is not to be supposed that all the members of the Corporation's board looked with favor on their chairman's frequent visits to the White House. As a matter of fact, some of them were so bitter towards Roosevelt that they vehemently resented them. Mr. Morgan did not like them because he did not like Roosevelt, and he and the man he had chosen to direct the Steel Trust had many warm though friendly arguments over the President. It was quite natural Mr. Morgan should not have approved of Roosevelt. In 1902 he had been as much startled as he probably ever allowed himself to be by Roosevelt's sudden announcement that the government would bring suit against the Northern Securities Company which Morgan had recently financed.

There was an element of egotistical wantonness in the way Roosevelt handled that matter, which Mr. Morgan rightfully resented. He had "sprung it" on the country. That is, nobody except his Attorney-General, Philander Knox—not even the members of his Cabinet— knew what he proposed to do until the morning papers announced it. It was quite proper that Mr. Morgan should appear promptly at the White House, inquiring what the President expected to do about the other aggregations that he was backing, as Roosevelt relates rather gleefully in his autobiography.

When the suit was won by the government in 1904, and Mr. Morgan and his associates had to retire from the Northern Securities Company, there was immense anger against the administration and all its friends. It broke out at a meeting of the Steel Corporation Board— a member offering a resolution directing the chairman to make no more visits to the White House and to give out no interviews to the public which had not first been passed on by the finance committee.

Never in the tempestuous history of the organization had Gary been so aroused. He felt more strongly than ever that the only security for the Corporation lay in recognizing the government's right to investigate and supervise as well as summarily correct any practice to which it objected, whether in the judgment of the board that practice was justified or not. And all this he now said with a heat, a firmness and an authority quite unlike the conciliatory tone he generally took in conferences.

They listened to him. And when he stopped, H. H. Rogers—Rogers of the Standard Oil Company!—said:

"Gentlemen, Judge Gary has handled this Corporation very well to date. I believe that he should be his own judge as to what is wise and necessary in the present situation." The resolution was tabled. I have heard Judge Gary say that he thought this was the most important happening in the history of the Steel Corporation!

Their faith in their chairman was soon to receive a severe jolt, however, for in 1905, came a congressional order to investigate the Corporation. What was the use of a friend at the White House if he could not prevent or stop such an order? Roosevelt knew better than to try, even if he had wanted to do so, of which there is no evidence.

He and Judge Gary had already discussed the possibility of an investigation. He was enlarging at one of their interviews on the sins of Big Business with an emphasis which the Judge seemed to think was rather personal. He finally ended by saying, "If I don't do something I am afraid the mob will."

"I don't know, Mr. President," said the Judge, "whether you are trying to hit me over the shoulders of the companies of which you speak, but I make you this promise. If at any time you feel that the Steel Corporation should be investigated, you shall have an opportunity to examine the books and records of all our companies, and if you find anything in them that you think is wrong, we will convince you that we are right or we will correct the wrong."

"Well," replied Roosevelt, "that seems to me to be about the fair thing."

The Judge was to be taken at his word, for soon after the resolution referred to above was passed—in January of 1905—James R. Garfield, the commissioner in charge of the Bureau of Corporations, called on Judge Gary at his office in New York.

"The President tells me," he said, "that some months ago you said that, if at any time the administration felt that it should investigate the Steel Corporation, your books were open to us."

"Yes," said Judge Gary, "I did. And they are."

Of course there was much discussion. Just what did the government want to do? What did it propose to do with what it found? In order to have the understanding clear, Judge Gary went to Washington, for a conference with the President, Secretary of Commerce Metcalf, and Commissioner Garfield. The gentlemen concerned took care to have a memorandum of what was said prepared, signed and filed in the Department of Commerce and Labor. The position of Judge Gary is clearly stated here. He did not raise the question of the constitutionality of the law, he told the President. Moreover, he desired to coöperate with the government in every possible way that was consistent with the protection of the interests of his stockholders. The thing that he was concerned about was the disposition of detailed information that might be given out, the possibility of its misuse if it were left as a permanent record in the Bureau.

It was finally determined that all information requested would be furnished by the Corporation, the fullest opportunity would be given for examining the books and records, and that any questions which might arise as to the use, publication and disposition of the material which Judge Gary deemed confidential would be considered by him and Commissioner Garfield; and, in case of disagreement, it should be referred to the Secretary of Commerce, and, if necessary, to the President for a decision.

It is an interesting comment on government procedure that this pledge not to hand over material without notifying the Corporation was later disregarded, though not by Roosevelt or Garfield. It was not the publication of which Gary still complains, but the lack of faith. Probably that lack of faith was due to ignorance, ignorance of the existence of the letter, though at the moment the material was used there was a general feeling in the government that keeping faith with any corporation was dangerous business—and poor politics!

Judge Gary faced the proposed investigation with a good degree of confidence. Ever since the question of who was to rule had been practically settled in August, of 1903, he had been trying not only to familiarize himself with the multiform practices of the companies that had been brought together, and that he was trying to unify, but he had been instructing the heads of these companies as to what the Gary policies meant, and also as to his determination to have them carried out. Many of these gentlemen had no sympathy with him and no intention of changing their ways. Mr. Schwab himself testified frankly in the United States suit against the Steel Corporation to this:

"When I was president of the Steel Corporation," he said, "one of the things that I had to contend with was Judge Gary's opposition to these things that I had been so long accustomed to."

"How did you manage it?" the examiner asked.

"I did it without his knowing anything about it."

There were others doing things to which they had been "long accustomed," "without his knowing anything about it.'' It would be surprising if it did not still happen now and then!

The difficulties were of course enormous. Men trained in the industrial world of the last quarter of the nineteenth century, as these men had been, were not given to nice distinctions. They enjoyed outwitting a competitor by fair or foul means. Business was war, and all was fair in war. In the Carnegie concern they were absolutely frank about it. Indeed, frankness was the redeeming feature of Mr. Carnegie's competitive methods. Not many men so trained will obey unquestioningly what they consider milk and water methods or be persuaded easily by preachments which they have been taught have no part in business.

But Judge Gary has never been daunted by a first or a twentieth failure to get what he was after in the conduct of the Steel Corporation. He kept up his reforming even in 1904, the year of the greatest difficulties the Corporation had experienced—the lowest earnings, no common dividends, no hope of bonus—the time the executives naturally felt every advantage possible should be seized.

It was in 1904 that he set to work to break up the pools in which many of the subsidiaries were partners, and which they contended were necessary to business. An outside lawyer was sent out to examine the books of all the companies and to report any illegal or suspicious practice found. President Corey was directed at the same time to send a letter dictated by Gary to the presidents of the subsidiaries ordering them to clean out all combinations to which the investigating counsel objected.

When evidence began to come to his attention about this time that, in spite of past orders, rebates were being taken, he wrote the following letter which he directed

President Corey to sign and send to the presidents of some twenty-seven different railroads:

As you know, this Corporation long since adopted the unalterable policy of recommending to subsidiary companies in which it is interested that under no circumstances should rebates be solicited or received contrary to law. This policy will be strictly adhered to, and it is hoped and expected your subordinates will be advised and instructed accordingly.

If any one should at any time violate his instructions in this respect, notice of the same should be promptly given to the President of the subsidiary company interested and also to the undersigned.

There is, I think, ample documentary proof of varied character to show that Judge Gary in these early years of the Corporation was, in spite of lack of understanding and sympathy and even in spite of the willful violation of his orders, doing his utmost to clean his enormous and rambling house. He had more faith that the work was being efficiently done than later facts seem to justify. Nevertheless his ideas took hold—made converts. The converts grew as faith in the man's ability as a business leader grew. There are those in the Corporation to-day who will tell you quite definitely of the occasion when they first realized that what they heard talked of as "the Gary policies" were to be taken seriously. "I was at a meeting of executives at our plant," I heard a man of important position in the Corporation say once, "and one of the fellows was telling gleefully of how, through the oversight of a repair gang, he was getting city water which did not go through the meter. 'You correct that at once,' the superintendent said to him sternly, 'it is not right and you know it. We are not going any longer to have such practices in this plant.' " "And then," said the gentleman, "I realized that a new spirit was abroad."

George G. Crawford, president of the Tennessee Coal, Iron and Railroad Company says that his mind first awakened to a new régime at a meeting of executives in New York. "We were accustomed to boasting about advantages that we had obtained over our competitors at these gatherings, to enjoying one another's triumphs. Judge Gary, listening to us, said quizzically, 'I see that you gentlemen will take care of your competitors. I think I shall have to make it my business to take care of the public and the employees.' It was these little remarks of his that gradually brought me to a realization that Judge Gary intended to bring about a new order of things."

It was what he had tried to do to put the Corporation right in the eyes of the law that made Gary confident the investigation of the government would do the Corporation no harm. He may have felt, too, that it might force action where he could not without a fight, which would be perilous to the organization in its present condition.

Mr. Garfield's Bureau began its work in 1905. According to his testimony, given more than once on the stand, the agreement which Judge Gary had made with the government was carried out punctiliously—all the books of the Corporation were opened to Mr. Garfield and his associates. The information they asked for was given. This went on for three or four years, and from time to time Mr. Garfield made verbal reports to the President of his findings. Compared with what he was discovering in other corporations under investigation at that time, the Steel Corporation seems to have convinced him that its chairman's contention that it was a "good trust" was justified. Not only did he not find anything of importance to criticize in his three or four years' work, but he testified in the government suit that he did not find a single competitor of the Steel Corporation who complained of unfair competition—and he looked for them! President Roosevelt's testimony in the same suit corroborated Mr. Garfield.

In spite of prophecies, the investigation did not disturb the business of the Corporation. I have already referred to the hard sledding that it had had in 1903-1904, how its earnings fell off, how it passed its common dividend. In 1905, the year the investigation began, business began to pick up, though no dividends were paid; 1906 was a good year, the highest earnings the Corporation had ever had; 1907 opened finely—Judge Gary was feeling good. He had weathered serious storms, as we have seen, and began to feel that he was getting a grip on his complicated situation.

Others thought so, too, among them Mr. Morgan, who at a senatorial dinner which he had attended in January of 1907 heard such praise of Gary for backing the President in his efforts to control business that he came home to insist that the Judge at once take the chairmanship of the finance committee, replacing his partner, Mr. Perkins.

Then there was a letter which brought him no little satisfaction, from no less a person than Andrew Carnegie. Carnegie had not always been pleased with Gary's handling of the Corporation, but by 1906 he felt that the "policies" had won, and was just enough to tell him so.

Nov 28th 1906

TWO EAST NINETY-FIRST STREET
NEW YORK

My Dear Judge.

Thanks for kind note. Delighted always to see you, have always felt drawn to you, & from the first you won my confidence. The "boom" has placed the Steel Co. on solid ground. What a future is hers. If you continue at its head.

Shall be at home tomorrow afternoon. or Friday. glad to see you. My greetings to your dear wife. I read of your union with much pleasure. for without a good woman to

look after us judging from myself we are poor creatures.*

Sincerely yours

Andrew Carnegie

---

* Judge Gary's first wife, Julia E. Graves, of Aurora, Ill., died in June of 1902. In December of 1905, he married Emma Townsend, of New York City.

Thus things were improving on all sides, and promising well for the future, when the fear and resentment against Big Business which, as we have seen, Roosevelt had stirred up in 1901 and which had culminated in the Bureau of Corporations with the attendant investigations, was brought to the boiling point again by the suits which the government instituted in November, 1906, against the Tobacco Trust and the Standard Oil Company.

Business was the more agitated because it had been going through a period of reckless speculation which those on the inside knew very well was straining the credit of many big financial institutions. They wanted nothing so much as quiet until the strain was relieved, and quiet was the last thing that Theodore Roosevelt was disposed to give them. Indeed, it was the last thing which the public at large, which knew more or less of the manipulations, would have permitted. From all sides—the business world, the press, leaders of public opinion—there came such a berating of the President as a man has rarely had to endure. Many of the letters written at this time have been published by Mr. Bishop in his *Letters of Theodore Roosevelt,* but many more are to be found in the Roosevelt papers now in the manuscript department of the Congressional Library; and it is obvious from them that scores must have been destroyed. As a matter of fact, the virulence and the volume of the attack on President Roosevelt in 1907 can hardly be overestimated. I have been through the manuscript correspondence and have been amazed to find that the only man of importance in the business world who at that time wrote him even one friendly letter—at least which has been preserved—was Judge Gary. Here is the letter:

ELBERT H. GARY
71 BROADWAY
NEW YORK

March 15th, 1907.

MY DEAR MR. PRESIDENT:

It is doubtful if you have time to read the opinion of a mere constituent. However, thanks to your disposition, every one has a right to give expression.

Notwithstanding I hear from some of my acquaintances who are men of experience and great ability that the present agitation, investigations and prosecutions have a tendency to depress values and slacken prosperity, it is my opinion that sooner or later, probably sooner, the results will be beneficial. I think the attitude of the present administration, as frequently stated in your utterances, is exactly what this country needs. I do not intend to be a hypocrite. If any company in which I am interested is wrong, it must get right. All of us must be measured by the standard of right. The application of this principle, from which as President I think you have never deviated, is building for you a monument which will be permanent and will be the lasting pride of all your friends. It is embodied in the sentiment expressed by you: A square deal for all. I do not hesitate to say that your influence as President of this great republic has been of benefit to me personally and I feel equally certain that it is beginning to have a good effect upon others who have been reluctant to see their faults.

Sincerely yours,

E. H. GARY.

To His Excellency
    Theodore Roosevelt,
        White House, Washington, D. C.

In reply the President wrote: *

THE WHITE HOUSE
WASHINGTON

Personal

March 16, 1907.

My dear Judge Gary:

I wonder if you realize what a friendly and kind and, as I believe, wise, letter you have written.   It pleases me very much.   Let me see you whenever you come on here.

With great regard,

Sincerely yours,

Theodore Roosevelt

Hon. E. H. Gary,
    Empire Building,
        71 Broadway,
            New York.

---

* These letters are reproduced from the files of the Steel Corporation, though I found them both in the Roosevelt manuscripts in the Congressional Library, which collection I was permitted to examine through the courtesy of Mrs. Edith Kermit Roosevelt.

One sentence in Judge Gary's letter had an interesting origin. He was having many tilts with his associates over Roosevelt at the moment, and one day Frick, who as usual was berating the President, violently cried out, "What man has he ever helped?"

"Here is one," said Judge Gary. "He has helped me ever since the beginning of my acquaintanceship with him."

It was not only to his associates that Judge Gary openly defended the President. He took pains to do it freely in the press.

The soundness of his views as they were frequently expressed to newspaper representatives and in public talks was such that even the *New York World* codified them:

Public sentiment is the great rectifier of wrongs.

Being good after you have been driven to it does not breed much public confidence.

When men come to the conclusion that it pays in dollars and cents to be honest, then we shall have good corporation conditions.

It would be a good thing for the business interests of the country to divorce Wall Street.

A disposition on the part of men who occupy positions of responsibility and influence to improve their methods will put them above reproach and attack.

The attack on Roosevelt grew through 1907. It came from all sides: presidents of colleges, business men of all descriptions, the press. His letters in reply are remarkable reading. That he was a little worried there is no doubt—that is, for him; but on the whole the letters give evidence of a righteous enjoyment of the excitement. The uproar grew as it became more and more obvious that the business situation was in a terribly shaky condition. Roosevelt was entirely right when he said that it was not he that had carried on the speculation or strained credit on unsound securities, but it was he that had persistently called attention to the danger and the wrong of such practices, and possibly, as he admitted, hastened the time of an inevitable settlement.

The time came in the third week of October, in a panic of startling proportions. So serious were the failures of banks and trust companies not only in New York City but in other parts of the country that credit was practically suspended. As for borrowing money, it was not to be had. The rates quoted at one time on the New York Stock Exchange were as high as 75 to 100 per cent! In this extremity the whole business world turned for help and leadership to J. Pierpont Morgan.

He had had eight days of trial when on Friday morning, November 1, Lewis Cass Ledyard, a well-known lawyer, brought him a fresh disquieting story. The firm of Moore and Schley, one of the chief stockbrokers of the city, was bound to go into bankruptcy unless a substantial sum of money—several millions—could be found for it.

It needed no argument to convince Mr. Morgan that if Moore and Schley failed they would bring down a few more stories of the tottering financial pyramid. Mr. Ledyard had a suggestion. The brokers held a great quantity of Tennessee Coal, Iron and Railroad Company stock, which was pooled and therefore unsatisfactory as collateral. The only escape that Mr. Ledyard could see for saving the firm was for the United States Steel Corporation to buy the company outright. He believed that the members of the syndicate controlling it—all important men in the financial world—would sell to save the situation.

Mr. Morgan sent for Judge Gary, who came at once, and gave a prompt "No" to the proposition.

He was not answering without knowledge of the T. C. and I., as it was familiarly called. As a matter of fact, so picturesque and dramatic had been the history of that concern since its name first appeared that everybody in the iron and steel world knew more or less about it.

In the forty years since its organization it had had probably twenty different managers. Much money and much ability had been applied to its problems, but there had been also much reckless financing. The skyrocketing of T. C. and I. stock was notorious. Dividends had been paid at times out of borrowed money. Its annals tell of one president who was known to have kept checks on twenty-seven banks in the air at the same time. As for making money, old-timers tell you that the only department in the concern that ever ran at a profit was the company's stores! And yet nowhere in the world is there such an extraordinary juxtaposition of the raw materials needed for the making of steel as in northern Alabama, the home of the Tennessee Coal, Iron and Railroad Company. Vast quantities of ore lie in the mountains, part of it self-fluxing; that is, carrying lime; and side by side with it lie that which is needed for reducing the ore—coal, in as great quantities, and dolomite, if an extra flux is needed. It is the only place in the world, so far as I have ever heard, where a blast furnace has its raw material in its back yard.

These vast quantities of easily assembled essential materials had long led those who learned of them for the first time and knew nothing of the history of the territory to believe that it was one of those sure things which every steel man would jump at the opportunity of acquiring. But not only had this wealth of natural resources broken group after group of financiers who had undertaken to develop it, but it had been, as was the common saying in the industry, "a graveyard of metallurgical reputations," for the ore was of a low grade, containing an amount of phosphorus which so far had stood in the way of producing a first-class steel. Freight rates put the T. C. and I. at a disadvantage in the northern market —its natural market, the South, was still too prostrated from the war to take its products in quantity. Nevertheless, there was confidence among many steel men that if money in sufficient quantities could be found and if there was a willingness to trust to a long future, the T. C. and I. would finally become a paying enterprise. It was this faith that induced a new syndicate to take over the plant in 1906. It embraced several men of money, and if John W. Gates was one of them, there were others of more conservative methods. They had put a good and experienced man in the presidency, John A. Topping of the Republic Iron and Steel Company.

Eight million dollars had been set aside for the rehabilitation of the plant by this syndicate, and by the time of the panic it was practically all gone. There were some four million dollars of floating debt, one and a half millions of which were overdue; and an expert that had recently appraised the plant claimed twenty millions were needed to make it a paying proposition. And that amount the syndicate was not prepared to advance.

Now, Judge Gary knew all this. Again and again persons interested in the T. C. and I. had sounded out the Steel Corporation, telling an officer or a director, "You

ought to buy it," and always they had refused as they
had refused most of the other big independent plants in
the country. It was as hard for its competitors as for
the public, to believe at that time that the Steel Corporation meant what its chairman had repeatedly said:
"We are not attempting to build a monopoly, but to perfect a large-scale, rounded proposition."

During the panic Judge Gary had already had an experience with the T. C. and I., Moore and Schley having
come to him for a loan, and he had exchanged $1,200,000
of steel gold bonds for $2,000,000 of their stock. That
is, when Mr. Morgan summoned him on that dark Friday
of November 1, 1907, he knew the stock at that moment
was worth little in the market and that Moore and
Schley's trouble largely came from the fact that others
had done what he had done, only on a much larger scale,
that is, loaned the firm large quantities of salable securities for unsalable T. C. and I., and the time had come
when the loaners were anxious for their sound securities.
He knew what he was talking about when he said "No"
to the proposition to take over the company.

But Mr. Morgan and those with him pleaded the situation of the Street. Mr. Frick was called, but Mr. Frick
was equally positive against purchase—why not loan the
firm five million dollars? He would consent to that, but
the firm said that was not enough. The finance committee
was summoned, but was unconvinced.

The committee conferences continued on Saturday and
Sunday morning in Mr. Morgan's library, which by this
time had become Panic Headquarters. Those intent on
saving Moore and Schley urged Mr. Morgan to bring
more pressure to bear on Judge Gary and his associates.
"I have done what I can," he told them. "I have never

been more concerned over a situation than I am over this. I think this is the most serious thing we have had to meet in this panic yet, but I cannot urge upon the Steel Corporation to take this property. I hope they will do it, but I do not think I have the right to urge them or force it upon them if I could. They must deal with it as they see fit. I have gone with it as far as I can.''

The gravity of the situation finally overcame the opposition of Judge Gary and Mr. Frick. If the panic went much further it was bound to involve the Steel Corporation. Already it was causing them loss and uneasiness— some companies indeed were issuing scrip in payment of wages. So, finally at a meeting of the finance committee, held at nine o'clock Sunday evening, November 3, the purchase was decided upon—the whole subject matter being referred to the chairman with power.

''Before we go ahead with this,'' Judge Gary told Mr. Morgan, ''we must consult President Roosevelt.''

''But what has the President to do with it?'' demanded the banker.

''If we do this without consulting the administration,'' persisted Judge Gary, ''a bill in equity might stop the sale, and in that case more harm than good would be done. He cannot say that we may or may not purchase, but we ought to know his attitude since he has a general direction of the law department of the United States.''

''Can you go at once?'' asked Mr. Morgan.

Of course he could, and he and Mr. Frick were at the White House at eight o'clock the next morning. Roosevelt saw no one before ten, Mr. Loeb, his secretary, told them. ''But,'' persisted Judge Gary, ''this is a serious matter, and I think that if you will tell him just what Mr. Frick and I are here for, he will see us.''

At this moment Secretary Garfield came up and to him the two tormented gentlemen confided their errand. Roosevelt did leave his breakfast table to see them at once, and they soon had told him their story. Attorney-General Bonaparte being out of the city, the President sent for Mr. Root, then Secretary of State, and together they went over the matter. A good many questions were asked. Mr. Root was frank with the President: "You have no legal right to consent to this sale or purchase, but I should think it was a question of policy." And that is what it was to the President. He felt that he could not make any objection to the sale, and then and there dictated a letter to the Attorney-General, the substance of which Judge Gary a few minutes later telephoned to Mr. Morgan.

Judge Gary was not unaware that the purchase might make trouble for him in the future and he took pains to secure immediately from President Roosevelt and Secretary Root confirmation of what had happened in the interview. The correspondence shows how they looked at the sale in November, 1907.

UNITED STATES STEEL CORPORATION
NEW YORK

November 7th, 1907.

CHAIRMAN'S OFFICE
Personal

MY DEAR MR. SECRETARY:

At the recent interview at the White House between the President, yourself, Mr. Frick and myself, I stated, in substance, that our Corporation had the opportunity of acquiring more than one-half of the capital stock of the Tennessee Coal, Iron and Railroad Company at a price somewhat in excess of what we believed to be its real value; and that it has been represented that if the purchase should be made it would be of great benefit to financial conditions, and would probably save from failure an important business concern; that under the circumstances Mr. Frick and I had decided to favor the proposed purchase unless the President objected to same. I further stated that the total productive capacity of our Companies would not be materially increased by the ownership of the properties of the Tennessee Company, and, after the purchase, would probably not amount to more than sixty per cent of the total steel production in this country, which was about the percentage of our Companies at the time of the organization of the U. S. Steel Corporation; that our policy was opposed to securing a monopoly in our lines or even a material increase of our relative capacity.

I understood the President to say that while he would not and could not legally make any binding promise or agreement, he did not hesitate to say from all the circumstances as presented he certainly would not advise against the proposed purchase.

If consistent, will you kindly write me if the above statement is in accordance with your understanding and recollection.

Sincerely yours,

[Signed]   E. H. GARY.

Hon. Elihu Root
    Secretary of State
        Washington, D. C.

DEPARTMENT OF STATE
WASHINGTON

Nov. 11, 1907.

MY DEAR MR. GARY:

I have your letter of November 7th.

It fully agrees with my recollection of the interview to which you refer, in which you stated to the President the circumstances under which the United States Steel Corporation had been asked to relieve the financial situation by purchasing a majority of the stock of the Tennessee Coal, Iron and Railroad Company. I have sent a copy of your letter with this answer to the President with a recommendation that it be transmitted to the Department of Justice for filing there.

Very sincerely yours,

[Signed]   ELIHU ROOT.

E. H. Gary, Esquire,
    United States Steel Corporation,
        New York, N. Y.

THE WHITE HOUSE
WASHINGTON

Nov. 19, 1907.

MY DEAR MR. SECRETARY:

I am in receipt of your letter of the 11th instant and enclosures, and have forwarded them to the Attorney General to be placed on the files of the Department of Justice, together with a copy of this letter. Mr. Gary states the facts as I remember them.

Very truly yours,

[Signed]   THEODORE ROOSEVELT.

Hon. Elihu Root
    Secretary of State.

Mr. Root immediately sent a letter to Judge Gary, in which he said:

I enclose a copy of a letter which I have sent to the President, enclosing a copy of your letter of November 7th (second edition) and a copy of the President's answer.

You now have a complete copy of what you will be able to find upon the files of the Department of Justice, if any occasion arise.

There were to be several occasions arising in the future when Judge Gary must have congratulated himself on his foresight in securing this official record.

The purchase of the T. C. and I. did materially ease the situation in New York, but it did not end the panic. Confidence had been so shaken that money stayed in hiding and rumors of future disaster kept everybody suspicious and cautious. Those who knew business history since the Civil War warned that industry was now in for a period of depression similar to those after the panics of '73, of '79 and of '93, when failure followed failure, prices and wages fell to the bottom, and general demoralization prevailed.

These periods had not been all loss to the strong. Many of them indeed had been quite willing to let the bottom fall out, since much irritating competition went with it, and often, too, it gave them an opportunity to gather in useful properties. If Judge Gary had been disposed to monopoly he could have added much more to the Steel Corporation in November, 1907, than the 4 per cent investment he got in buying the T. C. and I.

But he made it clear at once that he had no such intention, although he acknowledged that the power was in his hands. In an interview given the *Chicago Tribune* about this time he said:

It is clear that the United States Steel Corporation, with its extensive resources, could use its giant strength, like other corporations, to crush competition. But in the end would the game be worth the candle? The Corporation would become an object of attack. In my judgment such a policy would be the undoing of our Corporation in which billions of dollars are invested.

Too many men have learned too late that the friendship of the public and the confidence of one's competitors are the most desirable elements in business.

What he did propose was very different, that the power of the Corporation should be used to prevent the demoralization in the iron and steel industry that had usually followed panics. In his judgment what was now needed was coöperation to prevent a further stampede. Iron and steel men ought to stand together, and to preach his doctrine, he gave a dinner, destined to become historic in industrial annals—the first of the famous "Gary Dinners"—gave it to his competitors!

Judge J. H. Reed of Pittsburgh, who was present, gave a lively report of what Judge Gary said to his guests at this and subsequent similar dinners, when he was a witness in the government suit against the Corporation. According to Judge Reed it simmered down to something like this:

"We must keep our heads, go slow, let jobbers work off their goods, let the country storekeepers get rid of their stocks, take what business naturally comes to us at decent prices; keep our men working. Let us not go out and raid the country, trying to get everything into our own mill, regardless of price. This will soon be over."

"He exhorted us like a Methodist preacher at a camp meeting," declared Judge Reed. That is, Judge Gary now extended to the trade at large those Methodist counsels and exhortations which up to this time he had directed to the board of the Steel Corporation! Particularly did he emphasize his conviction about prices—one that he had been fighting for in the Corporation from its beginning. "Prices should *always* be reasonable," he said. "The mere fact that the demand is greater than the supply does not justify an increase in price, nor does the fact that the demand is less than the supply justify lowering prices. What we want is stability—the avoidance of violent fluctuations!"

Judge Gary's thirty or so guests, almost to a man, had always held and practiced the exact opposite of this doctrine. It was a tribute to his theory as well as a remarkable proof of their confidence in him that they now rallied to his exhortations and agreed that they would follow his leadership in the troubled period which they saw before them.

Judge Reed, commenting on the result of the dinners, said, "I think it is fair to say that he saved thousands of men from bankruptcy in this country in the panic of 1907."

But that is a judgment pronounced long after the event —in 1913. In November, 1907, the results of both the T. C. and I. purchase and the attempt to rally his competitors to join the Steel Corporation in coöperative effort to hold their industry steady were uncertain. One sure thing was that both undertakings were suspected by a considerable group of the public and that if the attack on the Corporation which Judge Gary had realized from the beginning to be possible should crystallize under the anger the panic had stirred in the public against all business—Big Business particularly—his efforts at stabilization were sure to receive sharp and hostile attention.

CHAPTER IX

THE ATTACK

PANICS, like wars, have their aftermaths. Frequently they are longer, more difficult and quite as bitter in feeling as the catastrophies which gave them birth, and always they are anxious times for governments and the organized agencies which support them. The public holds these agencies responsible for its losses and disorders. If they are to continue to exist they must at least appear to be reconstructing affairs so that a like calamity can never again happen. These reconstruction periods are also open seasons for people who believe that the existing forms of government are inadequate. The disaster serves them finely as a demonstration of their theory and gives them the chance to exploit the particular substitute in which they believe. Every variety of reform, of panacea, of grievance gets a hearing in this unsettled period. In a general reconstruction the more complaints voiced, the better chance there is of some radical change, consequently those with grievances and those with remedies, however irreconcilable at bottom, flock together.

The aftermath of the panic of 1907 was no exception to the rule. Business was responsible for the shock and the suffering. Business must be reconstructed, and an attack on its structure, its practices and its leaders at once developed in the Congress of the United States. It was joined by every agency that was seeking a hearing —the unionist, the single taxer, the Socialist, the tariff reformer. They found an open forum in the popular magazine, at that date at the height of its power and its courage. It was inevitable that the Steel Corporation and its spokesman, Judge Gary, should share in the suspicion and criticism which thickened and spread with every week. The Judge, however, had something to do at this juncture besides considering the criticism crystallizing around him. He was the responsible head of the world's greatest industrial corporation. The panic had forced two new and serious practical problems upon that Corporation. The first was, What were they going to do with the Tennessee Coal, Iron and Railroad Company which, as we have seen, they had taken over the first week of November, 1907, after three days of active opposition on Judge Gary's part?

The purchase of the T. C. and I. threw a new burden of labor on men already heavily loaded with magnificent and costly plans for expansion. Two years before the panic, the Corporation had decided to establish a new iron and steel center. The spot chosen was a long stretch of sand dunes on Lake Michigan in northern Indiana, a point in direct water connection with the Wisconsin and Minnesota ore mines and admirably placed to feed economically the greedy market of the Middle West and Northwest. Here they were building what they were ambitious to make the finest industrial plant and town that the United States had ever seen. Judge Gary particularly was interested in the new undertaking. He had a personal pride in it, for it had been named in his honor.

Fifty million dollars had been put into Gary before the panic of 1907, and it was known that thirty millions more must be spent before the twenty-eight open-hearth furnaces building would be ready for operation. And here

in the middle of this gigantic enterprise was dropped the
T. C. and I.—a thing of splendid future potentialities
no doubt, but potentialities which could only be realized
by the expenditure of at least twenty-five million dollars,
so President Corey and his associates, who immediately
after the purchase went down to Birmingham to see what
they had, came back to tell the finance committee—a purchase which required also that they immediately find the
sum of three million dollars to meet the overdue bills of
the concern they had bought.

The first thing was a man. One who reviews the hectic
early history of the T. C. and I. cannot but feel that at
last Providence was interfering in its favor, for if ever
a man was found fit for a trying job it was the one that,
on Judge Gary's insistence, the Steel Corporation now
chose to direct its difficult purchase, George C. Crawford, at that time manager of the National Tube Company at McKeesport, Pennsylvania.

Mr. Crawford was a native of Georgia, a graduate of
its school of technology, and later a student at Tübingen,
Germany. He had begun his practical education in steel
at Birmingham, but had left after three months because
of the unsatisfactory conditions. From Birmingham he
went to Pittsburgh, entering the Carnegie Steel Company
in 1892 as a chemist. In the fifteen years since, he had
deliberately changed from one position to another that he
might have practical experience in the entire complicated
range of steel making.

Called to New York after the purchase of the T. C.
and I. and offered the position, he at first refused. He
held the Pittsburgh idea of Birmingham—that it was a
hopeless proposition—an idea which probably had always
had more or less of jealousy in it, for Pittsburgh had

no inexhaustible deposits of iron ore, coal, and lime in its back yard! Mr. Crawford more or less agreed with what Andrew Carnegie once told the Birmingham people at a great banquet they had given him in the hope of persuading him to come to their rescue: "Cotton used to be king," he said. "Steel is now king. You have here all of the elements—ore, coal, dolomite—but," and having raised their hopes, he dashed them—"but," he added, "you cannot make steel."

Now, Mr. Crawford sympathized with that point of view. Iron, yes—but steel was doubtful. The attempt to make it there had, he knew, ruined the metallurgical reputation of more than one man. He had no desire to go to Birmingham, but President Corey insisted. "We took this thing, not for the deposits, as Pittsburgh thinks," he said, "but solely because Mr. Morgan felt that we should. We were pushed to it by the condition of the country. The operating department feels like a man who, having had a millstone hung about his neck, has been thrown into a rushing current and told to swim upstream. But you are the man for this place." And Mr. Crawford took it, and what he did there belongs to a later period of this story.

But Judge Gary, as we have seen, had assumed another responsibility in the panic, and that was to keep the bottom from falling out of the industry. He had set out to rouse in the Steel Corporation and among his competitors a sense of their responsibility to keep their industry steady, to sacrifice their opportunity to grow through the misfortunes of the weaker as had been the practice of the strong in previous periods of distrust. At the first of the Gary dinners, given November 20, and at others which followed in 1908, he had urged upon his guests, who represented fully 90 per cent of the industry, that they coöperate in holding prices where they were.

"Violent fluctuations," he told his guests, "resulting in abnormal high prices when the demand exceeds the supply and in unreasonably low prices when the reverse is true, are to be deplored. A friendly exchange of views rather than unreasonable and destructive competition is what our trade needs at the moment.

"This very meeting proves," he went on, "that there can be active, sharp competition in business without unfriendly and bitter warfare that in the end will be injurious to the manufacturer, the consumer and to hundreds of thousands of employees, dependent as they are upon the success of the industry for work and fair wages."

Portions, at least, of the public could not and did not believe that the leaders of the steel and iron industry were getting together for anything but a sinister purpose. They were "fixing prices"—"destroying competition." Again and again Judge Gary denied and explained. Possibly as emphatic a statement as he ever made in regard to the Gary dinners and the meetings of the Iron and Steel Institute which grew out of them was in 1911 at the Stanley investigation:

There is just one question involved in those dinners, it seems to me [he said]; that is whether it is good law and good morals to endeavor by intercourse such as you see described in those proceedings to maintain to a reasonable extent the equilibrium of business, to prevent utter demoralization of business and destructive competition. Prices were not attempted to be fixed, were not fixed, could not be fixed, and there was no possible way of fixing them or maintaining them, unless you have some way of having them fixed under Government control, or you are allowed to do it by positive agreements. It never has been possible. It never could be possible. We have never succeeded in doing so. But we have, by this friendly intercourse, prevented demoralization—sudden, wild, extreme fluctuations—destructive competition that would drive large numbers of them entirely out of business, and that would be ruinous to the customers of the steel people who had large stocks of goods on hand from time to time, and which would spread to other lines of industry. We have made no secret about it, and the public has known exactly what we have done; and if the Department of Justice, for instance, or the President, or Congress, should say, "This is not the wise thing to do or the right thing to do," you may be certain it would not be continued for one moment.

As a matter of fact, Gary had taken the criticisms to Attorney-General Bonaparte at the start, asking an opinion on the legality of the movement that he was fostering.

Large corporations [he wrote Bonaparte in February, 1908] are confronted with two extreme opposite points of view. Public sentiment as well as the laws are opposed to combinations in restraint of trade which I suppose would include positive agreements between large interests to maintain prices, restrict output, divide territory, etc., etc., in accordance with the practice of other countries. On the other hand, public sentiment is bitterly opposed to such competition as will result in the destruction of the business of competitors whose opportunities or resources are weak in comparison, because in the end it is certain to secure an absolute monopoly and in the meantime bring great harm to the employees and others.

We have endeavored to maintain a position between the two extremes. We are perfectly satisfied to limit the amount of our business to our proportion of capacity and to do everything possible we can to promote the interests of our competitors; and by frequent meetings and the interchange of opinions we have thus far been able to accomplish this result without making any agreements of any kind.

President Roosevelt and the Attorney-General gave careful consideration to Gary's letters as well as to criticisms which were coming to them from many directions, and finally, the end of May, gave the Gary dinners what we may call a clean bill of health. "I do not perceive," wrote the Attorney-General, "that the facts received from you render any suggestions to you from this Department appropriate, and while I submitted these communications to the President, he did not consider that they called for any official comment on his part."

That is, Attorney-General Bonaparte seems to have taken the same view of the meeting of competitors in a trade to discuss their problems, exchange information, advice and exhortation, that the Supreme Court voiced in June of this year (1925):

It is not open to question [said the Supreme Court] that the dissemination of pertinent information concerning any trade or business tends to stabilize that trade or business and to produce uniformity of prices and trade practices. . . .

We decide only that trade associations or combinations of persons or corporations which openly and fairly gather and disseminate information as to the cost of their product, the volume of production, the actual price which the product has brought in past transactions, stocks of merchandise on hand, approximate cost of transportation from the principal point of shipment to the principal points of consumption, as did these defendants, and who, as they did, meet and discuss such information and statistics without, however, reaching or attempting to reach any agreement or any concerted action with respect to prices or production or restraining competition, do not thereby engage in unlawful restraint of commerce.

But while this coöperation of the leading men in the industry prevented a violent and sudden crash at this time, things did go from bad to worse. The October panic had immediately reduced the number of blast furnaces active in the country from 329 to 314. At the end of

November there were 226 stacks blowing, by December 31, 154, and by January 31, 139—and no relief in sight. As 1908 went on, prices, in spite of their best efforts, sagged.

Prompt cutting of wages had always hitherto been the practice in the steel and iron industry when prices fell. Before the end of the year many of the big independents —the Lackawanna, Cambria, Pennsylvania, had begun to post reductions. The presidents of the subsidiaries naturally enough were restless under this disadvantage. Early in 1909 they circulated a petition calling for a wage readjustment. President Corey was with them; a majority of the finance committee was ready to agree. Judge Gary was opposed. He believed the depression was passing—a revival in sight—that a wage cut was unwise and unnecessary, and asked for time.

It will be recalled that back in 1902, when Judge Gary told Mr. Morgan that he thought his day of usefulness in the Steel Corporation was over, the banker had promised that if in future emergencies he wanted his support, to tell him what to do and he would do it—not to explain. The Judge took advantage of the promise now, calling by cable on Mr. Morgan, who was at Aix les Bains, for support in his opposition to a wage cut. He also asked Mr. Morgan to see Mr. Frick and Mr. Widener, who were then in Nice and had cabled that they favored the proposed reduction.

Mr. Morgan followed the suggestion, wiring Frick and Widener to meet him in Paris, with the result that the three men signed a cablegram sustaining Judge Gary. This was submitted to the finance committee, and wages were not dropped. As a matter of fact, the general average of wages and salaries was raised in 1909 to the highest point that the Corporation had yet seen, for Judge Gary had been right in his prophecy of business revival. Before the summer was ended the Corporation had taken on 30,000 workmen and its earnings were sufficient to resume the quarterly dividend on the common stock.

His long-sighted handling of affairs in these two tempestuous years made a deep impression on his colleagues. "I recall an interesting conversation with George W. Perkins at his house at dinner," writes Bradford Merrill, a well-known New York publisher, "about the value of the services of certain executives to certain corporations. It was a man's dinner with only five or six persons present. I think it was Senator Beveridge of Indiana who asked Mr. Perkins how many men were really worth the salaries of from $100,000 to $250,000 a year which great corporations were then paying to their chief executives.

"Mr. Perkins, who had been many years Chairman of the finance committee of the United States Steel Corporation, by way of answer recalled a single decision by Chairman Gary, made against great opposition, which Mr. Perkins said was, in his opinion, worth one hundred times all the salary that the Steel Corporation would ever pay Mr. Gary in his lifetime." It was the above decision concerning wages.

Mr. Perkins told his guests of Gary's long, earnest argument to the members of the finance committee. "He told them that the present unprofitable business of the Corporation would not last many months, in his opinion, and that it was the duty of the Corporation to try to improve conditions, to relieve distress, to keep up employment and wages *even if the stockholders were forced temporarily to suspend* dividends. But they could not see the situation as Judge Gary did. A majority of them were in favor of reducing wages.

"Judge Gary realized that if the matter immediately came to a vote, it would be decided against him, and he suddenly asked the directors if they would do him a favor. Would they agree to postpone the whole question for thirty days? They could not deny such a request from such an executive as Judge Gary."

The way he used the reprieve and the result I have recited.

With the reëstablishment of something like normal business, the iron and steel trade wakened to the fact that the "Gary movement," as it was called, had actually prevented the "cut-and-slash" demoralization that had followed previous panics. It is probable that the spirits of the steel men had been so chastened by the disastrous after effects of the panic of 1907 that they were peculiarly receptive to the evangelistic fervor of Gary's appeals to steadiness and to decent and friendly competition, however vigorous that competition might be. They had yielded to his advice to their own surprise, and in 1909, when things began to revive, they were almost buoyantly exultant over their virtue. "Who would have thought we could have been so decent?" was the gist of their talks at luncheons and dinners!

They had come to love one another like brothers. It was Gary who had converted them to this policy, and in October of 1909 a large number of his competitors showed their appreciation by giving him what I think is one of the most remarkable dinners in our business annals—remarkable because of its sincerity as well as the kind of thing it celebrated.

It was Mr. Schwab who said the great word at the dinner:

Several times during the past week I have endeavored to write something that I might say to you on this occasion that would be appropriate, Judge Gary, and that would express the sentiment of your friends here assembled, but each time I tore it up as unsatisfactory, and I made up my mind that I would say to you exactly what I personally felt, feeling assured that in the saying of it I would express what was in the hearts and minds of every gentleman here.

I am thankful for this opportunity of saying one thing, Judge. You and I have been associated in business, or we were, for some years; we have had many differences, and I am glad of this opportunity to say publicly that with my bounding enthusiasm and optimism I was wrong in most instances—indeed in all instances—and you were right. The broad principles that you brought into this business were new to all of us who had been trained in a somewhat different school. Their effect was marvelous, their success unquestioned. It was a renaissance and a newness of things in this business that were necessary and invigorating. Judge, we feel that your position in the steel industry is unique. I have been present at many gatherings where men have been honored for scientific attainments in steel. I have been present at gatherings where men have been honored by reason of their operative ability in the manufacture of steel; but, sir, this is the first time in the history of the industry when the great heads of all the big concerns in the United States and Canada have gathered to do honor to a man who has introduced a new and successful principle in our great industry.

I doubt, if in looking back on his long warring on things which he felt were wrong, there is any experience which Judge Gary treasures more than what Mr. Schwab said at this dinner, unless it be, indeed, what Mr. Morgan said.

Mr. Morgan was at his right. ''They will want to hear

you say something," the Judge told him. Mr. Morgan, confused as a boy, replied, "I never could make a speech." But they called him out, and with one hand on Judge Gary's shoulder and another on his chair, he spoke fewer than two hundred words, the gist of which was in one sentence: "What I might say at another time would be pretty poor, but to-night I am very much overcome by all that I have heard said, for Judge Gary and I have been working together now for ten years in a way perhaps none of you appreciate, or how much it has meant to me."

It is easy to see that it was a great emotional moment in the love feast! And not the least memorable thing to Judge Gary in the occasion was when he thanked Morgan for his speech, and Mr. Morgan answered, "You know I never could have said a word if I had not had a chair and your shoulder to lean on."

The policies were going on, but inside the Corporation there was still grumbling that the chairman of the board and of the finance committee outranked the president in authority. It came to a focus and was settled for good and all in the spring of 1910.

In the fall of the preceding year, Judge Gary had commissioned an executive in a western mine to look up certain information. When this came to the ears of the president of the subsidiary company, he promptly dismissed the man. The man complained to Judge Gary, who ordered him reinstated. President Corey resented the action, contending—and in this he was backed by the presidents of many of the subsidiaries, that the chairman had no right to go over the head of the president in reinstating an officer, that if he did so it would ruin discipline.

Considerable excitement developed, and one member of the finance committee, who sided with the president, went to Mr. Morgan with it. If the finance committee pronounced in favor of Gary in this matter, he reported, the presidents of the subsidiaries threatened to resign in a body.

"Tell them," answered Mr. Morgan, "that their resignations will be accepted."

The matter was thoroughly threshed out before the committee and the chairman unanimously sustained. After the vote had been taken, Mr. Perkins, turning to Judge Gary, said, "Is there anything further that you would like to have us do?"

"Yes," he said, "I would like a resolution more definitely fixing my status in this Corporation." He got it, for on March 1, 1910, the directors added the following section to the by-laws of the Corporation:

The chairman of the Board of Directors shall be the chief executive officer of the corporation and, subject to the Board of Directors and Finance Committee, shall be in general charge of the affairs of the corporation.

It is doubtful if this added to Judge Gary's power and authority, for already his position as chairman of the Board of Directors and of the finance committee gave him all of the power of the finance committee when it was not in session; but the new section did make the matter clearer, more positive.

It was time the matter was settled, for the Corporation was entering on a period which called for an executive who had not only brains and firmness, but one who believed the purpose of the undertaking was legitimate, and that this could be demonstrated if its conduct could be kept within certain well-defined legal and ethical lines.

The suspicion which the organization of the Steel Corporation had awakened in 1901 grew rapidly after the panic of 1907, and, by the time Mr. Taft's administration took hold of things in the spring of 1909, the points of attack were fairly well defined.

There was the tariff. The cry for revision was loud and general. To put down the duties on iron and steel was the real way to curb the power of the Steel Trust. Now, Judge Gary had clear ideas on the tariff. At his first interview with Roosevelt in 1902, the President said to him that he felt that something ought to be done about the tariff, but he was not clear in his mind on the subject. How did the Judge feel? The Judge told him facetiously that he was a free trader in everything except iron and steel.

"They ridiculed Hancock for calling the tariff a local issue," laughed Roosevelt, "but that is what it is."

"In my judgment," Gary told the President, "we must have a protection in our industry in order to compete, particularly with Germany, but I believe that the duties should be fixed at the point where they would protect from but not prohibit foreign competition, and at the same time prevent injustice to the consumer."

"Well," said Roosevelt, "until I find that point I think I shall say nothing about the matter."

From that time on, whenever interviewed on the tariff or questioned by the Ways and Means Committee, as he was more than once, Judge Gary held to these views. I have before me the notes of an interview with him in March of 1908 in which he reiterated his belief in the doctrine, declaring that all stable countries had adopted tariffs and that England would be in better condition if she had one. He said with great positiveness that, while he thought steel and iron needed protection, he believed it to be a great mistake for the Steel Trust to fight a revision, that in this matter, as in all others, public opinion was the true guide. Judge Gary at this interview insisted that what was needed for sound tariff revision was a commission of experts, outside of politics, competent and honest enough to gather full information and to fix the point where protection left off and prohibition began. That is, at this time Judge Gary advocated a handling of the tariff with which a patient reformer—even a patient free trader—could be satisfied—as a beginning! But he knew, of course, that his view was as unpopular in the steel and iron industry as many of his other views had been. The great majority of the trade at that moment, as in the past, cried for prohibitive tariffs, and so did the organized steel and iron workers. They had been taught and believed that it was high protection which filled their dinner pails. Indeed some of the most effective high tariff agitators in the preceding years had been labor leaders.

Consequently, the tariff reformer received no support from organized labor in the agitation which developed in the Taft administration. But if organized labor did not help the tariff reformer, it backed the "Trust Buster," as he was called. The strongest sector of the line forming for attack occupied itself, not with the Corporation's conduct, not with its views, but with what we might call its mechanics, the form of combination under which it was doing business. This, its critics claimed, was monopolistic in its very nature—its very existence was a restraint of trade, therefore the steel aggregation was illegal under the Sherman Antitrust Law. Organized labor gladly joined this line of the attack.

As we have already seen, the Amalgamated Iron and Steel Workers had agreed, in 1901, not to attempt to organize further inside the Corporation if the Corporation on its side would continue to bargain with the groups already existing. The agreement had worked out badly for the Amalgamated. It was a weak body in 1901, that is, weak when its entire membership, 13,900, is compared with the whole number of workers in iron, steel, and tin and their products. The census of 1910 gives 393,125 as the number in iron and steel in 1900—70,505 in tin. It was a little larger by the time the corporation was formed. Many thousands of these workers were outside of the Amalgamated's field. Of the "whole number," amounting to 433,630, the Corporation employed, in 1901, about 168,000.

By 1910, the number in iron, steel, tin and their products had grown to 993,116 (census total), whereas the membership of the Amalgamated had fallen to 8,300. How many of this 8,300 were in the Corporation and how many in independent concerns, we do not know. The number of employees belonging to the Amalgamated did not, however, represent all the unionists in the Steel Corporation. Among its foundrymen, machinists, railroad workers, miners, there were many members of their respective unions, and in case of trouble they gave more or less sympathy and support.

As for Judge Gary, he had publicly expressed his attitude towards unionism more than once. It is what he still holds:

"I am of the opinion, and always have been," he said in an interview in 1906, "that labor unions, properly managed, are a benefit to the workingmen. No reasonable man would say otherwise, for coöperation and organization of the right sort can result in nothing but good to those concerned. But the trouble with labor unions has been that they have too often come under the control of men who did not hesitate to resort to turbulent methods to gain their ends. The majority of men belonging to unions do not want to strike, and they do not vote to bring a strike about. Those at all familiar with the workings of labor organizations know how this is. The leaders gather a few of the more turbulent members around them and they do the voting. When the strike is declared the conservative men feel that it is their duty to the union to stand by what has been done, but they never resort to violence. Yet the effect of the strike is bad for the good men, and they are compelled to suffer for what the others have done.''

The Amalgamated charged its growing weakness in the industry at large to the Corporation's opposition to its further extension in its plants. It declared that, if a man was known to belong to the union, he would not be given work, that men were discharged when it was discovered that they were members, and that plants in which thriving lodges had once existed, had been shut down for the express purpose of breaking up the groups.

The Corporation made a general denial, but it is probable that many superintendents and foremen, particularly in former Carnegie plants, used their full authority against the union, just as the labor organizers used all their ingenuity in getting into the plants and carrying on their propaganda. Each side suspected the other, spied on the other, hated the other. That is, the war still existed, spreading bitterness and suspicion between men and management. More than once between 1901 and 1909, strikes had been attempted by the Amalgamated, but had always failed. In 1910, Samuel Gompers, the president of the American Federation of Labor, tried a novel stratagem—one in support of the main attack on the Corporation. In effect, he called upon the Attorney-General to disband it because it was oppressing labor by preventing men from joining the union. It was therefore, according to Mr. Gompers' argument, a conspiracy in restraint of trade. He pointed out, what was true in some places, that plants were surrounded by high walls over which it was impossible for organizers to climb and that the police and municipal forces in industrial towns of the Corporation were used to break up the meetings of organizers. He charged that it was intentionally employing foreign laborers to the displacement of Americans. What Mr. Gompers really asked was that the Steel Corporation be dissolved because it would not adopt the policy of the closed shop. But, as this was not a government policy, the Attorney-General could hardly heed the plea, and he did not.

Mr. Gompers' purpose, however, was admirably served. He emphasized the open-shop attitude of the Corporation and its interference with workmen, eager, as he claimed, to organize. If, however, there had been as strong a desire among iron and steel workers in 1910 for organization as Mr. Gompers would like to have had the country believe, there certainly would have been more than 8,300 members of the Amalgamated in a body of upwards of 1,000,000 workers, not a fourth of which belonged to the Corporation, whatever the percentage of that million outside of the Amalgamated's field or enrolled in other unions.

One of Mr. Gompers' complaints against the Corporation was that it was weaning men away by a labor policy which he characterized as a sham. What was this labor policy by 1910? We dropped it in this narrative in 1904 with two planks firmly nailed down: (1) the open shop and (2) a stock subscription scheme open to all employees with a bonus for special services, in all ranks. And at that time various other problems were under discussion—safety, relief, hours, conditions. It was safety that first crystallized.

When the Corporation was formed, all of the companies had what they called "casualty managers," looking after the settlement of claims of injured employees. These casualty managers had been gathered into one group under the general solicitor of the Corporation. There was a growing conviction, however, that this method of handling injuries was unsatisfactory, very expensive and rarely just.

One of the most valuable intangibles that the Corporation had inherited was a slogan and a safety policy, originated by Thomas Lynch, the president of the Frick Coke and Coal Companies. The slogan was "Safety a First Consideration" and the policy was "To —— with rescue work—prevent accidents." The Illinois Steel Company turned the slogan into the terse and compelling "Safety First"—the cry which now heads the National Safety Movement. Other subsidiaries contributed ideas, devices.

Early in 1906 the casualty managers came together in New York, in a first concerted effort to unify the contributions. By March of 1908 they had their plans sufficiently under way to announce a committee of safety, ready to make an organized attack on accidents. Judge

Gary started the committee off with a hearty endorsement.

"Some of the gentlemen present, if not all of them, know," he said, "that I am in hearty sympathy with the movement. There is not any doubt that our Corporation will promptly and fully approve every suggestion that is made for the betterment of conditions in this respect. We will not hesitate to make the necessary appropriations in money to carry into effect every suggestion that seems to us to be practical for the improvement of our mills so far as the question of taking care of our employees is concerned."

The promise has been faithfully carried out. By the time we have reached in our narrative 1910, the committee of safety had grown into a bureau of safety, relief, sanitation and welfare. Its organization reached down to the last man in the shop, its most valuable committees being made up of workmen, the members of which changed periodically so that each man in a plant would sooner or later be called upon to exercise personal responsibility in preventing accidents—a plan for coöperative action in their own interest which had already proved of genuine educational and coöperative value. From a half million to a million dollars a year had been spent in accident prevention, with the result that there had been a decrease of accidents from a little over 10 per cent in 1907 to 43½ per cent in 1910.

Dovetailed into the bureau was an elaborate plan of relief and pensions. Outside of the American Steel and Wire none of the subsidiaries had contributed anything of importance to this plan. That concern, however, had brought into the Corporation an excellent accident and pension department which the company itself supported

QUEBEC BRIDGE, ACROSS THE ST. LAWRENCE RIVER. THE LONGEST AND BY FAR THE HEAVIEST SINGLE SPAN YET BUILT. CENTRAL OPENING 1,800 FEET, CENTER TO CENTER OF PIERS. CANTILEVER CONSTRUCTION

by depositing from month to month a sum equivalent to one per cent of the pay roll, and from the start the finance committee heard much of this from Mr. Edenborn, with whom it had originated. Mr. Carnegie also had celebrated his retirement in 1901 by setting aside four million dollars, to be known as "The Carnegie Relief Fund," to be used exclusively for the employees of the Carnegie Steel Company. It was on this that the Corporation had begun to build. It had already set aside some eight million dollars as a pension fund. It was already voting annually many hundreds of thousands of dollars for the relief of those injured and it had under consideration at this time, 1910, a greatly enlarged relief and pension plan.

If we put down this safety and relief work as the third plank in the labor policy, the fourth deals with its attack on the seven-day week, which was practically universal in the iron and steel industry when the Corporation was formed. It was one of the results of the continuous processes which had been adopted in steel making. In other years when furnaces were small the practice had been to let them cool off on Sunday, but as they increased in size the loss from the shutdown, the difficulty of getting back to a normal product on Monday morning had resulted in a seven-day week, with a most brutal feature— a twenty-four hour turn every two weeks.

Public opinion was condemning the seven-day week and the matter had been more or less worrying the finance committee for some time. There was no general opposition among the workers, for it meant to them an extra day's pay. When Judge Gary and other officers talked of a six-day week to the executives of the various subsidiaries they scoffed at the idea, nevertheless in April of 1907 the finance committee was sufficiently concerned to recommend that all work be suspended on Sunday at all steel works, rolling mills, shops, quarries and docks.

It is understood [their resolution said] that it is not at present practical to apply the recommendation to all departments, notably the blast furnaces, but it is desirable that the spirit of the recommendation be observed to the fullest extent within reason.

The order was issued the next day. An immediate and whole-hearted obedience was perhaps too much to expect. There were executives who treated it as they had the order to stop pooling, to take no more rebates. In 1910, at the time that the *Pittsburgh Survey* was calling particular attention to the laxity of the Corporation in regard to the seven-day week, Judge Gary and President Corey issued a peremptory order that a way be found to put an end to it, and very rapidly after that the seven-day week was brought to a practical minimum in the Corporation. When the order was put into effect four thousand men left the Corporation plants in one district, going where they could work the full week—a proof that there had been something in the contention of the executives that the men *wanted* to work seven days, an argument loudly ridiculed outside of the industry. What they wanted was the money, not perpetual labor.

Another labor policy that should not be overlooked in this general consideration was Judge Gary's effort to keep up wages. He had, as we have seen, fought every cut proposed, and had lectured his associates in and out of the Corporation on their obligation at all times to sustain wages. He had always been willing to sacrifice dividends before wages. Indeed, one of the chief reasons that he gave for his consistent advocacy of stabilizing prices was that it meant steadier wages.

The point here is that, by the time Mr. Gompers called on the Attorney-General in the name of organized labor to dissolve the Steel Corporation, it had developed a fairly well-rounded labor policy, planned to meet some of the most serious and the most justified complaints of workers. Labor complained that it had no opportunity to acquire ownership in the industry to which it gave its time. Here was one—safe and liberal as investments go. They had sensed this, and every year there had been thousands of subscribers to the stock. The abolishing of the seven-day week gave them one day's leisure—the safety rule from the beginning made life surer, while the compensation eased the hardship which accidents brought to them and their families. The pensions helped take care of old age. It was a policy that had required serious study to inaugurate and to administer, on which they had already spent many millions of dollars and which they considered far from complete. That is, they had no idea of stopping where they were. It was a policy that, for any degree of success, required faith and coöperation on the part of the worker.

But Mr. Gompers characterized the program as a sham.

Now in this period when the complaints against the Corporation were crystallizing, Judge Gary had been diligently pursuing the policy in relation to the government that he had adopted in 1901. This had amounted to telling President Roosevelt and his Attorney-General, Mr. Bonaparte, that he considered it their business to see that corporations did not oppress their competitors, their employees or the public, and the Corporation's business to find out what the government regarded as oppressive, illegal and contrary to the public good and to put itself in harmony with that policy.

The new Attorney-General, Mr. George Wickersham, an eminent New York lawyer, knew Judge Gary's ideas on corporate conduct, for he had carried on for him in 1905-1906 an investigation of the way the Corporation was conducting itself, particularly in relation to pools, and his advice had then been taken. When in 1910 Mr. Gompers became active it was possible for Judge Gary to write to the Attorney-General, without fear of misunderstanding, that as a matter of course they would be glad to furnish him or his representative at any time all the data in their possession or within their reach, bearing upon the subject matter of the complaint. "My understanding is," he concluded, "that our men generally are very well satisfied with the treatment received, notwithstanding Mr. Gompers and others have unsuccessfully attempted from time to time to get their support."

The acquaintance made it natural for Judge Gary to meet and to talk with the Attorney-General as he had with Mr. Roosevelt. As late as March of 1911 he dined with Mr. Wickersham at his home in Washington. They talked over the business situation much as he and Roosevelt had done, and he said to Mr. Wickersham as he had to the former President in a similar discussion, "I don't know whether you have any complaints against the Steel Corporation, but I want to say to you, as you know that I did to Mr. Roosevelt, if there is anything that we are doing that seems to you inimical to your policy, let us know and we will correct it." And Mr. Wickersham had replied, "I hope you don't think that there is any reference to your Corporation in what I have been saying."

But the public was pressing hard, and early in 1911, on the resolution of Representative Augustus Stanley of Kentucky, an investigation was ordered. The Stanley investigation, although inevitable in the general suspicion and ignorance of the work of the Corporation and its relation to the industry, has always been blackened by the supposed connection with it of one of the most notorious men of the last twenty years, David Lamar.

Lamar is charged with having had interviews with Mr. Stanley before the investigation was called. If this is true, Mr. Stanley did not of course know that the fellow also had wormed his way into Judge Gary's office and said to him: "This Stanley investigation is going to be a serious thing for the Steel Corporation. I know Stanley. I am the only man in the country that can stop him"—at which point Mr. Lamar was shown the door.

Richard Lindabury, chief counsellor of the Corporation, told me only a few days before his death in July of this year, that soon after Lamar saw Judge Gary, he came to his office in Newark, repeating the identical proposition, and with the same promptness was sent on his way.

I am not sure, however, that Judge Gary deplored the Stanley investigation. It gave him the best chance he had ever had to tell the public what he was trying to do, and he used it brilliantly to emphasize certain facts which were not yet fixed in the public mind.

The statement which attracted the most attention was one which Judge Gary had repeatedly made but which never before had so taken hold—chiefly because never before had everybody listened.

"I realize as fully, I think, as this committee that it is very important to consider how the people shall be protected against imposition or oppression as the possible result of great aggregations of capital, whether in the possession of corporations or individuals. I believe that is a very important question, and personally I believe that the Sherman Act does not meet and will never fully prevent that. I believe we must come to enforced publicity and governmental control, even as to prices, and, so far as I am concerned, speaking for our company, so far as I have the right, I would be very glad if we had some place where we could go, to a responsible governmental authority, and say to them, 'Here are our facts and figures, here is our property, here our cost of production; now you tell us what we have the right to do and what prices we have the right to charge.' I know this is a very extreme view, and I know that the railroads objected to it for a long time; but whether the mere standpoint of making the most money is concerned or not, whether it is the wise thing, I believe it is the necessary thing, and it seems to me corporations have no right to disregard these public questions and these public interests.''

"Your idea then," said Martin Littleton of the committee, "is that coöperation is bound to take the place of competition and that coöperation requires strict governmental supervision?"

"That is a very good statement," replied the Judge.

Another statement that called forth surprised comment concerned Mr. Morgan's power:

"I believe," said Judge Gary, "any man of Mr. Morgan's wealth and strength of character and courage can do a great deal of harm in banking circles as well as a great deal of good. I believe that with power and privilege there is necessarily involved responsibility and obligation. That applies to the individual or the corporation and also applies to the Government. I do not think I would be frank and sincere with this Committee if I should say that Mr. Morgan, under such circumstances, could not do a great deal of harm if he had the disposition to do so. That is true of other individuals, and that is one of the reasons why I say that this country, if it keeps up with other countries, in view of our great wealth and growing wealth, has got to come to the position, in my judgment, where there is coöperation between the Government and the individual.''

This was getting a good deal more than the committee bargained for, but it still had nuts much harder for Judge Gary to crack—the purchase of the T. C. and I., the increase in the Corporation's ore lands, the prices at home and abroad, its profits, its competitors. They were not easily disposed of, and in spite of frank and interesting testimony, a considerable group of the public questioned the explanations.

Through all this, a demand had been growing stronger and stronger that the Attorney-General's office test the validity of the Steel Corporation as it had that of the Standard Oil Company and the Tobacco Trust. The charge was made by the more irresponsible of the press that the government was shielding the Steel Corporation; and that Mr. Wickersham ought to be impeached! A report was widely circulated that Judge Gary had told a reporter that the Corporation was immune from examination and punishment. Certainly not from examination! For nearly six years now, the bureau of corporations had had the run of the Steel Corporation books and the free service of auditors, twenty or thirty extra ones frequently being employed to compile the statistics to answer the

Bureau's questions. Judge Gary told the Stanley Committee that the Corporation had spent hundreds of thousands of dollars in the effort to give the information wanted.

As for punishment, there was nobody inside the Steel Corporation's offices that did not think that the examination had been punishment enough for any corporation!

Now, this repeated charge that the administration was favoring the Steel Corporation while dissolving the Standard Oil and the Tobacco Trust, as it had in May of this year (1911), probably was encouraged, or at least not discouraged, by the corporations that had been punished. Naturally enough, they had no love for the Gary policies. It also had a certain backing in anti-Roosevelt circles. Roosevelt had consented to the T. C. and I. purchase, and therefore it must have been wrong. It would be understandable if there had been a certain sympathy with this anti-Roosevelt feeling in the Taft administration. At all events, in the early summer of 1911 Mr. Wickersham said to Judge Gary at a public dinner in Washington, where the two men were seated side by side, "I have something on my mind which I think I ought to tell you. There is such excitement over that Stanley investigation, such hostility to the Steel Corporation, so many charges that the administration is favoring it, that we believe that we must proceed to a searching examination."

"Do you mean a suit?" asked Judge Gary.

"Yes," said the Attorney-General.

"Well," said the Judge, "this is so different from what I have believed to be your view of our Corporation that I am overwhelmed. But you must make your own decision—take your own course."

The decision of the government to prosecute the Steel Corporation was unquestionably a terrible blow to Judge Gary. I have heard one of his presidents say that the only time in all his twenty or more years of association that he ever saw the Judge's emotions get the better of him was when he had to tell them they were to be tried by the government, on a charge of conspiracy in restraint of trade.

These presidents knew what he tried to do. They also knew—some of them—how at the start they and their executives had jeered at his efforts, how little sympathy they had had with his attempts to control and regulate their conduct. They had now proof of how much greater than theirs had been his wisdom and foresight.

Not a few of the leading lawyers, now consulted by the Corporation, insisted that an effort should be made to settle rather than allow the suit to go to trial. They came to Judge Gary—consent to lop off here and there, give up this or that—anything but a trial, they told him.

"No," he said, resolutely, "I will never consent to that. This Corporation is not a conspiracy, it is not a monopoly, it is not restraining trade, and its intent has been from the start to avoid these things. The facts prove that we have done so, we have constantly corrected practices which we found to be in contradiction to the law as determined from time to time, we have helped rather than hindered our competitors. They have grown faster than we have. We have improved the condition of our employees, their wages, their prospects in life; we have stabilized business. We have made a demonstration of what a corporation ought to do. I will never consent to a settlement of this suit."

The only drastic change on which he insisted was the

cancellation of what was known as the "Hill lease."
Early in the history of the Corporation Mr. James Hill,
president of the Great Northern Railroad, had suggested
to Mr. Morgan, who was associated with him in various
enterprises in the Northwest, that the Steel Corporation
lease a tract of some thirty-nine million acres of ore land
which his road controlled. Mr. Morgan wanted to oblige
Mr. Hill. Mr. Gayley, head of the Corporation's ore department, approved, but Judge Gary objected. He
thought the royalty too large and that it was unwise as
policy, since it looked like an attempt to monopolize the
ore of the region. The discussion of the lease ran over
two or three years, Judge Gary not withdrawing his
objection until a clause was inserted in the contract
giving the Corporation the privilege of canceling it on
January 1, 1915, by giving at least a two-year notice.
A notice was actually given October 26, 1911.

The Judge's associates had another proof before them
of the long-headedness of their chief executive.

The government went ahead, filing its petition on
October 26, 1911, praying that eight of the subsidiaries
as well as the Steel Corporation itself be held "unlawful
monopolies" and dissolved.

Judge Gary's whole mind now was given to making
the defense as complete and as strong as possible. The
legal battery selected was of the first class, including,
besides the chief counsel of the Corporation, Mr. Lindabury, and his associates, an admirable man, Raynal C.
Bolling, who was later to lose his life in France; Joseph
H. Choate; John G. Johnson; Francis Lynde Stetson;
David A. Reed, now Senator Reed; and Cordenio A.
Severance. Judge Gary himself watched, supervised,
suggested at every point, such suggestions as that in the

following letter, which proved of great value in the end. This letter was written in August of 1913, from Cologne to Raynal Bolling:

MY DEAR BOLLING:

The more I think of the subject, the more convinced I am that we should introduce a *large number* of witnesses who are our competitors in one line or another and who have never coöperated with us, to testify to their business success; or at least a number who can testify as to themselves and their business and also others. It will look well in the record, even if the total tonnage is not so large, and will demonstrate the flourishing condition of the trade in spite of our domineering (?) disposition.

The case for the government was in the hands of J. M. Dickinson, former Secretary of War, a Democrat—as able a man as Mr. Wickersham could select. The case was tried in the United States District Court for the district of New Jersey before four well-known circuit judges—Buffington, Hunt, McPherson and Woolley.

The taking of testimony began in May of 1912, and continued at intervals for over two years. Four hundred and two witnesses were called. Theodore Roosevelt and ex-Secretary Garfield appeared, so did other characters in the T. C. and I. drama—Oakleigh N. Thorne, Lewis Ledyard, John A. Topping, the company's president at the time of the purchase. There were at least two hundred competitors, big and little, topped by the president or vice president of the biggest independents: Schwab, now chairman of the Bethlehem; Campbell, of the Youngstown Sheet and Tube; Willis King, of Jones and Laughlin; Powell Stackhouse, of the Cambria. The officers and directors of the Corporation itself with many executives of the subsidiaries spent days on the stand—

Judge Gary was there for a week. In all, one hundred and eighty-nine full days were required to find out what this small army knew about the Corporation. Put into print the testimony filled thirty volumes—12,151 pages of about four hundred words each. In addition to this there was close to 4,000 pages of government and Corporation exhibits. This was what the four judges had to listen to and digest!

The briefs and statements—admirable analyses of the testimony from the opposing points of view—were not presented until October of 1914.

In the meantime many things had happened besides the suit to engage the attention of the chief executive officer of the Steel Corporation. There had been two years of business—months of it the worst they had ever had—with lower earnings, bad fluctuations in stock; there had been internal changes, one in particular of great moment and great sorrow to Judge Gary. This was the death of Mr. Morgan in March of 1913. The two men, as we have seen, had been brought into close association, first in 1898, in the Federal Steel Company and later in the Steel Corporation, where they had shared in the most gigantic industrial responsibility which men in this country had ever dared assume. The relation had grown steadily in confidence and affection. I think it is not too much to say that Mr. Morgan had not only come to feel that he could not, as he once told Judge Gary, do a thing in steel without him, but he had come to have a thorough respect for his point of view, to which he often did not subscribe. "He is too good a man to oppose," he is known to have said more than once when he and his directors disagreed with Gary. Moreover, Mr. Morgan had come to feel genuine personal affection for Judge

Gary. He was a man of ardent temperament and found satisfaction in surrounding himself in business hours with men he liked. He liked Judge Gary. In the early days it often happened that a Morgan partner would come over to the Steel Corporation to say, "Senior" (the office name for the older Morgan) "Senior wants to know why you have not been over." As years went on, it became Judge Gary's habit when Mr. Morgan was in New York to go frequently at Mr. Morgan's request to his house or library for conference, and he has more than one anecdote to tell of the great banker's private life.

In the summers when Mr. Morgan was abroad, Judge Gary on his annual trip always visited him. He saw him gradually going down physically and the last time he was at Dover House—the Morgan country place in England—he was painfully aware of the difficulty Mr. Morgan had in getting up steps when called to the house from the garden where the two were sitting.

The day before Mr. Morgan sailed in January, 1913, on what turned out to be his last trip, Judge Gary stopped at his request at his library. After a long talk he started several times to go but Mr. Morgan called him back, evidently reluctant to say good-by; and when finally he withdrew, saying "Come back to us well and strong, Mr. Morgan," he shook his head, "I don't know. I may never come back." And in March the news came that he was not coming back.

It was a severe blow to Judge Gary, particularly in the matter of the suit. He wanted his policies justified in his friend's eyes—his friend who through this period of trial had been standing splendidly by him.

But that was not to be. Moreover, it was to be literally years before Judge Gary himself was to know the end of the attack which had given him so much anxiety, for when, as I have said, the testimony and the briefs were before the judges in the fall of 1914, neither Judge Gary nor the world at large had their minds centered on the results of lawsuits. Something greater had broken out in the world. The head of the Steel Corporation had a new subject for anxiety—war.

CHAPTER X

GARY AND THE WAR

LEADERSHIP demands fitness—physical fitness—
else the resolution, patience, equable temper of
the leader becomes jaded, unreliable. Head-
aches have played a part in the loss of more battles than
Waterloo.

The chief executive of the Steel Corporation, whatever
his conflicts and his uncertainties, had always taken good
care to keep his body fit, his mind clear. Two months
of Europe had been his chief relief and tonic from 1906
to 1914, the point we have reached in this narrative, two
months properly voted by the finance committee, for in
August of 1903 that body had deemed it wise to pass a
by-law requiring official permission for vacations. Judge
Gary, even now, never takes a vacation without this
official permission.

The spring of 1914 found him in special need of the
relief of Europe. The long ordeal of testimony-taking
in the government's suit against the Corporation was
over, but the briefs were not yet in. It would be many
months before an opinion could be expected from the
Circuit Court, and after that there was a possibility,
indeed a probability, of an appeal to the Supreme Court.
It is not action but waiting that pulls hardest on men's
nerves. A long continued depression in iron and steel
had added to the strain of the government's suit. Judge

Gary had been going through an experience not unlike that of 1907-1908, when he had assumed leadership of a panicky industry and by his counsel and example had kept his own executives as well as his competitors' from losing their heads and bringing a general smash in iron and steel.

He had been counseling steadiness and patience in the very months he and his associates were spending long days on the witness stand, trying to justify their handling of their gigantic and suspected enterprise.

Again and again in these months he had advised against cuts in what were believed to be "reasonable prices"; again and again he had fought the lowering of wages.

The country was sound at bottom, he told the members of the Institute, the depression was temporary. "Keep your heads, go slow and have faith." But there was not much to reassure even him, in the spring of 1914. Times were worse than at any period in the preceding decade, worse than in 1904, in 1908. He had to admit at the May semiannual meeting of the Institute—where his talks on business conditions, then as now, were always listened to with respect—that the prophecy he had made them six months before of "the approach of the dawn of prosperity" had proved to be mistaken. But his inveterate faith asserted itself. "Don't forget, gentlemen," he said, "that we are six months nearer the dawn."

He needed Europe, and late in June he and Mrs. Gary sailed. It was their custom to make Paris their headquarters, motoring in whatever direction they pleased. In their trips they had become thoroughly familiar with western and central Europe and with Great Britain—

scenery, folks, towns, cathedrals, and especially pictures, for that first picture pilgrimage of Judge Gary, made in 1897, of which I have already spoken, had developed into a settled interest. He studied pictures and had become an intelligent and careful buyer.

An interesting angle of the social side of these annual tours was the contact with the European leaders in iron and steel—a superior and highly trained scientific and business group. Judge Gary had been intent from the start of the Corporation on cultivating friendly relations with foreign industrialists. The Corporation proposed to build up a regular foreign trade; the foreign manufacturer would be its competitor in various lands. They must meet on either militant or coöperative grounds; must be enemies or friends; must suspect, defy, injure, or trust, accept, and help. He preferred the second alternative and adopted the same tactics abroad that had proved so successful at home. He sought his foreign competitors, discussed with them, opened his mind frankly, and soon was on good terms with great numbers of them. They liked him apparently and trusted him as men did on this side of the water.

In the autumn of 1908, the British Iron and Steel Institute gave him a complimentary dinner in London, at which he told them of the efforts of the American iron and steel trade to put itself on a coöperative basis, and suggested that this might not be a chimerical idea for international as well as national trade.

In 1910 a large number of foreign delegates visited this country and the idea of an International Institute was discussed. A committee was appointed and it was planned to meet in June of 1911 in Brussels to organize. The suggestion sounded sinister to the superheated imaginations of the professional trust-busters. Representative Stanley told Judge Gary, when he was before his committee in the spring of 1911, that one of his reasons for calling for an investigation of the Steel Corporation was this proposed international gathering. He dreaded, he said, lest the proposed institute should succeed in making prices for the world as he believed the Iron and Steel Institute was making them for this country. Judge Gary was entirely frank in answering Mr. Stanley. He pointed out that all of the discussions regarding the international institute had been published, and he said emphatically that unless something came up to make it appear to him and to the others interested that they should not, from a legal or moral standpoint, carry out what they planned, they would go ahead.

"I will not intentionally be put in a position where any one has the right to say that I intend to violate any law or oppose the best interests of the public," Judge Gary told Mr. Stanley. "I intend to say that modestly, but these are my views and the views of the members of the finance committee, the governing body of the United States Steel Corporation."

"This international association," he went on to say, "will consider the same sort of technical questions to which the British Iron and Steel Institute devotes its time. It will also," he said, "consider many other questions—ethical questions, psychological questions—questions that nowadays thinking people believe to be as important as the mere question of making a little money."

As usual when there was a serious question of one of his policies, Judge Gary put it flatly up to the administration, and he now appealed to Attorney-General Wickersham. Did he see anything wrong in the proposed international iron and steel institute? The Attorney-General answered that he did not.

Judge Gary was simply running ahead of his time, as he had so often before in his business policies, when he set out to build up friendly relations between the iron and steel interests of this and other lands. The international coöperation he saw then as necessary to a stable and prosperous world is as inevitable in industry as it is in science, transportation, labor, and governments.

Among the friends Judge Gary had made in this association with European leaders in iron and steel was the head of the commercial department of Krupps, Baron von Bodenhausen. The two men had first met in London in 1908 and had repeatedly seen each other since. There had long been talk of a visit at the Baron's Bavarian estate. There had been invitations from the Garys for Paris, but it was not until the summer of 1914 that the pleasant plans matured, and Baron von Bodenhausen and his wife came to Paris, arriving about July 20. Three days later, July 23, Austria presented her ultimatum to Serbia. Baron von Bodenhausen was thrown into the deepest depression by the text. It meant war, he told his host, for, in his judgment, Serbia could not, or would not, give an answer satisfactory to the Austrians.

"How will it begin?" Judge Gary asked him.

"When Austria declares war, Russia will act. She cannot allow Serbia to be destroyed. When Russia mobilizes, so will Germany, and as France will support Russia, Germany will begin by attacking France."

"And England?" Judge Gary asked his friend.

"She will keep her hands off."

"If she does not?"

"Then," said the Baron, "I fear the destruction of Germany."

Judge Gary was, of course, familiar enough with the talk of war which for years had agitated the high political, military, and industrial circles of Europe. He had come to believe from what he had seen and heard in these years, that war between France and Germany was inevitable, so when three days later, at five o'clock in the morning of Sunday, July 26, the Baron knocked loudly at his chamber door, announcing joyfully, "There will be no war—Serbia has sent an answer so conciliating that it cannot be refused," the Judge shook his head.

"I hope you are right, but I don't see it. I think Germany *wants* war"—yet he did not see it so near as immediately to change his plan of starting on Thursday of that week for Carlsbad. On Wednesday he went to his bank for a supply of German and Austrian currency only to be told that no rates of exchange were quoted. Judge Gary was too money-wise not to see the portentous meaning behind the information. He decided to postpone his trip.

Tense and terrible days followed, days when the city of Paris waited for the war which she felt rather than knew was now a certainty. Judge Gary made himself one of the great crowds which overflowed boulevards and squares, seeing and hearing everything. At midnight of Saturday after the Jaurès assassination, he visited the offices of the great newspapers, eager as a boy for the last word of news, the most authoritative opinion. He followed the mobs that formed to *conspuer* the President of the Republic or some other distracted official, only to see them melt before police or military.

He watched with a professional eye the perfection of

that quiet mobilization: tens of thousands upon tens of thousands of soldiers gathering from every direction— a common order universally obeyed—and so quiet, so matter of fact; even the women and children, who followed the marching men to their very railway carriage, made no sound. Paris had accepted war—all Paris, for in those running thousands there was now no distinction because of opinion—socialists whose hearts bled for Jaurès marched side by side with those whose hate had killed him.

The mobilization left a new Paris: no taxicabs, no groups of excited people, streets empty, scores of shops and restaurants closed, those which were open without clerks or waiters; and to cap the change, the lights were put out at eight o'clock. From being a busy, crowded city, Paris, wrote Judge Gary at the time, became a deserted village.

And now a new and distressing anxiety arose. France and central Europe were alive with American travelers, who hurried to Paris as rapidly as transportation turned overnight from peace to war purposes could take them. They arrived half distracted from the hardships and alarms they had suffered, often sans luggage or money, only to find the ships on which they had return passage had been commandeered.

The American Ambassador to France, Myron Herrick, came at once to the rescue of his stranded compatriots. One of his first moves was to ask Judge Gary to form and act as chairman of a committee to assist the beleaguered. This committee was organized on August 4, the day after Germany declared war on France, and until the end of the month held daily meetings. There are hundreds of Americans who have reason to be thankful that in August of 1914 the head of the United States Steel Corporation was giving his time and trained ability to arrange for their safe and prompt return to their own land. As for Ambassador Herrick, he has said more than once in public, "I don't know what I would have done without Gary."

While laboring for his compatriots, the Judge was watching the stripping and arming of Paris. He saw art treasures disappear into vaults and crypts, or shipped to the south; warehouses stored with food, great flocks of sheep and cattle herded in the parks; hospitals built within the fortifications; defenses on all sides strengthened, and finally he heard the order to remove the government to Bordeaux.

His work was done, it was time he was going, but before he left he motored a hundred miles along the rear of the battle front. "Taking good care to keep within the safety zone," he is sure to add when he tells you of the expedition—such is his dislike of seeming to boast of going into places of danger! Next day the German army seized the road to Compiègne, and so at the last moment he left for his ship, sailing on September 6 from Havre.

He reached New York at a moment when a horrified and amazed public was trying to get its thoughts into order and when it sought eagerly the word of the last returned. There was no little wisdom in his talks in these months and one piece of real prophecy.

Here is his idea of the cause of the war:

"The struggle for commercial supremacy was the underlying cause of the war, or at least had a decided influence upon its precipitation; the questions at issue largely relate to dollars and cents."

Could it have been prevented?

"Proper publicity would have prevented the present war. If before wars were started the masses of the people of the different countries had been informed that wars were to be started and the reasons or lack of reasons for starting them, would they have submitted to their precipitation?

"It is not too much to demand that the people should know the reasons for the commencement and the continuance of the pending wars and they should understand the awful consequences. Those who are directly affected and must bear the burdens are, in a large measure, ignorant of the facts which have been suppressed, partly at least because knowledge of those facts would prevent a continuance of the most stupendous, if not the most unreasonable, destruction of life and property the world has ever witnessed."

What can be done to prevent like catastrophe?

"It is not too much to believe that, after the close of the war, there will be a feeling almost universal that there must be established and maintained a court of arbitration—simple, comprehensive, effective and permanent—that will secure the adjustment of all future differences without any protracted or general contest by armed forces. A majority of the nations will, to use an ordinary paradox, 'secure and maintain peace if they have to fight for it.' "

Should we go in?

"Up to the present time, the attitude of the President with respect to this question has been admirable. He has shown himself to be a true patriot and a wise statesman. In my opinion, the United States has not been called upon to do or say anything with reference to the war or any of the participants which has not been said or done. Every duty devolving upon the United States has been performed. We may have sympathies or prejudices or notions concerning specific acts or expressions on the part of some or many of the foreign nations, but, in my judgment, they have not required and do not require any act or expression on our part which has not been done or made. We have fulfilled every obligation imposed upon us by all treaties or agreements expressed or implied.''

And here is the prophecy.

''The people, as distinguished from the rulers, will have a voice in bringing the war to a close and in the settlements which are to be made. The doctrine of 'the divine right of kings' will be only a recollection. It is a good guess that many kings and kingdoms will be occupying space on the Transition Slide.''

Judge Gary came back from the exciting work of rescuing American tourists from the path of war to find the United States in the grip of the worst depression that he or any one of his generation had seen. Tens of thousands of people in New York City alone were out of employment. All over the country men were walking the streets looking for work. He immediately threw himself into the relief movements on foot and at the same time took upon himself particularly the work of encouraging and counseling his associates in the Corporation.

They needed it, for never had they been so heavy hearted as in 1914. Their earnings were lower than in 1904 or 1908—the periods they had always looked back to as the worst they would ever be asked to weather! Again the dividends on common stock had to be passed, again men had to be laid off—nearly 50,000 of them in the Corporation—and yet, difficult as things were, wages were not lowered in 1914. There was a determination that that should be the last move.

It was the war, coming on the top of two years of depression, which made the situation so disastrous; but it was the war which brought them out of unemployment and depression, for early in 1915 the warring countries began calling on our resources—food, ammunition, clothing, shoes—all that armies and navies required were sought in this country. Iron and steel and their products are basic needs in wars; and nowhere in the world outside of the warring countries was there any group so splendidly equipped to supply the demand as the United States Steel Corporation.

It will be recalled that one of the arguments Judge Gary had persistently used with Mr. Morgan in the two years that the Carnegie interests were trying to persuade the banker to buy them out, was that with the resources of the Carnegie Steel Company they would have the capacity to develop a systematic foreign trade, something the Federal Steel Company had not been able to do, although that was one of the reasons for its organization. Building a foreign trade had been one of Mr. Schwab's most forceful arguments in the speech in December of 1900 which finally had brought Mr. Morgan to the buying point.

As soon as the Corporation was in harness, it began to talk foreign extension, "The idea being," according to the minutes, "that our export trade is not for the purpose of disposing of surplus products and thereby making the business to a certain extent a temporary one, but that it is the intention to supply at all times as large a market as our facilities will permit.''

Luckily for the idea, they had acquired in one of the subsidiaries the ablest and most experienced man in the country for this particular work, James A. Farrell, at that time foreign sales agent of the American Steel and Wire Company, but who, on January 1, 1911, at the insistence of Judge Gary, was made president of the United States Steel Corporation, a position he still holds.

Mr. Farrell was a product of the wire end of the steel business. He had gone to work as a laborer in a wire mill at fifteen, had become a mechanic, and after four years' experience, a wire drawer. He had risen from his machine to the position he held when the Steel Corporation was organized—one of those ''intangibles'' whose money value could not be estimated like ore, but which gave those on the inside faith in the ''water'' of the Steel Corporation.

Under Mr. Farrell's direction the various branches of foreign business in the subsidiaries were soon united, operation and management being centered in 1903 in a new company, a subsidiary of the Federal Steel, called the United States Steel Products Company. Steadily and quietly this company went about its business. Mr. Farrell was called upon in 1913 in the course of the government suit against the Corporation to explain what they were doing abroad. His story amazed and impressed every student of international commerce; and it was so different from the popular notion that all the Steel Corporation was doing was dumping its surplus in countries well equipped to supply their own needs. As a matter of fact, so Mr. Farrell claimed, these products were not offered for use in England, France, or Germany. They had agencies in most of the great European capitals, but this was because they were the trading markets of the world, the points to which the representatives of countries which were just beginning to develop their resources came in order to make the best bargains.

They had offices in the world's great market places and they had warehouses at its chief distributing centers. Thus there were better shipping opportunities in Antwerp for many points the Corporation wanted to reach than there were in New York; accordingly, it had there an enormous warehouse. Mr. Farrell told the examiners in the suit that the Corporation had sixty agencies scattered throughout the world, with warehouses in South Africa, China, South America, and Australia. They had made what their customers needed and wanted—Java wanted square nails and got them, but Australia would not use anything but oval, and oval it was. Costa Rica built a railroad, but she must have steel ties and telegraph poles as well as steel rails, otherwise the ants would eat them; and they were sent her.

Mr. Farrell was able to state that in eleven years this foreign trade had grown to $90,000,000 a year, and that its cost had been reduced from between 8 and 11 per cent to 0.8 of 1 per cent.

Moreover, the relations of the United States Steel Products Company with its competitors were as satisfactory abroad as at home, so it was natural that when the warring nations of Europe looked outside for help in steel and iron, they thought first of the Steel Corporation. It was not long before their demands were taxing the full resources not only of the Corporation, but of the entire American industry.

Work—work for everybody—brought relief even if

that relief came through the horrors of war. The tragedy of unemployment which had lain over the country throughout the fall and early winter of 1914-1915 passed. Prosperity had returned.

A genuine satisfaction was soon added to Judge Gary's relief in the break of the long depression, for in June (1915) the four judges who had heard the testimony in the suit the government had brought nearly four years before returned their opinion.

The government had asked for the dissolution not only of the Steel Corporation, but of each of the companies which had gone into its making. It was alleged that they were all "illegal monopolies"—the American Bridge Company, American Steel and Wire Company, Carnegie Company, the Federal Steel Company—each of the groups put together in 1901. The reason they were called illegal was that in each case it was said competition had been destroyed; that is, substantial concerns formerly in interstate competition had, by the amalgamation, become coöperative. The fact that in each the union had been voluntary, by bargaining and not by intrigue and force as in other combinations with which the courts had recently dealt, did not change the law; the fact that there was not complete monopoly in any of the concerns made no difference. It was charged that by getting together they had each limited competition and were therefore criminals; that the Corporation was a crime of crimes, since it was a criminal made up of criminals.

The government's lawyers in their brief contended that if two combinations had been created at the same time, "identical in character except as to constituents, and one used its power or position to advance or control prices, pursuing unfair methods of business or competition toward its competitors, and increasing its percentage of control, and the other did the opposite of all these things, they were alike illegal and so remained as long as such combination continued.'' There was no such thing as a ''good trust,'' the brief went on to say, they were all ''bad.''

This would mean, of course, that Judge Gary's theory, laid down to Mr. Morgan at the start, was unsound in the government's judgment. He had contended that conduct, not size, not the former competitive condition of the companies united should decide whether or not a trust should be allowed to live; and we have traced his continued effort to correct the practices of the Steel Corporation, to find out whether or no the government disapproved of this or that transaction or policy. He was certain that in the end the law governing corporations would be developed to prevent predatory competition, but allow voluntary, natural combinations; to prevent practices which were oppressive but allow those which were economically sound and in harmony with the forces of integration, and that sooner or later the law would accept his views and permit the ''good'' trust to live.

But had the time come?

The opinions handed down in June, 1915 (there were two of them reaching the same end but by different routes), proved that the law had gone a long way toward meeting Judge Gary's contention. The four judges agreed that the government had not made out a case that should be followed by a decree of dissolution. Their reading of the Sherman Antitrust Law was different from the government's and much closer both to the text of that law and to the various opinions which had been laid down up to that time in the effort toward its interpretation.

The act was meant to protect trade, they pointed out. It was not aimed at size or power, but their possible abuses. It was not intended to force competition, but to prevent interferences with competition. It was not concerned with combinations, however monopolistic in their original intent, if that intent had proved abortive or had been abandoned, but at monopolies which destroyed the "potentiality of competition."

It was on this reading of the law that Judge Buffington, of the Circuit Court, based his opinion, one of the ablest and most exhaustive digests of an appalling amount of testimony and statistics, as well as one of the clearest and most sensible pieces of argument to be found in the important opinions interpreting the Sherman law.

Judge Buffington came to the case with an understanding and a background which unfortunately few judges bring to industrial cases. He knew the steel business, had worked as a boy in his vacations in steel mills—and loved them. Out of sheer interest he had continued, after entering the law, following the changing processes in the industry, and had come to believe that economic forces were compelling integration.

Reading the law as we have seen and distinguishing clearly between monopoly and integration, the steel case became for Judge Buffington one of business facts. He sought in the testimony answers to two questions:

"First: Was the Steel Corporation, when this bill was filed in 1911, prejudicing the public interests by unduly restricting competition, or unduly obstructing the course of the steel and iron trade, between the States or with foreign nations? If this question be answered, yes—the law was then being violated and an injunction should issue to restrain present and future violations.

"Second: Did the Steel Corporation, when it was formed in 1901, by the intent of those forming it, or by the inherent nature of that company's contemplated acts, prejudice the public interests by unduly restricting competition or unduly obstructing the course of the steel and iron trade, interstate or foreign? If this question be answered, yes—then the law was violated, and the Steel Corporation must be adjudged originally illegal. If illegal, it must be dissolved."

The facts he marshaled from the testimony in answer to his questions came like news to many of those who read them. Judge Buffington was certainly right in saying as he did in his opinion, that when the steel business of the United States was referred to, people thought only of the United States Steel Corporation. The government attorneys had evidently so thought in preparing the suit. But he pointed out the surprising fact that while in 1901 the Corporation had made and sold about 60 per cent of the steel and iron produced in the United States, in 1911, when the suit was brought, its competitors had the 60 per cent of production and the Corporation the 40 per cent. Nor had the change in percentage been forced upon it, as one of the judges in the case intimated, for Judge Gary had intentionally curtailed the production. His conclusion was not to allow in any branch over 50 per cent of the business, and oddly enough, it was William Jennings Bryan who set this per cent for him! Along in 1906 Bryan was advocating 50 per cent as a legal limit for the size of a business, and Judge Gary had seized the figure. "If we confine ourselves voluntarily to a size approved by the most popular and trusted of radicals, we surely cannot be attacked for monopoly," he had told his associates. They had acquiesced and had succeeded fairly well in keeping the percentage down, even in the leading products.

The Steel Corporation was not a monopoly in 1911, for its competitors had a majority of the total production. To be sure, it had grown. It was mining a little over $13,000,000 worth of ore in 1901, and about $20,-000,000 worth in 1911; the gross receipts were $560,000,-000 in 1901 and $615,000,000 in 1911. Everything considered, there had been about a 40 per cent increase in its business in the ten years. But its chief competitors had all made a higher proportionate gain: 90 per cent for the Republic Iron and Steel; 155 per cent for the Cambria; 206 per cent for Jones and Laughlen; 3779 per cent for the Bethlehem. Its own growth had come partially, too, from developing a foreign trade in countries where heretofore no nation had had much trade. Judge Buffington made a detailed and brilliant picture of the legitimate foreign trade developed by the Corporation, to which I have referred above, pointing out that this was not a seizure of what had once belonged to somebody else, but a legitimate extension by its own energy and ability and patience. This was news to many of those who read his opinion.

Competitor after competitor testified that while the Corporation was a hard-headed one, it was fair, often generous and that *nobody feared attack from it,* a striking contrast to those great combinations where strength was so systematically used to injure that competitors lived in a kind of chronic panic, without confidence or peace, frequently "seeing things" where there was nothing.

The changes its methods had brought had affected not only the steel industry but others related to steel. It was news to many people that in 1911 there could be found many competitors willing to say to the government what this one did:

"Before the formation of the Steel Corporation, business ethics, I might say, were in very bad shape; competitors had no confidence in each other; they resorted to subterfuges, misrepresentation and false statements. That same lack of confidence existed between sellers and many purchasing agents. It was a very undesirable condition in which to do business. For the past seven or ten years—in later times at any rate—all that misunderstanding or misgiving has been displaced by manly, straightforward dealing. I do not think it could have been brought about without the Steel Corporation's influence and example."

One of the exhibits on which the government had depended to establish its charge was a monopolistic control of ore. This was examined at length and the four judges agreed that the Corporation did not have a monopoly of raw materials.

Another piece of evidence which was pretty generally held to be conclusive of the government's case was the purchase of the Tennessee Coal, Iron and Railroad Company, yet the decision was that this, as well as other challenged sales, were "made in fair business course."

Considerable stress was put by the government on the prices of iron and steel products after 1901; yet the Judges asserted that there was no evidence that the Corporation had ever set an "arbitrary, exorbitant, unfair or controlling price." The answer then to the first question Judge Buffington had asked was, "No." The United

States Steel Corporation was not in 1911 a monopoly unduly restraining trade.

But how about the second question? Was it the intent in 1901 to monopolize and restrict trade? Judge Gary had always contended not. They sought a "rounded proposition." Robert Bacon, certainly a witness of character and at the center of negotiations, said: "It was said by all those gentlemen present—I believe by all of them; I know by Mr. Morgan—that under no considerations would they take part in anything which was or might be considered to be a monopoly, or any attempt to restrain competition. I know that that was one thing furthest from his willingness to participate in."

Mr. Schwab was equally emphatic as to Mr. Morgan's idea in forming the Corporation: "From the moment when I first started with Mr. Morgan, the question of our gaining a monopoly or in any way controlling the steel industry was never mentioned. My whole argument with him, as advocating this company, was the economic development of the same, and the matter, to the best of my knowledge, never came up thereafter."

What, then, were they attempting? Judge Gary explained it once in these words: "There was an effort made to acquire properties that would be useful to each other—and by that I mean to acquire a plant that furnished certain commodities to another plant which we were acquiring, and to acquire the latter because it could, at good advantage, secure the products which it needed for its uses, and so all through the line, from the ore down to the conversion from one product into another and the final distribution of the finished product."

That, of course, is the process later known to the public as "integration," though in 1901 the word was not in popular use. Indeed, Judge Woolley, who wrote the second of the two opinions, pointed out what is true, that the word was not used once in the testimony reporting what was said by Mr. Morgan, Mr. Schwab and the others engaged in forming the Steel Corporation. Therefore, he argued, they must have meant monopoly—which does not follow. They used a near equivalent, "rounded proposition," and Mr. Percival Roberts, Jr., used no other word than "integration" in his testimony.

Reviewing the testimony—analyzing ably and succinctly the forces of integration—Judge Buffington gave a "No" to his second question.

But if the Steel Corporation was not criminal in 1911, nor had a criminal intent in coming together, one of its practices abandoned in 1911 was condemned in both opinions as a restraint of trade. "The Gary dinners," wrote Judge Woolley, "were in effect pools."

"But the period of coöperation had passed away before the bill was filed, and as far as we can see it is not likely to be repeated. We do not think the Gary movement [the "Gary dinners"] would justify us in imposing so drastic a penalty as the dissolution of the corporation, but we will, if the Government moves for such action, retain the bill for the purpose of restraining any similar movement by the defendants that might be contemplated hereafter."

There was great rejoicing in steel circles. Many congratulations on all sides for "the good trust." Nothing Judge Gary received pleased him better than the following characteristic letter from Theodore Roosevelt:

Personal.   OYSTER BAY.
                      LONG ISLAND. N.Y.   June 5th, 1915

My dear Judge Gary:

      I want to congratulate you most heartily upon the outcome of the suit against the United States Steel Corporation.   It is a great personal victory for you, because one of the main counts of the suit was the action of the Steel Corporation in acquiring the Tennessee Coal & Iron Company; and you were directly accused of deception in connection with that purchase.   The Court has now declared that your action in this matter was absolutely legal and honorable.   Personally I was able to declare when I testified in the suit that my subsequent investigation showed that your statements to me were absolutely true.   As you know, the investigation which I had the Bureau of Corporations make into the affairs of the Steel Corporation convinced me that there was no warrant for the suit against you.   I appreciate the important part that your counsel has had in establishing the course of conduct of the Corporation; and I therefore congratulate you on the vindication you have received at the hands of the Circuit Court.

      With best wishes, I am

          Faithfully yours,

Hon. E. H. Gary,   *Theodore Roosevelt*

   71 Broadway,
      New York City.

The immediate effect of the opinions handed down by the judges was greatly to encourage Judge Gary in his belief that in the end the conduct of the Corporation would save it. A long period of waiting was still before him, however. The government carried the case to the Supreme Court, and it was not until March, 1917, it was heard. Seven judges heard the case, but failed to return a majority opinion, and a reargument was ordered.

Almost simultaneously with this order came a request from the government to Judge Gary, as president of the Iron and Steel Institute, to form and head a committee of steel men to mobilize the nation's industry for the war which was now a certainty. It was a position of tremendous responsibility. Steel is a first essential in war. In the last two years the American industry had been making money on foreign orders at an unheard-of rate. The Steel Corporation's earnings in 1916 had been more than twice what they had been in any previous year in its history—over $333,500,000. All its competitors were prospering equally. Would they accept the lower prices the government was sure to insist on—increase their plants—make the gigantic effort it asked?

Judge Gary had not a doubt of it. He proposed that the Corporation should coöperate to the limit, and he believed that the majority of the trade outside would do what the government asked.

The legal department of the Corporation, foreseeing the enlargement of plants, the launching of new enterprises, the extraordinary expenditures which war meant for the Corporation, pressed for a prompt decision in the suit. See the position we are left in, they argued; the loss to stockholders, if after the war we are dissolved.

But the government decided it was not to the public interest to hear the appeal in the war.

It seems to have made no difference in the energy or the wisdom of the chairman of the steel committee.

He had a nice task. The government was grimly determined from the start to get its supplies at what might be called reasonable war prices. The first business of the chairman of the steel committee was to bring his associates to accept a list of prices the President would approve. The Corporation itself had already given proof of its intention to meet the government's prices, even though it might think them too low, for on the very day that war was declared, Secretary Daniels had sent out a bulletin boasting of making a contract which, he said, had saved the government $18,000,000. It was a contract with the Steel Corporation for plates at $2.90 per hundred pounds, although, as Judge Gary told his stockholders at a meeting held a few days later, they could have sold the same in the open market at eight, nine, or ten dollars; but, as he said, they would not, under any consideration, have thought of accepting those terms. The price they put on plates at that time to the Allies was from $4.00 to $4.50 per hundred pounds. That is, he had been holding since the war began, as he had held in peace times, that prices should always be reasonable, and he had done much talking both in and out of the Corporation on the sound economy of not letting the war run away with prices.

Few of his competitors agreed with him; generally they were for taking all they could get, and as for subordinating themselves now to the government's decisions, there was more than one strong and important man who believed in the beginning that it would be the surest way to decrease production. It was not strange. The handling of the industrial side of the war was based at the start on a muddle of military, legalistic, doctrinaire, political, and business or practical notions and shibboleths. The great ability, disinterestedness, and devotion which the civilians brought to the government's problems were still mixed with so much vanity and greed, ignorance and suspicion, bumptiousness and self-seeking, that at times the whole war machine was threatened with destructive delays.

The country was soon ringing with stories of the confusion at Washington, and almost every business man that came back told some experience like this, which actually happened to a high official of the Steel Corporation at one of the first meetings of the General Munitions Board.

He was explaining that there was at the moment—early April—a shortage of ore, due to the late ore shipping season. "Why," said a visiting member of a related committee sternly, "did you allow a late season in such a crisis?" Practical men controlled their smiles, and the reproved gentleman said the lakes were full of ice. "Why then," continued his critic, "did you not ship by rail?" "Even if it had been practical," he replied, "to ship great quantities of ore by rail—which it is not because of the weight—the railroads run in the wrong direction."

Judge Gary realized the demoralizing effect of the criticisms and the ridicule running over the country, and in May, at the first meeting of the Iron and Steel Institute held after war was declared, he cautioned the members against a loose acceptance of hearsay.

"You have heard some criticism concerning the conduct of the Government's business affairs," he said. "It has been said that confusion or at least lack of system or coöperation sometimes appears; but it must be remembered that there has been suddenly thrust upon the Government officials an enormous amount of business, extraordinary in volume and character, and the strength and capacity of all are taxed to the utmost and often beyond physical endurance. Besides, rules of law or of departments established to fit other conditions sometimes appear and prevent the exercise of judgment which would bring better results if more latitude were permitted. Officials in Washington are entitled to credit and praise for their management, under existing circumstances, and so far I believe there is no just ground for severe criticism.

"And then there is a disposition on the part of Government officials to coöperate with the business men in promoting the welfare of the country. This is what all of us have desired and advocated, and now we will probably have as much opportunity in this direction as we have ever desired."

They were to have just that and there were not a few of them who were to receive their first lessons in the meaning of government coöperation. They discovered that it meant placing the general good above private ambition.

It was not the work the government asked of them at which they balked. They were willing to a man to tackle anything however untried, whatever the expenditure it required, however certain that, the war over, the equipment would be scrapped; but they demanded to be paid; and in the months between the May and October meeting of the Institute there were many exciting tussles over

JUDGE GARY ON HIS FARM

MEMBERS OF THE FINANCE COMMITTEE, UNITED STATES STEEL CORPORATION, VISITING BAYVIEW, ALABAMA, JUNE 7, 1917. LEFT TO RIGHT, GEORGE F. BAKER, HENRY C. FRICK, GEORGE W. PERKINS, PERCIVAL ROBERTS, JR., HON. ELBERT H. GARY.

prices between the committees representing the iron and
steel industry and those representing the government.
Judge Gary was spokesman of the steel men—not of the
government. It was his business to see that the industry
received what was fair, but he would not fight for more;
and there were certain strong leaders in the industry
that did. More than once the meeting broke up in those
early months of the war because certain steel men stood
out for higher prices than the government was willing
to pay.

"Wait," said Gary to the government committee one
day when the recalcitrant steel men had walked out of
the meeting. "I will bring those men back." "You are
asking more than you ought to have," he told his associates, and after half an hour's discussion, he kept his
promise. The committee reconvened, with the result that
the debated price was referred to him, with power.

By October the committee was working in fair harmony, but when the regular semiannual meeting of the
Institute was held, Judge Gary took his chance for
further counsel.

"Many of you," he said, "were disappointed when
the prices of the commodities in which you are particularly interested were announced. You had expected
larger figures. You had been receiving from your customers, in the ordinary course of trade, much more
favorable results. Your profits will be less than you
have believed you are entitled to. Your costs of production and construction are increasing by leaps and bounds.
Many manufacturers have struggled for existence in
periods when business conditions were bad, trusting to
the future for improvement, and they have argued that,
if the law of supply and demand should govern under

such circumstances, it should control at this time and all times. However, all these things have been considered by the iron and steel committees, and by the representatives of the Government as well. It is only stating facts to say that the former have endeavored to represent the manufacturers conscientiously, intelligently and forcefully, and that the members of the War Industries Board have at all the hearings given patient attention, thorough investigation and careful consideration to every claim presented, with the sole purpose of doing justice both to the government and to the individual."

Throughout the war he kept up these exhortations. All of those who worked close to the Judge and his executives in the war have testified to both the efficiency and the willingness of his coöperation. Colonel F. A. Scott of Cleveland, Ohio, who, at the suggestion of Secretary Baker, was made chairman of the General Munitions Board on March 31, 1917, and later, in July, chairman of the War Industries Board, from the start dealt with Judge Gary and Mr. Farrell. Major General Crozier, Chief of Ordnance, describes Colonel Scott as a "man of sanity" whose coming into the "turbulent situation" at the beginning of the war was a "great good fortune to the Government." He was with Mr. Farrell when he made the contract with the Navy Department which so pleased Secretary Daniels, and he speaks warmly of the help that he received from the Corporation. He pays a high compliment to Judge Gary —one that not many men earn in such situations—that in all of these early negotiations he "showed the patience of a statesman who understood that you must give time to allow the mental column to close up."

R. S. Brookings, who in the spring of 1918 was made

chairman of the price-fixing committee which covered the products of some two hundred factories and who constantly came into contact with Gary at the meetings where the prices of steel products were settled, says in a letter to the writer:

As Chairman of the Price Fixing Committee it was my privilege to be very closely associated during the war with Judge Gary, who was spokesman for the entire steel industry. As steel was the keystone of our war needs and maximum production at a fair price was no easy problem, I have only the greatest admiration for the fairness and skill with which Judge Gary met the views of the Government and at the same time, reconciled and satisfied the great variety of interests which he represented.

Mr. Replogle, who in April of 1918 was made director of steel supply and who at once began to whip up the delinquents (supposed and real) in the industry, said at a gathering of the steel committees held at Judge Gary's offices:

In the early stages of the game, when we were in great distress for some material for General Pershing, we came to Judge Gary and Mr. Farrell; and despite the fact that they were loaded up, they turned in—they had taken seventy per cent of all the Government orders placed at that time, which was far in excess of their capacity, and yet they absolutely took that without question and gave General Pershing the material when and as he needed it.

Now, this was the public side of the work of the Judge in this period, but as chief executive of the Corporation he had an even heavier responsibility. The Corporation was on its mettle, proving not only its efficiency and usefulness in a time of stress, but its good will. An unprejudiced examination of the available material from the various agencies charged with the conduct of the war proves that everything asked of it was done. Not only that but, according to Colonel Scott, certainly for many months in a position to know, "If there was a difficult and undesirable job to be done, the Corporation took it."

This is the more praiseworthy, because they were in a position to select their own tasks. Mr. Farrell had been made chairman of the "Sub-committee for Ascertaining Capacities and Supervising Allotments of Orders to Manufacturers." He never spared his own people; never failed to help a competitor. Frequently a concern found itself short of materials required for an order allotted and to be delivered by a certain date. Mr. Farrell, under Judge Gary's instructions, supplied them, whether it was billets or nuts, and at a price below his own cost if the other concern stood to lose on the contract, as was sometimes the case. They must be allowed to make a little money if they were to carry on. Such transactions were frequent throughout the war.

There were voluntary acts of foresight which prevented disasters. For example, the Washington purchasing bureau refused to provide extra supplies of manganese. It would not be needed. Judge Gary and Mr. Farrell knew better and the Corporation laid in 600,000 tons. When the shortage came, they sold to their competitors at the price they had paid. The close of the war found them with 200,000 tons on hand.

The government agencies came to them in tight places. At one time it looked as if the reserve of block tin for food containers was near exhaustion. A big credit was needed in London to insure a supply. The Corporation was asked to put up one million pounds, sterling, to carry on the trade which was with the Malay Straits. It did so and the generosity not only saved the situation but rebounded to the benefit of the country from which the supply came.

Incredible quantities of an incredible number of different things were furnished. Take wire alone. The army, the navy, the bureau of aircraft, the signal corps, the shipbuilding plants, each had its separate and special needs: they ran from wire so fine it almost needed a magnifying glass to see it, to the great submarine cables —and the quantities! The American Steel and Wire Company made in the war some 20,000 tons of bookbinding wire for binding government productions—"principally questionnaires"!—which is easier for the layman with his war experience to visualize than 75,000 kegs of horseshoes, or 500,000 kegs of iron nails for cantonments and buildings!

Extraordinary tasks were put upon the Corporation— tasks in which they had had no experience—which demanded huge sums of money and which would be dropped at the end of the war, such as building ships.

They were asked in the summer of 1917 to assist in meeting what was realized as one of the most formidable weaknesses of the situation. "We did not wish to go into the business of building ships," Judge Gary told his stockholders at their next meeting April, 1918. "It was entirely out of our line; but we were approached by Government representatives to see if we could assist in building ships at a time when they were so much needed. And after making a careful study of the situation we decided we could build them at least as cheaply as any one else, and at least as rapidly as any one else, that we could get into the business as soon as any one else, and that we could build a style and character of ship that would be practical, efficient and satisfactory to the Government.''

Two plants were started, one on the Hackensack River, the other at Mobile, Alabama. When Judge Gary talked to his stockholders he told them, ''amid applause,'' that the first ship was to be launched in May—nine months after they broke ground—and that, beginning in July, the Corporation's two plants would furnish a complete ship every ten days.

It was this record of efficiency and this spirit of prompt coöperation which led Secretary Baker to wire Judge Gary on April 20, 1918, that he was sending the Assistant Secretary of War to New York ''to take up with you a matter of the very greatest urgency and importance to the Government in the prosecution of the war. The project which he will present to you will involve the immediate and thorough-going coöperation of the Steel Corporation, and perhaps to some extent a departure from its lines of policy as heretofore projected, but the subject has been earnestly studied from every point of view and the conclusion reached that the Government must depend upon the action of the Steel Corporation in this matter, there being no other agency to which we can turn in the emergency.''

The project presented to Judge Gary was formidable: to build an ordnance and munitions plant with a capacity of ''Twelve 14-inch 50-caliber guns—or equivalent—and of 40,000 shells per month.''

It was a staggering undertaking for a group which for months now had been working under the lash of a desperate government; but when Judge Gary had laid it before his associates, they agreed with him, as he wired Secretary Baker on the twenty-fifth, that there was an obligation to undertake the work. On the heels of his consent followed a contract, "intended," so the Judge said, to be "simple, thoroughly explicit and comprehensive." The contract provided that the Corporation should take entire charge of the design, construction, and operation of the plant, subject to approval of general plans by the Secretary of War, and that it should be reimbursed for only the exact cost of outlays made directly for the work which, in accordance with the offer of the Corporation, included no compensation for the service of its officials, experts, or its general organization in supervising the work; nor for the interest upon considerable sums advanced for the payment of labor, material, and other construction expenditures.

A special department for the work was organized. Neville Island, in the Ohio River, just below Pittsburgh, was selected for a site, and by September they were getting ready to make guns, though the plant was, of course, far from complete.

The promptness with which this difficult project was tackled was but a reflection of the desperation felt at that moment by all those responsible for handling any essential factor in the prosecution of war. Judge Gary at this period certainly felt more alarm for the result of the war than he ever had before and he expressed his fear more freely. He had come to feel that the Allies had their backs to the wall. On June 13, 1918, in a speech at Duluth, he voiced his fear—but with a prophecy:

"I venture the assertion that the allied armies, together with those of the United States, are or soon will be standing with their backs to the entrenchments which they have constructed, their faces fronting the enemy, with teeth set, weapons in place, and a fixed and defiant purpose that will never yield nor retreat. We need not be surprised if in the near future the tide of battle shall change, and that threatened defeat and disaster shall be turned into glorious victory for our forces.''

His prophecy was to be realized quicker than he dared hope. On July 19 the turn came—the German armies retreated across the Marne, and they never after reestablished their military line. On November 11 the Armistice was signed. Even before November 11 the government dropped its whip; the stream of production began to fall. Secretary Baker sent word that the plans for the Neville Island arsenal should be curtailed —a small plant would do. "Why should the government build any plant?" replied Gary. "The war is over." And after careful consideration that was the final decision.

The Steel Corporation had already contracted up to fifty million dollars towards the undertaking. The government reimbursed them for their actual outlay, not for their services—they donated them and took the steel they had made off the government's hands.

Taking it all in all, the coöperation which the United States Steel Corporation gave the government of the United States, from the hour that it first appealed to it in March of 1917, before the declaration of war, was whole-hearted and of the highest efficiency. Judge Gary asked of his associates that they set the pace for production—give the model for willing compliance with demands, and to do it even if what was demanded might seem to them impractical, unnecessary. No one was omniscient, he told them, mistakes would be made in so gigantic and hurried an enterprise. Generous coöperation in whatever was undertaken was the surest way to win the government's confidence.

At the head of the steel committee, charged with keeping the industry in line, his work through the Iron and Steel Institute was patient and tactful, but determined. Many of the great independents were like Price McKinney of Cleveland, and George Verity of the Amico, who asked only "Tell us what to do—as for price, what the government sets." But there were laggards and bargainers in the industry. The government was harsh with them, as was necessary, and too often it threatened the whole industry because of what a few were doing; often, too, the forming and reforming committees of the Council of Defense, intent on making a record without fully informing themselves, charged the steel industry with delays of which it was not guilty, shortages when there were none. It was Judge Gary's business to find the truth, appraise, stir up the laggards and mollify— and sometimes inform—the harassed representatives of the government.

He was amazingly patient and adroit in most difficult situations. In April of 1918, when defeat seemed impending and the pressure of the government was harshest, a meeting of the full steel committee was called at his office in New York to meet Mr. Replogle, the newly appointed steel director. Forty-four concerns beside the Steel Corporation were represented. Judge Gary realized the difficulties ahead of the meeting and sought to set the key for it.

Gentlemen [he said, in opening], this is an important meeting. . . . It is unnecessary to emphasize the fact that the Allies engaged in the Battle of all Ages are calling upon this country for all the help that can be given. . . . They need more men, more food, more munitions of war, more guns, and various other things, and ships to carry them across the seas when needed. And all these things must be provided at the very earliest moment. The furnishing of necessary supplies promptly means the saving of millions of lives. So far as I am personally concerned, while I have great hopes for the future and a feeling of grim determination to win this war, yet I have a feeling of fear for catastrophes, a fear for results that we cannot recover from. And that arises not from the fact that we have not enough men or money or materials, but rather from the fact that there is danger that these will not be provided as promptly as they might be and as appears to be absolutely necessary if we are to do everything we ought to do and that we can do.

I feel it is not necessary in talking to Americans to deal in language of patriotism or duty. Many of your boys and your relatives and your friends are already on the battle lines or on their way to those places, and more and more will be called and are going. And the more diligent we are in the performance of our duty the less will be the number that are called upon to make the supreme sacrifice which war, and war alone, asks of the people, of the country.

. . . The question of making money, while always important and necessary for the nation, is of no importance when compared to the immediate necessities of the government for the production and delivery of the things which it demands and finds necessary for military purposes.

A stormy session followed, marked by outspoken charges of delays and indifference from Mr. Replogle, by delinquents named, and by equally outspoken denials by the accused. At a moment when it looked as if the meeting was getting out of hand, Judge Gary suddenly laid before the members of the committee a pledge:

"For myself, my Corporation or my firm, I pledge the prompt production and delivery of the largest possible quantity of material in our departments that is, or shall be required by the United States Government for the necessities of itself and its allies, and agree that all other lines of our business shall be subordinated to this pledge, and all this in accordance with the request of the War Industries Board.''

There was not a man present that would have dared— even if he wished to, of which there is no evidence—to have refused to sign, and every man present voted ''Yes'' when the roll was called. Everybody was in line —all Mr. Replogle had now to do was to give his orders. A more tactful, effective, and legitimate way of saving a difficult situation it would be hard to cite. But it was typical of his handling of the steel committee throughout the war.

The war was over, but before the Armistice was signed new problems confronted the Steel Corporation. Here it was with shipyards; with an arsenal building; with immense expansion of all kinds in and out of what it considered its line. What should it do? How contract? And was it to be allowed to live?

The government's plea for its dissolution was on the docket of the Supreme Court. In a few months it might be ordered to go out of business as a corporation— returned to the hundred or so companies from which its subsidiaries originally were formed. It was a staggering idea, but they must face it, waiting the government's time.

A more immediate problem, one all signs showed it must take up as soon as the war machine stopped, was the old one of labor. Organized labor was preparing war on the open shop. It had given full and intelligent co-operation in the war; now it proposed to assert its claims for recognition by all industries. The steel industry was its chief opponent, and the Steel Corporation with its

40 to 45 per cent of the business was the point in the industry it was certain to attack.

To that attack the Corporation opposed its own labor policy much in the same way as it had opposed its conduct to the government's legalistic pleas for its dissolution.

How about their labor policy? What was it and how was it working at the end of the Great War?

CHAPTER XI

GARY AND LABOR

A CONSPICUOUS phenomenon of the Great War was the use made of the desperate straits in which governments found themselves by advocates of this or that change in the political, social, or industrial structure. The mass in every country served the War with singleness of purpose— "Win the War" was its slogan. But in every country those wedded to special reforms or systems watched for moments when they might take advantage of situations to strengthen their particular cause.

American organized labor, adopted this venerable political strategy when it set out in 1918 to extend unionism over the country. The particular industry which it chose for attack was the one in which it was the weakest —steel; and the particular section of steel which it chose was the one which was strongest and the one that for sixteen years had consistently held to the policy of the open shop—the United States Steel Corporation.

When the movement for the nationalization of the steel industry cropped up in Washington in that year, it had at least a tentative backing from labor. The sporadic strikes which occurred in certain steel plants were probably engineered by labor leaders who believed in the nationalization of steel, and hoped to bring about such interference with war production that the government

279

would have to take over the industry. If this happened, unionization of labor was inevitable. But the movement for nationalization never took hold. No more did its supporters receive substantial aid from labor; the mass of the workers were more interested in the war than in unionism.

The first effective move in the agitation came in June of 1918 when at the convention of the American Federation of Labor held in St. Paul, Minnesota, the following resolution was adopted:

Resolved, That the executive officers of the American Federation of Labor stand instructed to call a conference, during this convention, of delegates of all international unions whose interests are involved in the steel industries, and of all the State Federations and City Central bodies in the steel districts, for the purpose of uniting all these organizations into one mighty drive to organize the steel plants of America.

Organizers went to work in the chief steel centers in August following this meeting. The skilled men in and out of the union were lukewarm. The chief response came from the rank and file—foreigners of little experience in the United States, many of them not speaking English. Steel managers everywhere of course followed the movement, estimating its growth and temper. There is no doubt that they had their agents in the shops as the unions did their organizers. Under-cover agitators always breed under-cover men in human activities. As the months went on, suspicion grew into passion; by spring the steel plants and towns were thick with it. Public sentiment began to be aroused. In and around Pittsburgh, where the memories of the strikes of 1892 and 1909 were still alive and bitter, the press, churches,

business organizations called loudly on the authorities
to prevent disorder.

The leaders knew by the early summer of 1919 that
the movement was not as strong as it must be if they were
to succeed, and at the convention of the Federation held
in June at Atlantic City, it was decided that the force
in the field was altogether inadequate to carry on the
work in the vigorous manner the situation demanded,
and President Gompers was requested to secure the assistance of all the international unions affiliated with the
American Federation of Labor, whose members were directly or indirectly connected with steel. This was done,
a strike committee from twenty-four different organizations being appointed.

Judge Gary's help in the movement was now sought,
Mr. Gompers, the president of the Federation, writing
him that the American Federation of Labor had decided
to bring about a thorough organization of iron and steel
and wanted to confer with him. Mr. Tighe, president
of the Amalgamated, wrote him. Mr. Foster and Mr.
Fitzpatrick, who had been the active men in the movement from the start, sought conferences. It was sound
political strategy on their part, for if Judge Gary received them as leaders, as they asked, it was a recognition on his part that they represented the employees of
the Corporation and it could not but stimulate organization in the United States Steel plants where it was
lagging badly. Corporation officials claimed that there
were not over 15 per cent of the men in unions, which
seems probable, as at the height of the movement there
was not over 25 per cent in all the various trade groups
in the whole steel industry.

Judge Gary is no mean politician himself. He realized

the boost a conference with him would give the movement and he refused to see the gentlemen who sought him—not as individuals as he tried to make clear—but as representatives of a movement in which he did not believe and which he had no intention of encouraging directly or indirectly.

The refusal came as a surprise to many of the public. The great mass had not realized the steady effort that had been going on for over a year to organize the steel industry. The great mass of people never see anything coming. They notice it when it arrives. The first serious attention they gave the labor disturbance was when Judge Gary refused to see the labor leaders. It amazed them that this could happen at a time when "getting together around the table" had become the favorite formula for settling disagreements. Judge Gary, who all through the troubled period of the War had been constantly employed in "getting together around the table" in order to relieve difficult situations, had refused, and many people, big and little, besought him to reconsider his decision. The president asked him to confer. I do not know his answer, but he did not confer.

What were his reasons? He gave them repeatedly. The gist of them was that the men did not represent the workers of the Steel Corporation, that no one of them had ever been in its employ, and that no man in its employ had asked him to see them.

"These men are volunteers, outsiders entirely. I don't think our men asked them to represent them. I have no idea they did because if our men were dissatisfied in any respect we would have heard of it and if we were wrong we would have corrected it. If they had come to me and said, 'We represent 15 per cent of your men and because we represent 15 per cent of your men we should like to talk to you about that 15 per cent,' I am not prepared to say that I would say 'no' to that. But they did not do that. Our 85 per cent are working side by side with 15 per cent who are members of the union. They have no controversy over it, all they want is an open shop. They say to the union men, 'Get all you can; we recognize that position, but do not interfere with our right to work in this shop.'

"This is a movement for a 'closed shop.' We are not willing to do anything which we believe, after consideration, amounts to the establishment of a closed shop as against an open shop, or that tends to do that. We stand firmly on the proposition that industry must be allowed to proceed untrammeled by the dictates of labor unions or any one else except the employer, the employees and the Government. That is where we stand." And that is where he continued to stand, in spite of attacks from many sides.

In the meantime the movement was getting away from its leaders. From every steel center organizers began to insist that there be action—a strike—some proof that what the men had been promised, or thought they had been promised, was going to happen. If the membership was to be held they must act—and to act meant to strike. In the emergency the leaders used Judge Gary adroitly. They called a strike on September 22, 1919, and the reason Mr. Fitzpatrick gave later was "the refusal on the part of Judge Gary to meet a conference."

But Judge Gary would not budge and he was in better case to hold his position because he thought it certain that the strike could not succeed. Indeed, it had the feel of failure from the start. Mr. Gompers felt this, so did Mr. Tighe, so did all of the experienced labor men in the conservative unions. It was a strike which never fully believed in itself, which was saturated on the inside from the start with suspicion—suspicion of the radical for the conservative; of the conservative for the radical. The members of the committee organized in June to invigorate the movement, pulled at cross purposes from the beginning, actuated as they were by their different notions of industrial organization. It was a committee perfectly described by a union official as having the "cohesiveness of a load of furniture."

While the organization of the entire steel industry was the goal of the labor leaders, its chief attack was on the Steel Corporation; Pittsburgh and vicinity was a vital point of this attack; but the strike never had solid footing in that district. True, large bodies stayed away from work in the plants around Pittsburgh in the early days of the trouble—some out of sympathy, some out of fear. There was violence at some points, clashes between strikers, men going to work, and police anxious to keep order, but, in spite of this, the majority soon came back. Organized bodies, like the switchers and the carmen, stayed at their posts. In the third week of the strike, a Senate committee which had promptly undertaken an investigation and which went to the Pittsburgh field, found 9,044 out of a normal force of 11,500 at work at Homestead; 5,370 out of 5,700 at Duquesne; 6,500 out of 7,000 at the Natural Tube Works, McKeesport; 2,600 out of 4,000 at Clairton. Four plants down the Ohio, near Wheeling and Steubenville, were closed on an average for two full months. The plant which suffered most severely in the strike was the Central Furnaces of Cleveland, employing some five or six hundred men. It was out five full months. A majority of the workers, many of them non-English speaking foreigners, seem to have been persuaded that if they held out the plant was certain to come under their management. So sure were they of this that they were reported to have portioned out among their numbers the executive jobs and to have tried to persuade the clerical staff in the company offices to join them. "We are going to run the plant and we shall need clerks," they are said to have told them. "If you come with us, you will get the jobs."

The best evidence that there was no deep or general determination among the employees of the Corporation to force organization, was the fact that life went on in the steel communities without serious dislocation. Production kept up fairly well, which was the test of management. Order was fairly well maintained, in spite of occasional violence on both sides. All the manifold social and educational activities of the towns went on. Schools were in session, churches were filled, prizes were awarded as usual for the best gardens, plant ball teams played one another, picnics and tournaments were held. We even read of one plant picnic at a tense moment in the drama at which 20,000 ears of corn and 600 gallons of ice cream were consumed!

A most conclusive proof that the body of steel workers had not lost confidence in the Corporation is the fact that in this disturbed year of 1919, 61,324 subscribed for steel stock and 46,676 of these were men receiving from $800 to $2,500 a year. The year following, 1920, with the after effects of the strike hanging over the labor body, 66,311 workers subscribed to steel stock.

The effort to unionize failed. In January the strike was called off. Judge Gary's contention, made so repeatedly during the trouble, to all sorts of critics and questioners, seems to have been sustained: "They (the organizers) did not represent our employees—they were not authorized to speak for them. We were absolutely certain they did not represent the sentiment of the large majority of our people, if any of them."

But if the strike was dead one problem it had raised was very much alive. Although the agitation had been started for the purpose of unionization it became necessary to give to the public reasons why unionization was desirable. This was done in the form of twelve demands—one of which was the eight-hour day. The strikers and their sympathizers declared that Judge Gary's opposition to the unionization of the Corporation's plants came mainly from his determination to preserve a twelve-hour day. There were persons who in the bitterness of the controversy intimated, and perhaps honestly believed, that Judge Gary had himself personally committed the industry to this schedule of hours and that he now was fighting to preserve his work.

It is possible to say now, though in 1920 there were people who would not listen to the statement, that the Steel Corporation and Judge Gary, its leader, never had anything to do with the arrangement of hours to which so many people in and out of the industry rightfully objected. These hours came into operation years before the Corporation was organized. As a matter of fact, they were practically forced on the steel industry in the 'eighties and 'nineties by workers in opposition to the employers, who were insisting on eight-hour shifts in the interest of more tonnage.

The proceedings of the Amalgamated Iron, Steel and

Tin Workers show that when the Federation of Labor began its campaign for an eight-hour day, the Amalgamated Council instructed its representatives to take no active part in the propaganda. The Council knew that it dared not run the risk of antagonizing members who had helped put the twelve-hour day into force. Why should they have held to twelve hours?

J. S. Robinson, who has made the only detailed study of the Amalgamated proceedings which has ever been published, says that their objection to the eight-hour day was twofold. "In the first place," explains Mr. Robinson, "earnings are less, since it is not easy to make five heats in eight hours, and it is imperative that the puddler has his heat out by the time the next turn comes on. Secondly, the workman enjoys less freedom under an eight-hour system. The puddler always has been accustomed to arrange for himself the time of starting and quitting. He objects to being hurried in order to produce a 'reasonable output.'"

A third reason, which crops up in the reports of the proceedings, was the fear that the eight-hour shift would bring in new labor, increase the competition in jobs, and there would not be work enough to go around. This fear was so strong that in the early days when three shifts were allowed by the union, it was the understanding that the output of each man should be limited.

Judge Gary has been criticized for declaring that the twelve-hour day in the steel industry was established by the men themselves, but he was right. A stock-holding workman who resented this criticism once declared at the annual stockholders' meeting: "I helped to establish it, and every working man who helped to build up the iron business helped to establish it. And the refusal in many cases to grant the twelve-hour day would have been a sufficient cause for a walk-out, many a time.''

These men who had established the twelve-hour day had adjusted their lives to the practice, particularly in the skilled branches of the trade. No twelve-hour man worked continuously; he probably was not employed over two-thirds of the time. No one who has been much about steel plants but has seen men in certain departments playing cards, sleeping, gardening, reading, eating a lunch with wife or children—a whistle blew and every man sprang to his place. Twenty to forty minutes of intensive work followed—then came leisure again. The unskilled twelve-hour man has his rest periods too, as every observer knows though they are less regular.

But as the steel industry grew, the evils inherent in such long hours became more and more apparent, particularly in congested districts like Pittsburgh and its vicinity. Social workers, pastors of churches, industrial investigators pointed out that the twelve-hour day, with the time consumed in going back and forth from work, left no waking hours for the family, the church, citizenship. It kept men from out-of-door life, self-improvement. It was antisocial, unhealthy, and, as they saw clearly, was arousing in younger men who had no industrial traditions, knew nothing of the origin of the custom, a bitterness which could not safely be disregarded. The campaign against it became so strong that in 1911 Charles M. Cabot of Boston, a steel stockholder, who had been much disturbed by the agitation asked at the annual meeting for a committee which should investigate and report in regard to the twelve-hour day and other charges that had been made against the Corporation's labor policy.

Judge Gary always holds a large majority of proxies and could of course have quashed the resolution at the start, but he told the meeting that he intended to vote for it; and the result was that it was unanimously carried. A year later the committee reported.

They told the stockholders that they had ascertained by an examination of the records of employees that about one-fourth of the whole labor body—25¾ per cent, to be exact—was on a twelve-hour basis, that the largest proportion of these men were in rolling mills, open hearths, blast furnaces, where the work was more or less continuous. They declared that the exhausting drudgery of the earlier years of the iron and steel industry had been cut down so that there was actually less call for hard work in this long day than in many of the eight- and ten-hour positions. Notwithstanding this, the committee said, they were of the opinion that a twelve-hour day of labor, followed continuously by any group of men for any considerable number of years meant a decreasing of the efficiency and lessening of the vigor and virility of such men.

They criticized the social effects particularly and emphasized the necessity of conserving the strength of the working population in order to be assured of a healthy, productive, intelligent citizenship in the future. "We are not unmindful of the fact," the committee went on, "that the twelve-hour day has, by its general acceptance and practice over a considerable period of years, become firmly entrenched, and that any sudden or arbitrary change would involve a revolution in mill operations. Nor are we at all sure that it would be possible for any one employer, or any number of employers, to inaugurate a shorter hour system, unless a similar policy should be adopted by all employers engaged in the same industry.

"We do believe that following in the wake of other betterment of conditions in the steel industry, there will naturally come a shortening of the hours of labor and the eventual abolishment of the twelve-hour day, which will tend towards increasing the efficiency and resourcefulness of the working population, and for that reason bring benefit to both employer and employed.

"That steps should be taken now that shall have for their purpose and end a reasonable and just arrangement to all concerned, of the problems involved in this question—that of reducing the long hours of labor—we would respectfully recommend to the intelligent and thoughtful consideration of the proper officers of the Corporation."

These "proper officers"—the finance committee—to leave no room for doubt as to where they stood, promptly approved of the report and appointed a committee to study what, if any, arrangement could be made toward reducing the twelve-hour day, so far as it then existed. That is, in 1912, the governing body of the Corporation added to the labor program which it had begun to construct in 1901, the elimination, if possible, of one of the most firmly fixed practices of the industry.

But why "study"—why "if possible"—why not *order* that it be done away with? A summary change from twelve to eight hours meant a big increase in expenses. This increase would have to be added to prices or come out of wages or profits. Neither the public, the men, nor the stockholders would accept that cheerfully. A gradual change was believed possible by a few—not a majority—of the executives, if time was given to reorganize and reëducate. Scientific management might do it, but thirteen years ago, it must be remembered, scientific management was still a red rag to workers and a "frill" to many managers.

Nevertheless, the executives in the plants where twelve-hour shifts existed went to work, and two years later, that is in the spring of 1914, the Judge told his stockholders that there had been a 3 per cent reduction in the numbers working twelve hours a day, and that they were making further efforts to improve conditions. A stockholding employee present declared that he knew from his own experience as a worker that the Corporation was making a great effort to reduce the twelve-hour day, and that, in his judgment, it was about at a minimum at the present time. Those on the outside, this gentleman commented, could not understand that the change could not be rushed through all at once, that it was part of a system which had grown up with the industry, was in existence when the Corporation was formed, and that any change had got to be gradual. The workers, he said, realized this and resented the criticism of the public.

This is where matters stood in the spring of 1914. Then came the War with its demand for production— more and still more production. The 22 per cent of twelve-hour men in the Corporation plants in 1914 became 32 per cent. Then came the demand to unionize —the strike—the renewed attack on the long day. "Judge Gary could put an end to it if he would," men said, "but he will not listen." But they were wrong. As a matter of fact, one of the first labor subjects that Judge Gary took up after the War was, how to bring not only his Corporation, of which he was the chief executive officer, but the iron and steel industry, for which ever since 1908 he had been the chosen and respected spokesman, to adopt the eight-hour day. Talking to the Senate committee investigating the steel strike in October of 1919, he said that, for his part, he believed that eight hours were long enough for a man to work out of the twenty-four. He thought there were a good many employees, though by no means a majority, who believed the same thing. "As a matter of policy and principle," he said, "if we can make it practicable to adopt eight hours throughout our works universally, and the men themselves are willing to accept that basis, we would be very glad to adopt it, for the reason, if for no other, that we think there is a strong public sentiment in favor of it."

He continued through 1920 to keep the subject to the front. At every meeting of stockholders or presidents he brought it up. It was causing him a great deal of anxiety, he told them. President Buffington of the Illinois Steel Company tells me that again and again, after meetings at which the twelve-hour day had been discussed and difficulties and demurrers emphasized, Judge Gary would say as they left, "Gentlemen, it will have to be done. The twelve-hour day must go. Public opinion demands it."

The seriousness and insistence of his exhortations had their effect, for in April, 1922, he was able to say to the stockholders that the 32 per cent of twelve-hour work left by the War had been reduced to 14 per cent and he added, "we would like and hope to eliminate all of the twelve-hour work if practicable."

The report of what the Corporation had accomplished in the reduction of hours as well as this statement of their

wishes and hopes brought a powerful aid to Judge Gary's
real desire to see the practice eliminated, not only in his
own body but throughout the industry, for three days
after his announcement to his stockholders, he received
from the President of the United States a letter, obviously inspired by his announcement. In this letter President Harding said:

"I do not know whether the rumor is well founded,
but the story comes to me that you are contemplating the
discontinuance of the twelve-hour day in the steel plants
and the substitution of the eight-hour shift. If you really
have this important change in mind I would be perfectly
willing, if it seems desirable, to lend any consistent assistance in securing the acceptance of the same principle
in other large establishments. I write all this because
I do not believe there is anything that could be done
that would be of greater assistance in making for an
equitable readjustment of our economic situation. Your
lead in this matter would have a tremendously helpful
effect throughout the country, and I am only writing to
commend, and tender any prudent assistance if you
really have this plan in mind and you think it desirable
to have anything like a concerted effort in the direction
of this important change."

My own judgment is that nothing could have pleased
the Judge better. He acted on the suggestion immediately, saw the President and suggested a meeting with
leaders in the iron and steel industry. President Harding immediately arranged a dinner at which some forty
or fifty were present. What happened at this dinner,
Judge Gary reported a week later in an open session
of the annual meeting of the Iron and Steel Institute,
when he appointed a committee whose real business was

to convert the industry as a whole to a belief that the change was desirable and practicable.

There was no evasion or lukewarmness in Judge Gary's charge to this committee, and particularly to the body of iron and steel men who, he insisted, should share its responsibility in getting facts and adopting a worthy report. "Here is your opportunity to put yourselves on record," he told them, "to show your determination in advance to find ways and means of getting rid of the twelve-hour day, if it can be done. It depends a great deal upon how any one considering a question of this importance approaches the subject. If he is trying to find a way not to do a thing he is more apt to find that way than if he is disposed in advance to do it."

It can hardly be denied that there was perhaps a majority of the gentlemen to whom the Judge spoke who were not disposed to find a way. Their influence was certainly reflected in the report which the committee finally brought in. It was not a final report—Judge Gary took care that that was made clear at the start—but it was not an encouraging report to those who hoped the industry as a whole would go vigorously at the question. It rehearsed the difficulties in the situation, declared that if the twelve-hour day should be abandoned summarily it would increase the cost of production on an average of 15 per cent, and there would be at least 60,000 additional employees needed, and they were not to be had, such was the shortage of labor. But a loophole was left.

"If labor should become sufficient to permit it," continued the report, "the members of this committee would favor abolishing the twelve-hour day, provided the purchasing public would be satisfied with selling prices that justified it, and provided further that the employees would consent, and that industry generally, including the farmers, would approve.''

The report was bitterly criticized. It showed lukewarmness—indifference. The figures in regard to the increase of cost and the number of workmen which an immediate change would demand were ridiculed. But here the critics were wrong—that is, if European éxperience is to be trusted. Several of the European countries directly after the War abolished the twelve-hour day by law or by an arrangement with the unions, with the result that there was an immediate increase of men employed of from 30 to 50 per cent, and of course a considerable increase in costs.

The criticism of the report centered on Judge Gary. How did he take it? Well, I think as good a proof of the kind of leader that he is as can be found in a man's words—and practice and words go unusually well together in Judge Gary's case—is what he said to the presidents of the subsidiaries two weeks later.

The criticisms had been based, as a rule, he said, upon misrepresentation or misapprehension, some of the severest coming from those who evidently had never read the report. ''These unjustified criticisms,'' he said, ''naturally provoke a feeling of deep resentment on our part. We think they are undeserved.

''There is a possibility that some, perhaps all of us, may carry our feeling of resentment too far and thus become unreasonably antagonistic towards some of the criticisms or those who make them, and thereby do an injustice to others and to ourselves; and I make bold to offer for consideration conciliatory suggestions.

''Newspapers, magazines, public speakers, in fact all

persons, have the right to form, and, if done in good - faith, to express unfavorable judgment concerning the conduct of our affairs. Probably the whole iron and steel industry would agree to this, but in these remarks I am not attempting to speak for any one except myself. The great majority of publicists intend to be right and fair and to base conclusions on facts as they understand them. Their motives are good. They are honest and intelligent; therefore they are apt to be right and within the limits of propriety. Decidedly this does not apply to all of them; but this is beside the question.

"On this occasion I would urge and emphasize that on our part we must be fair and reasonable; that we should read and consider all criticisms that are made concerning our Corporation or its subsidiaries or their management or managers; that in so far as complaint is made concerning our attitude or action, which is supported by the facts, we must be prompt to adopt a corrective. Simply because we believe a part of a statement is unsupported by facts or that the motive for the whole or a portion of it is unworthy we must not reject or ignore anything which in honesty and propriety requires our approval."

And he told them after this little preachment: "As to the twelve-hour day in the iron and steel industry, I have not changed my mind, long since expressed. I think it should be completely abolished. My views are shared by our Board of Directors, our Finance Committee and our Presidents, therefore it is expected you will continue your efforts in good faith and vigorously to effect a total elimination."

By this time the President seems to have read the report, which his first comments show that he had not

done, and to have found the loophole; and, at the suggestion of his Secretary of Commerce, Herbert Hoover, who
had engineered the negotiations as well as suggested
them, he took advantage of it.

"I am impressed," he said, "that in the reasoning of
the report great weight should be attached to the fact
that in the present shortage of labor it would cripple
our entire prosperity if the change were abruptly made.
In the hope that this question could be disposed of, I
am wondering if it would not be possible for the steel
industry to consider giving an undertaking that before
there shall be any reduction in the staff or employees of
the industry through any recession of demand for steel
products, or at any time when there is a surplus of
labor available, that then the change should be made
from the two shifts to the three-shift basis."

When one follows Judge Gary's leadership in all the
various matters he has been called to direct, one realizes
that he has a sure sense of the moment when the "mental
column" he has been handling can be closed up. He
believed that the moment had come now to bring the
iron and steel industry as a whole to make a definite
and positive pledge, that no one could mistake, in regard
to the twelve-hour day. "I will immediately call a meeting of our committee," he wrote the President. And this
he did, and ten days later was able to announce, "We
are determined to exert every effort at our command to
secure in the iron and steel industry in this country a
total abolition of the twelve-hour day at the earliest time
practical—without an unjustifiable interruption to operations. The change cannot be effected overnight. It will
involve many adjustments, some of them complicated and
difficult, but we think it can be brought about without

undue delay when, as you stated, there is a surplus of labor available." The men signing this decision represented about 75 per cent of the whole iron and steel industry.

There were difficulties and delays but by September the Corporation at least had done away with the 10 or 12 per cent of twelve-hour labor which remained at the time the pledge was given, but for the elimination of which we have repeated documentary evidence that Judge Gary had long been working. It is indeed very doubtful whether the President himself could have secured the final pledge that he did from the industry if it had not been for Judge Gary's leadership. Secretary of Commerce Hoover, through whose courtesy I have been able to examine all of the departmental correspondence in the matter, says that Judge Gary "through his leadership and coöperation, made the largest contribution possible to the final solution of the twelve-hour day problem in the steel industry"—a comment which he permits me to quote.

A second serious charge against the labor policy of the Steel Corporation which the strike left in the public mind was that it "suppressed labor," had no form of collective bargaining, no channel by which a man or a group of men could make known to management their grievances, their opinions, their criticisms.

Two ways of bargaining collectively were recognized by the public at the moment—through trade unions and through company unions. The Federation of Labor refused to admit the adequacy of the latter and included in its strike-demands their entire abolishment. It was on this point that the first Industrial Conference, called in October of 1919 by President Wilson, went to pieces.

The public group, of which Judge Gary was a member, held to the principle of collective bargaining, but it insisted that any system which recognized the worker, as the various forms of plant organization did, satisfied the principle. Judge Gary gave his notions on the point to the Senate committee investigating the steel strike while the Industrial Conference was in battle:

"I think labor ought to be encouraged to deal collectively, and it ought not to be prohibited at any time from dealing collectively; but dealing collectively, in the form of committees, or however they themselves may decide, is one thing, and dealing collectively as insisted upon by the labor union leaders, which means that the union labor leaders shall decide all these questions, and shall represent the men, whether they are asked to or not, and will establish a basis for the closed shop which would shut out the individual voices of these men practically, is quite a different thing."

He was obdurate about trade unions but open-minded about the company union. One of the best collections of pamphlets, both theoretical and practical, which the writer has ever seen on the subject, she found on Judge Gary's table when she was one of the stream which flowed into his office to ask why in the world he was not seeing Mr. Foster and Mr. Fitzpatrick. "Much consideration of late has been given to the subject of shop committees," he told his stockholders in April, 1920, "we have made diligent investigation of these matters, and up to date we think no plan better, or more satisfactory to employees, than our own has been tried."

"But," declared his critics, "the Corporation has no plan. There is no way for the man at the bottom—

the man that we are interested in—to get the ear of the governing body.'' Judge Gary thought differently. He declared that any employee or any self-appointed group of employees, could make their wishes known at any time to the authorities, even to the top of the organization. Now, what is this plan in which Judge Gary believes? Is it really a plan? A thing of which you can make a blue print?—the ability to make a blue print of a policy being the test of its virtue in the minds of many people.

Begin at the bottom and work up. The unskilled workers in the Steel Corporation are organized for the most part into gangs, at the head of each being what is called a "straw boss." President Schiller tells me that in the National Tube Works the gangs formerly numbered six and the "straw boss" was a comparatively stationary executive. When the six-day took the place of the seven-day week, an extra man was put on and the practice of weekly rotation in bosses was adopted. This is one of the most profitable results of the six-day week from the point of view of management, he says, since it gives to unskilled men an opportunity to show whether or no they have executive ability.

The immediate superior officer of the gang is a foreman. If these men wish to bargain, complain, ask a change, they go to their foreman. And right here, the critics declare, the Corporation's plan—which of course is the oldest in industry—breaks down—one never gets by the foreman.

How about this? Thirteen years ago, an employee stockholder, who had come to a meeting in New York as the elected representative of a large body of stockholding workers, pointed out several improvements in the condition of labor which he claimed had been brought about by the Corporation. "The foremen are not abusive to men like they used to be in former days," he said, "the officials *won't stand for it.*"

At the Senate investigation of the steel strike, an old-time union man who had been called as a witness, said when questioned as to whether or not the employee could get his complaint past the foreman, "Why, the humblest man in the mill, foreign or American, does not have to accept finally anything from them (foremen). Any grievance he may want to make, he can make it to the foreman, and if the foreman won't take it up, he can just simply open the door of the main office and walk right in to the superintendent. That condition obtains to the best of my knowledge and belief—to my knowledge—all through the operations of the company. If grievances are felt, the humblest man in the mill can walk past the foreman right to the general superintendent and get things remedied very quickly."

In certain of the subsidiaries grievance committees exist. For example, in the Tennessee Coal, Iron and Railroad Company and the Oliver Iron Mining Company there is a so-called "Mutuality Committee." It is made up of from three to five men who are changed from month to month so that every man can get a chance. This committee is supposed to keep in close touch with the men. Any complaint which they consider legitimate they take to a foreman. If they do not get from him what they call fair treatment, they go to the superintendent. If he does not satisfy them, a hearing is held, a real hearing before the head of the employment bureau. If the decision at the trial is not satisfactory, then the Mutuality Committee can take it up to the president. "The men have been so fair in these trials," the head of the employment bureau of the T. C. and I. says, "the committees have been so serious about their work that foremen and superintendents have come to be very careful about refusing anything that is brought to them by a Mutuality Committee."

In some of the plants, notably the American Steel and Wire Company, there have been in operation for some time training courses for foremen, devised by the educational department of the plant itself. At the National Tube Works, courses have been established for which a fee is charged, and there are always more men seeking admittance than the directors have been able to accommodate.

It must not be forgotten that for fifteen years or more employees of the Steel Corporation have had a continuous representation in safety committees. These committees, on which probably at the present writing fully ten thousand men are serving, were originally appointed to coöperate with the management in developing and executing safety and sanitation measures. The members rotate in order to give the largest number possible an opportunity for service. Naturally all the grievances of a shop are known to this committee. They find expression there, and more and more the safety committees of plants have become, in practice at least, more or less effective channels of expression. It is doubtful indeed if there are many company unions in which there is more real expression of complaints and ambitions.

From the ranks of foremen come superintendents and their assistants. It is with these superintendents and their assistants that the top body of the subsidiary company, the president and vice president directly deal. It is through them that the president must get over the

Corporation's labor policy as he gets it from New York. And how does he get it from New York? And what has New York, that is, the governing body of the Steel Corporation, to give to the subsidiaries, scattered as they are, all over the country, carrying on as they do, a multitude of different kinds of industries: the mining of ore, coal, lime, manganese; the running of railroads and ships; the operating of blast furnaces, open hearths; the turning of the steel and iron which come from the furnaces into a multitude of structural forms, big and little, bridges and buildings as large as we find on the earth, wire, wheels, nuts so small that it almost requires a glass to see them. Two hundred and fifty thousand or more men do this work, men of varied nations, English-speaking and non-English-speaking, of varied races with varied kinds of industrial notions and various kinds of ideas about property and industrial rights. What can the governing body of the Steel Corporation, seated in New York, know about the real interests of this complicated multitude? How can it make labor policies for them, that its presidents can interpret to their superintendents and these superintendents get down in any practical way to foremen?

From the day in 1901 that the governing body of the Steel Corporation elected to become responsible for the labor policy of the Corporation, contrary to the judgment of many of its most experienced members who believed that labor could only be successfully handled by the individual subsidiaries, there have been very few of the weekly meetings in which a part of the time has not been given to the consideration of some phase of the life and interests of the workers. I have gone over many pages of the Corporation minutes and I cannot recall a single meeting in which some action was not taken showing that one phase or another of labor had been under consideration.

Usually this action called for the voting of money. The finance committee of the Steel Corporation votes no sum of money, large or small, without believing that it has a good reason. In the twenty-five years Judge Gary has been conducting the affairs of the Corporation, upward of $150,000,000 have been expended under authorization, for one labor purpose or another. It is Judge Gary who invariably presents these claims of labor, argues for them.

But how does Judge Gary know the causes or the objects for which money should be devoted? The presidents of the subsidiaries meet in New York monthly, or when called, and a good deal of their time is given to reporting and discussing workmen's interests. They present needs, make requests. Their presentations must pass what may be called the Corporation's labor bureau, known as the Bureau of Safety and Sanitation, whose director since its organization in 1910 has been Mr. Charles L. Close. In this bureau is centered safety work, town building, educational work, the administration of the pension and compensation funds, loans for home building, an activity which was first taken up in 1920.

This bureau has coming to it daily from every Corporation plant full records of the life and activities of the steel communities—their needs, their grievances, their ambitions. It has this information, and it has a most extraordinary picture gallery—men, women, children, towns. Very few days pass when there does not come to this office persons concerned in the labor interests of some particular plant—a social service worker, an official, or a worker off on a vacation, or perhaps a delegation from Gary or elsewhere, wanting a contribution for a church they are building, a community hall, a new athletic field, better equipment in this or that school.

All this activity, carried on constantly and as a matter of course, centers in Judge Gary. I do not believe that there is anything connected with the Corporation—finance, operation, expansion of foreign business—to which he gives more attention and from which he gets more pleasure than from the operation of these labor activities. He knows what is going on in Mr. Close's bureau, he sees many of the delegations that come, and always he hears from his presidents. He must do this in order to lead the governing body whose support, money, and understanding sympathy he must have for these policies if they are to go through.

This form of organization deals more intelligently with labor because from top to bottom the great majority of the executives concerned have come from the bottom and know the life and needs from experience. Advancement through proved ability is a rule of the Corporation. Foremen are made from "straw bosses" just as assistant superintendents are chosen from foremen, superintendents from assistant superintendents and presidents from superintendents.

Go through a steel plant and ask how this or that executive came into his position. Almost invariably it will be a story of a rise from office boy, water boy, or the labor gang. President Schiller of the National Tube Company started in as an office boy; the present president of the Corporation, Mr. Farrell, as a day laborer.

One often hears an old steel worker say, "Look at Jim Farrell. See what he has done. I knew him when he was drawing wire." These advancements, it is to be remembered, are not by accident or chance, but by a carefully supervised system based on merit. They are an everyday proof to the men that a share in management is open to them, waiting for them, if they prove their willingness and ability to take it.

But, it is objected, there is no system of bargaining in regard to wages—at least nothing comparable to the making of scales through the union. A grievance about wages is handled in the same way that a grievance about any other matter is, that is, a man or a group of men go to the superintendent with their request. As long, however, as the established policy of the Corporation in regard to wages is to keep them a little ahead of those paid by competitors, to raise them without request, and never to reduce them unless conditions make it obviously imperative—so imperative that the men themselves understand it—there is little chance of dissatisfaction on this score. It should not be overlooked that the Steel Corporation, through its stock subscription scheme, to which the men subscribe yearly in large numbers, gives a basis for considering the fairness of wages which practically no other organization in the country gives, and which the union unfortunately does not often have in making its claims.

Last year (1924) over 61,000 men took stock in the Steel Corporation. Now, to each of these went a copy of the annual report analyzing the business. Stockholders, who went in at the start and have held their stock, have the data for telling how the Corporation has used its money since the beginning, how it has built up

its capital, provided for future obligations, what it costs
to enlarge, to replace, to keep up to the times. They
see there what the production of iron ore and steel
ingots and finished steel costs per man. They have
the total net earnings before them and how they are
used. They can see, too, that the average wage has
been steadily upward, and they know, if they are holders
of common stock, that when it has been a choice between
cutting their wages and cutting dividends it has been
the latter that have suffered. Now, while there is no
doubt that many men do not study these reports, there
are at the same time many that do study them and discuss them in mines and mills and plants and homes all
over the country. They are as good textbooks in the
conduct of financial corporations as the country affords.

This is *their* business which the report analyzes, the
one which pays their wages and in which they have invested savings. It *reports* to them. They have the right
to go to stockholders' meetings and make any remarks
they please. Partnership, coöperation is offered them
instead of collective bargaining through the union.

The intelligent and persistent effort the Corporation
makes to regularize and stabilize employment is not lost
on the men. "It is better to keep men on pay rolls than
on relief and jail rolls" is a dictum Judge Gary laid
down years ago and every subsidiary has its own way
of following the council. Mountains of ore are piled
up in dull times, yards are filled with iron and steel
ingots, plants are repaired and extended, new ones are
built. The men know these are efforts to protect their
jobs and their stock. For illustration, the Minnesota
Steel Company began after the War, in a period of depression, to build a wire plant. The construction gang

was made up largely of men from closed mills. When the new plant was finished, twenty-five specialists were brought in to help start it. Practically every man who had worked on its construction who did not go back to his old job when his mill started again, went to work in the wire mill. When running full it employs 572 men, and there are only three wire drawers who did not learn the business there! One valuable feature of this policy of developing the labor at hand, whatever its experience, is that it often opens the way for the unskilled man at the bottom, a man for whom, as a rule, the skilled worker has no thought, whose competition he fears and whose training he often hinders, in the same way as the earlier trust builders feared and hindered the operation of smaller competitors.

Many, indeed one may say almost all, of the activities of the steel plants depend for success on the coöperation of management and workers; safety, sanitation, community life would be impossible if there was not a natural and interested response from the men. They serve regularly on committees in the towns as in the plants. The Corporation has been trying for years to make the steel communities desirable places in which to live, they succeed in proportion to the response of the workers.

It is not a simple problem. Many of the plants which the Corporation acquired, such as Homestead and those at Duquesne and McKeesport, were in established communities where the worker must depend upon the municipality for social life and the education of his children, and he must rent or build a house as workers in other industries of the town were obliged to do. There are ten thousand employees at Homestead, and the Corporation never owned more than four hundred houses there. As a rule, however, the steel town must be built by the Corporation. Mines are opened where ore or coal is found. Wild land must be developed if a great new plant like Gary is to be established. Thus, community building becomes a part of the Corporation's work. It has some $90,000,000 invested in houses, and since 1920 it has been loaning money to employees for buying or building. Some $8,000,000 has been loaned in this period, and I have had presidents of subsidiaries tell me that there has been no pressure from the men stronger than that for the Corporation's help in buying a home. Under this scheme a man can buy or build, in or out of the limits of the steel community. All of the comparatively few Homestead houses have been bought under this plan. Not a few men prefer to go where they can acquire larger tracts of land, depending upon their cars to take them back and forth. So common is the practice that it has been found necessary to establish in the yards of all the big plants extensive garages for workers' cars.

Great pains have been taken in remodeling the old communities, as in the towns of the Frick Coke and Coal Company near Pittsburgh; and in old as in new towns, a consistent and intelligent effort is made to provide decent, comfortable and attractive living places where the workers will have satisfactory opportunities for the education of their children and for social life— places where they can feel and act like citizens.

The towns of different companies differ because, as Mr. Crawford of the T. C. and I. says, each is the individual attempt of the management to translate Judge Gary's notions of what the American worker ought to have. Mr. Crawford's own translation was made in a community where the original native labor body was indolent, untrained, unreliable, and where there was no initial desire for regular employment, for schools or for decent orderly living.

It was seventeen years ago that the Steel Corporation bought the T. C. and I., under circumstances described in Chapter VIII. The labor problem at the start was difficult beyond belief. All the traditions were bad. Negro convicts farmed out by the state of Alabama had for years worked in the mines. The company stores were a scandal, swindling the workers and corrupting wholesale merchants, purchasing agents, politicians, and not infrequently labor leaders—all of whom found in these stores the only lucrative graft which Birmingham offered at that date. There were no decent houses, no decent schools. The air was full of mosquitoes in summer and of influenza germs in winter. It was a terrible position for a man who had a complicated metallurgical and developing problem thrust upon him and who needed steady, trustworthy labor if he was to succeed. There was nothing to do but import this labor from Europe or develop it from the material at hand. The policy of the Corporation has always been to take what you had on hand and work with that and that was what Mr. Crawford did. When the contract with the state for convicts ran out, he took up its renewal with Judge Gary. "Think of that!" I have heard the Judge say, "I, an Abolitionist from childhood, at the head of a concern working negroes in a chain gang, with a state representative punishing them at a whipping post!" "Tear up that contract," he ordered. "It is not necessary to consult anybody. I won't stand for it."

The old convict jail in the mountains near the mines

where the negroes lived has been made into a store-house. Mr. Crawford will tell you that they tried to make a boarding house of it but the men shunned it, and he respected their abhorrence. The old quarters are abandoned and to-day the hills are dotted with neat cottages. Near by in a big and commodious community house I watched last spring doctors and nurses examining babies and instructing mothers. Whites and blacks, each in their separate groups and quarters, receive the same care, the same instruction.

This town, with its community house, its men's clubs, its schools and their activities, is but one of some twenty or more which have been developed in the last seventeen years as the foundation of Mr. Crawford's steady labor body. Of them one of our best authorities on housing —a man whose knowledge of industrial towns and housing experiments included all that has been done in Europe as well as this country—Dr. F. L. Hoffman of the Prudential Life Insurance Company of America, wrote to Mr. Close, after an extended examination in 1918:

The work of your company in the Birmingham district is one of the most remarkable contributions to the ultimate solution of the labor problem of which I have knowledge. That problem, as I conceive it, involves no more and no less than the whole question of contentment, or absence of friction, on the part of the employee with any and all conditions giving unnecessary occasion for irritation, discomfort, etc. Now, of all that concerns laborers, there is nothing as vital as the houses in which they live, and the surroundings that go with them, and the conditions of family life that depend upon them. Your company, under your direction, has taken hold of this question with a thoroughness rarely met with in this country. . . . It is obvious that you are aiming at a provision for home life rather than for mere housing, and that is, after all, the most vital distinction to be made in matters of this kind. . . .

What pleased us most, however, was the fact that your company disregards racial lines, and aims in its home and housing provisions to provide the same comforts and surroundings for the negroes as for the whites. . . . Nothing has hindered the Negro as much as the deliberate policy on the part of the whites to provide him continuously with housing accommodations frequently unworthy of the name. While some progress has been made from the one-room cabin to two or more rooms, your company is the first, to my knowledge, which is providing a real home life on equality with the conditions under which the best white element lives for those of the colored race.

As for the schools that have been developed by the T. C. and I., they have warm approval from the highest authority in the country, the Federal Bureau of Education. In one of its bulletins, issued in 1920, an observer says:

One of the most interesting educational experiments in the bituminous coal region of the Appalachian system is conducted by the Tennessee Coal, Iron & Railroad Co. The work is done in complete coöperation with the county school board, which apportions funds to the mining town school on the same basis as to other schools. The superintendent of the schools in the mining towns is an assistant county superintendent, but is paid entirely by the company.

Social work is required by the company, and special stress is placed on personality and fitness for this additional service. The classroom work is of spendid quality. The teaching staff shows good organization, enthusiasm, loyalty and a high degree of professional spirit.

As a whole it is an object lesson in efficiency which may well be studied by other mining communities. It shows conclusively what can be done by the expenditure of reasonable funds, business encouragement, and professional service. Conditions are not different in any essentials from those of the surrounding territory. What can be accomplished here can be accomplished elsewhere, with similar management and expenditure.

No one who has studied the social service department under which the T. C. and I. schools and their activities come but will echo the enthusiasm of this Federal observer. A more carefully chosen or more scientifically directed body it would be hard to find anywhere in the multitude of social service organizations in this country. It is a band of highly trained people who appreciate to the full the real joy of getting their hands on human beings who need direction and of having in their work the full and sympathetic support of the organization which has brought them together.

One of the finest achievements in the T. C. and I.'s group of fine achievements is what has been done for the health of the community. The director, Dr. Noland, whom Mr. Crawford brought from the health department of the Panama Canal, where he had been working for a number of years under General Gorgas, found conditions in and around the plants and mines about as bad as they could be. To-day there are few, if any, healthier industrial communities in the world. And the whole remarkable organization is capped by a model Employees' Hospital, which in design, equipment, location, medical staff, and nurses' training schools is as good as can be found in the United States.

This noble institution gives to black and white, each of which has, under one roof, its own quarters, exactly the same food, care, physical surroundings. Judge Gary himself has given the highest endorsement possible to the Employees' Hospital of the T. C. and I. by going there himself for treatment and rest. Under the same roof with him, though out of his hearing, negro and white mothers bear their babies, negro and white workers are treated for burns and broken bones, negro and white children are nursed through measles and mumps.

What is done by the T. C. and I—schools, churches, housing, hospitals—is typical of what is done at the great number of plants of the United States Steel Corporations scattered over the country.

The manifold ramifications of the Steel Corporation's labor policies are administered with extreme care. Not long ago I came accidentally on an example of their method, at a luncheon given to a distinguished gentleman who was about to sail for Europe. The head of the Bureau of Safety and Sanitation was present. "What kind of a corporation is this to which he belongs?" the guest of honor said laughingly, pointing to Mr. Close. "I asked him if I could do anything for him in Europe. I thought he might ask me to bring back a present for his wife. He took me up eagerly. 'Yes,' he said, 'you are going near such and such a place. Will you not see the American consul and find out whether Mrs. —— is receiving all her pension money. We have all kinds of trouble in getting money to foreign beneficiaries of those who have been injured or killed in our plants. The law requires that we turn the money over to the consulates on this side. Time and again we find that the consul holds it back and when he sends it charges up a wicked amount to expense. In the case of the woman I want you to look up, we turned over a first remittance of $564.84 to the consul. It was months before he sent her a cent and when finally the remittance was received, it had been reduced by expenses he charged up to $242.03. Now, do go and see how much of her last remittance reached her, and if you can, find out if anybody on that side is robbing her as her country's consul on this side has been doing."

Any one who is much about the steel towns knows that this persistent following up of every case is an everyday matter in the administration. The workers know it.

The final test of a labor policy must be its power to hold men. Orthodox or not, deficient or not in modern industrial dogma, formulas, and terminology, the labor policies of the Steel Corporation work—they hold a substantial body of men, hold them through thick and thin as the strike of 1919 proved. These men are not fools. "It amounts practically to a slander of the workmen," said one of them a few years ago, "to give out the impression before the public that they don't appreciate these things." They judge a policy by actual results—the union itself has been their teacher in this—and when they see that their wages are a little better than in most of the plants of their kind about them, that efforts go on year in and year out to regularize and stabilize their jobs, when they see the opportunity given them not only to become stockholders with the privileges of the stockholders, but that money is loaned them on easy terms to buy homes wherever they wish, in or out of the Corporation communities; when they find their children getting opportunities for education and health which they have believed beyond the reach of the great mass of men; when they see men, who have worked beside them up to sixty-five, able to retire on pensions which helps keep them in modest comfort for the rest of their lives; and, when they know this is all done in no spirit of paternalism or charity but as a business proposition, they are willing to do their part to make it a success. They have common sense enough to see that a demonstration of what can be done profitably by a corporation should be of substantial value in working out the immensely difficult labor problem. They know that their coöperation is a factor in this, and many of them have no doubt come to believe that they are doing as much for the ultimate solution of the labor problem by giving their coöperation as they would be doing by warring through strikes for a particular form of labor organization.

This, I take it, must be about how a large group of the steel workers feel, else they would not stick at their posts as they have through these twenty-four years. It is this recognition of the Corporation's aims that has made it possible for Judge Gary to say, as he so often has to stockholders and subsidiary presidents: "We have great reason to be thankful to our workers that they have confidence in what we are trying to do and that they have stood by us, whatever the depression or the agitation."

CHAPTER XII

GARY—INDUSTRIAL LEADER

THE abandonment of the twelve-hour day in the steel industry ended an anxiety which Judge Gary had been carrying for more than a dozen years. Another long continued anxiety which had been ended by this time was that over the outcome of the government's suit against the Steel Corporation. It was in October, 1911, that the government first filed its petition praying that the Corporation be dissolved. Six months later the examiners began taking testimony—a task which filled nearly two years. The case was argued for eight days in October of 1914 in the United States Circuit Court of Appeals. Six months later, in April, 1915, two opinions were handed down. Both these opinions held that the Corporation was not and never had been a monopoly; that it did not and never had restrained trade, that it never tried to do so, and never had had power so to do; that as a result of the Gary Dinners, prices had been more or less maintained, but that the practice had been given up before the suit was brought. This abandonment was in accordance with Judge Gary's settled policy to change any practice whenever it was seriously complained of by governmental representatives. Both opinions united in dismissing the government's appeal.

The government took the case to the Supreme Court, where it was argued in March of 1917. As the bench was tied, it was ordered to be reargued—but the War was on, and in spite of the urgent appeal of the Corporation's counsel to grant an immediate hearing and decision, it was considered bad public policy in the emergency. Thus it was not until nearly a year after the Armistice that the case was reargued. This argument came at a busy moment for Judge Gary—the most exciting moment of the strike of 1919.

Six months later the final decision was handed down in an opinion delivered by Mr. Justice McKenna, three justices dissenting, who expressed the minority opinion, in substance, that the Corporation was illegal and should be dissolved because its dominating influence in the industry was dangerous to free competition and ought not to be allowed to continue.

The majority, after analyzing the opinion of the District Court, among others things, said:

We have seen that the judges of the District Court unanimously concurred in the view that the Corporation did not achieve monopoly and such is our deduction, and it is against monopoly that the statute is directed, not against the expectation of it, but against its realization, and it is certain that it was not realized. The opposing conditions were underestimated. The power attained was much greater than that possessed by any one competitor—it was not greater than that possessed by all of them. Monopoly, therefore, was not achieved, and competitors had to be persuaded by pools, associations, trade meetings, and through the social form of dinners, all of them it may be, violations of the law, but transient in their purpose and effect. They were scattered through the years from 1901 (the year of the formation of the Corporation), until 1911, but, after instances of success and failure, were abandoned nine months before this suit was brought. There is no evidence that the abandonment was in prophecy or dread of suit; and the illegal practices have not been resumed, nor is there any evidence of an intention to resume them, and certainly no "dangerous probability" of their resumption. . . .

What then can be urged against the Corporation? Can comparisons in other regards be made with its competitors and by such comparisons guilty or innocent existence be assigned it? It is greater in size and productive power than any of its competitors, equal or nearly equal to them all, but its power over prices was not and is not commensurate with its power to produce. . . . Against it competitors, dealers and customers of the Corporation testify in multitude that no adventitious interference was employed to either fix or maintain prices and that they were constant or varied according to natural conditions. Can this testimony be minimized or dismissed by inferring that, as intimated, it is an evidence of power not of weakness; and power exerted not only to suppress competition but to compel testimony, is the necessary inference, shading into perjury to deny its exertion? The situation is indeed singular, and we may wonder at it, wonder that the despotism of the Corporation, so baneful to the world in the representation of the Government, did not produce protesting victims. . . .

In conclusion we are unable to see that the public interest will be served by yielding to the contention of the Government respecting the dissolution of the company or the separation from it of some of its subsidiaries; and we do see in a contrary conclusion a risk of injury to the public interest, including a material disturbance of, and, it may be serious detriment to, the foreign trade. And in submission to the policy of the law and its fortifying prohibitions the public interest is of paramount regard.

We think, therefore, that the decree of the District Court should be affirmed.

The government had lost its suit. The "good trust" had won as Judge Gary always contended it would.

"How is the good trust, this morning?" ex-Speaker Tom Reed, who never lost an opportunity to banter a friend, used to say jokingly to Judge Gary when they met in the morning on their way down town, and the Judge, who found it difficult to jest about the criticisms of the public, would answer, in his serious way, "You will see, Mr. Reed, you will see!"

"Judge Gary?" said Mark Twain, when the Judge was first presented to him, "I know him. He is the good corporation."

"Mr. Clemens," retorted the Judge, "the time will come when you and every one else will see that there is a difference in corporations."

"I believe it now, Judge Gary," the great humorist consoled him.

The time seemed to have come. It was conduct which had won the suit. At least, Mr. Lindabury, the chief counsel of the Corporation in the contest, so believed. "It was the conduct of the Corporation which saved it," I have heard him say, "and that conduct was due to Judge Gary's farsightedness and his conviction that sound ethics are the basis of all sound business."

The Steel Corporation's lawyers in their arguments naturally made the most of the Gary policies and his struggles to incorporate them. This insistence led to one quite delightful bit of comment from the government's side. "In our presentation to the Supreme Court," said Mr. Lindabury, "we possibly overemphasized Gary—his ideals, his desire to have things right, his frankness, his ability, what he had done. When John W. Davis, who was solicitor-general, arose, he introduced his speech by saying, 'I entirely agree with the opposing counsel in their opinion of Judge Gary—his idealism, his fine efforts to have things right—but I should like to call the attention of the Court to the fact that the government is trying to dissolve the Steel Corporation and not Judge Gary.' "

But if the government had won, had ordered a dissolution, what would Judge Gary have done? I asked him once. "I had in mind a plan," he replied. "I might have said to the government, 'We propose that you consent to dividing the Corporation into two distinct companies, each having every line of business, fully integrated and fully diversified: one—The Federal Steel handling the West and Middle West territory; the other—The Carnegie Steel Company—handling the East.' This would have accomplished the government's purpose and would have been the least possible shock to business and to the foreign trade and would have protected investors."

The suit was disposed of and the eight-hour day established, but there were still problems and criticisms. There was "Pittsburgh Plus"—words which the great majority of the people of the country outside of the steel industry had never heard, until, in April of 1921, it was announced that the Federal Trade Commission had issued formal complaint against the United States Steel Corporation for an unfair business practice, a practice called "Pittsburgh Plus."

To the outsider it looked as if here was something which the Attorney-General's office, in spite of nine years' hard work, had failed to unearth. Now, what was "Pittsburgh Plus," and how did it happen that it had come to the attention of the Federal Trade Commission when neither the government in its suit nor the Bureau of Commerce and Labor which, as we know, had spent years investigating the practices of the Corporation had apparently ever heard of it, or at least taken exception to it?

"Pittsburgh Plus" is a trade practice in steel, forty or more years old. If one will run back in trade history to the 'thirties he will find the city of Philadelphia raising up its voice in protest against the rising industrial importance of the youthful Pittsburgh. Philadelphia in those days was the iron center of the country—the base point from which prices were calculated; but Pittsburgh, because of its location, its coal supplies, its increasing communication with ore deposits, rapidly took Philadelphia's place. Steel could be made cheaper there than anywhere else; it became the base for prices in all the territory which it served. Steel makers at other points quoted their prices plus the freight from Pittsburgh—it was their protection against their big rival. It was the only practical way of developing the steel industry in new territories. Buyers in the territory might pay more, but they were willing to do this because in the long run they believed their own industry would so develop that it could go on its own in prices.

The prices under "Pittsburgh Plus" were never absolute, but were shaded by demand, competition, the time that the goods must be delivered, supplies on hand, and all the various other circumstances which affect prices in active trade. As time went on, the new steel centers did develop, thus Chicago had come to a point by 1918 when it could satisfy, or nearly satisfy, all the demands of its natural territory. Consumers began to complain about "Pittsburgh Plus."

The first serious questioning came in the War; and for a few months two bases were established for prices on shapes, plates, and bars. But this created unexpected disturbance. Certain independent mills in the Chicago territory, cut off from the long established protection which "Pittsburgh Plus" gave them, and not able like the Steel Corporation plants, because of their size and economies, to produce steel as cheaply as Pittsburgh, found themselves unable profitably to produce steel for the government.

The War Industries Board decided that the two bases were working badly for its end—the greatest possible production—and returned to the single base.

When things had settled down after the War, the Western Association of Rolled Steel Manufacturers decided to contest "Pittsburgh Plus." They engaged a lawyer to see if it would be possible to remove what they claimed was a discrimination against their trade on the part of both Corporation and independents. The lawyer in the case, John S. Miller of Chicago, went directly to Judge Gary as the head of the Iron and Steel Institute. His clients, he said, would like to have the discrimination removed without friction, and if Judge Gary thought a conference between representatives of the interests concerned was desirable, he would be glad to represent his clients.

Judge Gary promptly replied that he had been studying the practice for some time, both from the point of view of economics and of what was fair and just. He had discussed it with his colleagues in the Corporation and with his competitors and their lawyers but had secured no unanimous opinion. He did not think it a legal question but he did think it was an ethical one. This was the beginning of considerable correspondence between the two gentlemen and resulted in Judge Gary's suggesting that he and Mr. Miller go to the Federal Trade Commission with their difficulty.

"The whole industry ought to be in here," he told the Commission. "You ought to have jurisdiction over the whole thing. It is one of the most important questions that you have ever had before you, or ever will have before you, if you take jurisdiction, as I think you ought and as I think you can. I believe it is a matter to be settled by this Commission. That is my judgment about it. . . . I am not trying to bring work to this Commission, because every one knows you have enough; but I am disposed to say that from my standpoint I would like to have this question fully heard on the evidence, so that the facts from the beginning to the present can be determined, and every interest heard that desires to be heard, and then the whole question settled, so that the Steel Corporation at least could say to anybody hereafter complaining, 'There is an adjudication of this question, and we are following the judgment and decree of the Federal Trade Commission.' If it is right to have this changed, I would like to have it done. I will say, speaking for our Corporation, that the matter of making a little more or a little less money on account of this basing price does not appeal to me at all.''

This suggestion of course was in line with Judge Gary's long established practice of taking promptly to the proper governmental department any questioned practice in the steel industry. It was the business of the government, he always contended, to help work out these problems.

A hearing was held and a majority of the Commission at first decided that they did not have the jurisdiction. With the shifting of its make-up, this opinion was changed and the Commission took up the case. But they did not take it up as a coöperating and correcting body —they took it up as a prosecuting body. And they prosecuted not the whole industry nor the whole group of manufacturers of which the Western Association of Rolled Steel Manufacturers had complained—they centered the attack on the United States Steel Corporation. Judge Gary, who had brought the matter to their attention, found his Corporation being prosecuted for unfair business practices.

The Federal Trade Commission· took thousands of pages of testimony, much of it duplicating what had been taken in the government's suit. It went over question after question on which both the Circuit Court and the United States Supreme Court had passed judgment. Its object seems to have been to prove that the Steel Corporation's handling of prices had been systematically unfair and discriminatory and that "Pittsburgh Plus" was only another example of its unfairness. The upshot of the suit was an order that "Pittsburgh Plus" be abandoned as a base and that henceforth every mill that made steel be its own base.

There were many of Judge Gary's competitors who would have been glad to join him in fighting the decision of the Federal Trade Commission, but he was for accepting the decision. He realized that the coöperation of the entire industry with the Commission which he had hoped for and which he believed practicable, had failed. The Commission had regarded prosecution and no coöperation as its business. It had found it simpler and perhaps more dramatic to concentrate on the Steel Corporation than on the whole industry. "But," as Gary told the Iron and Steel Institute when it met in October, "after giving the whole subject careful consideration, the respondents concluded to cheerfully accept and acquiesce in the decision. Many of the leading independents in the steel industry, and perhaps all of them, later followed suit." And he counseled that, as a body, they do the same.

"Many of you," he said, "were startled by the action of the Commission and temporarily, at least, entertained feelings of disappointment and dissatisfaction. More than that, your business activities and progress have been interrupted, impeded and in places almost demoralized. As yet, you have not been able to restore the natural trend of affairs. Sellers and purchasers alike have been groping for a course that would permit a basis for transactions which would furnish the stability and uniformity which every department of business effort desires and seeks. For the best success in industrial enterprises of any kind it is as necessary to have some standard to reckon from as it is to have a gold dollar basis to make comparison and computation concerning the values of money. You are encountering and will continue to encounter difficulties. You may decide to appeal to the courts for remedy; but you are beseeched to give the matter most patient and painstaking thought before doing so. . . .

"For one, your President entertains the opinion that there are involved questions more important than those which are of a legal nature. What is the fair, and equitable view to take? What is just as between producers and their purchasing acquaintances? . . .

"The highest and best rewards come from honest and proper practice. Bad results in the long run come from selfish, unfair and dishonest conduct."

And the industry decided to follow his counsel. The worst effect of the government's method of handling the case was that it added to the general cynicism of business men about the practicability of coöperating with the government in correcting practices which have come in the development of business to be unfair. The government, they say, does not want to coöperate—it loves to prosecute. There is little political capital in coöperation, there is much, though it may be short-lived, in prosecution.

Inside the industry there were many people who felt like a certain old-time editor in the metal trades. "I have been engaged in iron and steel trade journalism since February 22, 1892, and thus have been familiar with this system of making the market for practically thirty years. It never struck me as peculiar or out of line with natural trade practices. As I have learned more about the markets for other commodities, I find that the principle of having a basing point on which prices are arranged is a natural thing in commerce, and indeed more or less necessary for the orderly conduct of business.

"What strikes me as especially peculiar about the criticism of 'Pittsburgh Plus' is that it is directed particularly against the United States Steel Corporation. When the Steel Corporation was formed, April 1, 1901, I regarded myself as rather an 'old-timer' in the iron and steel industry. The practice had been general even before my time, and certainly I observed no change when the Corporation was formed. The system merely continued. I do not doubt that the Steel Corporation would prefer the system to continue but I am absolutely convinced that the independent steel producers, whether located in Pittsburgh, Chicago or elsewhere, are much more anxious. . . ."

The attitude of the Federal Trade Commission was perhaps a reflection of a feeling in the country that the Steel Corporation was making more money than was possible if all its practices were fair. The question of profits came in for severe criticism after the War; and both inside and outside of the Corporation there were examinations, and explanations of the whole financial history and situation. The findings are of course important in any review of Judge Gary's business life since they are so largely the result of the application of his business theories and ethics. It was proper that the War earnings of the Corporation should be studied by the government. It was necessary in order to meet the rather persistent charge of profiteering as well as to give the government a base for the handling of private industries in case of another like catastrophe.

Many of the charges of profiteering were highly fantastic, and those who made them overlooked the fact that the prices charged by the steel industry were fixed by the government itself. These prices were more advantageous for the Corporation of course than they were for nonintegrated, nondiversified concerns. It was necessary, however, that such concerns should be allowed to make money enough to keep them going, their product was needed. The government proposed to offset by high taxes the profits which the great steel companies made through the prices they fixed. There were periods of the War when the federal taxes on the Steel Corporation were a million dollars a day, which was not too much, considering what it was producing.

The following table comparing earnings and taxes in the years 1916 and 1917 shows the results of the government's policy on prices.

	1916	1917
Net Earnings for Investment before Paying Federal Taxes	$312,941,489	$487,073,637
Federal Income and Excess Profits Taxes	9,692,009	233,465,435
Balance of Earnings	$303,249,480	$253,608,202

Besides, the outlay of the Corporation for new properties was enormous—properties which would in all probability be discarded, the War over. There were shipyards, an ordnance plant, enormous additions to its own equipment, purely because of War demands. Moreover, the Corporation frequently helped out weak competitors and financed extra supplies of raw materials which it realized would be needed, such as manganese and block tin. Mr. Filbert, comptroller of the Corporation, says that in the five years beginning with 1915, $497,000,000 were spent in expansions and additions—almost as much as had been spent in the fifteen previous years.

The investigation of the War profits and costs in the steel industry was carried on by the Federal Trade Commission. It was interesting to note that they submitted the first drafts of their report to the officials of the United States Steel Corporation; and, in making this report public, the Commission gives credit to the constructive suggestions and criticisms which they received from Judge Gary and his associates. It was the first time that such a course had been pursued by the Commission in cost investigation.

The period looked into was from 1915 to 1918, and it estimated the earnings of the Corporation at 18.2 per cent *before* federal taxes were paid. This was less by 2 per cent than the average earnings in the industry as a whole.

Judge Gary set his foot firmly down on what he called "unreasonable profits." War was not an excuse, in his judgment, for letting the market run away any more than a panic was an excuse for letting its bottom drop out.

It was not until the fall of 1917, as we have already seen, that the government agencies and the steel industry came to an agreement on the prices for steel products—

prices which were considerably lower than those that
Judge Gary had considered reasonable before we went
into the War. The government asked that the prices
fixed should be extended to the allies.

This request caused a violent protest among the steel
producers generally. They had agreed to the government's shedule with much groaning, but to sacrifice what
they had been getting from the Allies in the last two
years they felt was too much to ask, and many of them
said emphatically that they would not do it. Indeed, it
was not until it became known that Judge Gary and his
associates proposed to agree to this proposition, whatever the rest of the trade did, that the government's request was heeded.

This stand of Judge Gary's and its effect upon the
prices in the steel industry as a whole became known to
the Allies and it brought him a handful of buttons and
medals of one kind or another; but I doubt if anybody
ever saw him wear one, unless it might be when courtesy
to a visiting foreigner whose government had decorated
him required it. "I don't like to be singled out," he
said, "there are others who deserved recognition as much
as I did or more and didn't get it."

The effect of the decision of the Corporation in this
matter is a good example of the way the Gary theory of
prices works. It can and does prevent prices going too
high, for any length of time. It is only in an emergency
like war, or when a sudden and unexpected demand for a
great quantity is made that the independent who holds
to the beneficence of peaks in prices, can operate. He
can always, of course, undersell, and often does, in spite
of the general conversion of the trade to Judge Gary's
ideas. Stability of business is undoubtedly fostered by

this practice. The only serious question is whether the price made by the Corporation is reasonable. On this point Judge Gary has talked much from the start, and has again and again said that he personally would be willing to leave the matter to some proper body in the government as railroad freight traffic prices are left to the Interstate Commerce Commission.

The high earnings of the Corporation in the War were shared with both stockholders and labor. Holders of steel common have never been too highly rewarded for their faith. Up to 1916 there had been three years in which the dividends had been entirely passed, and there had been other years in which the 5 per cent on common, which the Corporation has always aimed to pay, had been cut to 4, 3, and 1½ per cent. Then, in 1916, dividends of 7 per cent were paid; in 1917, of 16¾ per cent; in 1918, of 16 per cent. Since then they have fallen back to the peace rate of 5 per cent, though since December, 1923, an extra 2 per cent has been paid.

Labor's average rose with the boom, the rise being voluntary. In 1915, the average wage and salary per man was $925; two years later, $1,280; in 1920, $2,173. It has been receding since, and in 1924 the average per day for the year was $5.74 exclusive of the administrative and selling forces. With these forces they were $5.85 per day. Altogether, the most heartening thing about a study of the financial conduct of the Steel Corporation is the steady improvement it shows in the earnings of workers. This conduct has been from the start as open as day. The annual reports of the Steel Corporation give the fullest information, and if a stockholder or a student finds that anything has been omitted that he wants to know, all that has been necessary has been for him to

call on Judge Gary. The information or explanation follows. The result is that it is possible to tabulate the
financial history of the concern through the twenty-four
years of its life so that every essential figure is before a
student. The *Wall Street Journal* does this, publishing
annually a tabulated history of the Corporation's capitalization, production, and disposition of gross receipts.

This tabulated history gives an opportunity for many
illuminating comparisons. For instance, running back to
the first full year of business, 1902, we find that the gross
receipts were something over one half billion dollars
($560,510,479 to be exact). Twenty-one years later these
receipts were greater by a billion dollars ($1,571,414,-
483). In 1902, only about 16 per cent of these gross
receipts went to the employees; in 1923, 30 per cent.

The ups and downs of these twenty-one years are
graphically shown on the charts. Here are stories of
panics and recoveries, of strikes and reconciliations, of
wars and peace; but, whatever these vicissitudes have
done to earnings and dividends, wages have been the last
thing affected and always, proportionally, the least affected.

The table shows graphically the increase in the
Corporation's wealth and stability. Judge Gary's ambition has been to make the Corporation as nearly impregnable as an industrial enterprise can be made. This he
believes is not only due the stockholders and the employees, but the public. The Steel Corporation is a semipublic enterprise, he will tell you. It handles a basic
material. All industries, all commerce, agriculture itself
depend upon iron and steel. A concern handling as large
a proportion of a basic industry as the Steel Corporation
does becomes a barometer for the industry, and this in-

dustry is a barometer for all industries. Here is a responsibility not to be ignored or shirked. The Corporation ought to be so solidly based financially that no conceivable shock could upset its equilibrium, for let it rock and all other industries will rock with it. That is, Judge Gary had been trying for years to realize the prophecy which Lord Haldane recently made in a brilliant essay forecasting the future, "As industries become more and more interwoven so that a dislocation of one will paralyze a dozen others," he wrote, "the ideal of the leaders of industry under no matter what economic system will be directed less and less to the indefinite increase of production in the intervals between such dislocations, and more and more to stable and regular production—even at the cost of reduction of profits and output while the industry is proceeding normally."

Seventeen years ago Judge Gary said the same thing to the Ways and Means Committee: "I consider the action of the steel people more important to be considered in connection with general business conditions than the condition of the steel trade."

The Corporation has always been conducted financially with this view of its relation to other industries in mind. It started out twenty years ago with a capitalization of a little over a billion dollars and a bonded debt of about $380,000,000. Against this the government investigators a few years later claimed that there were but $680,000,000 of actual property. The finance committee of that date disagreed, for in its first report it put down its assets as $1,647,443,022. The estimate was severely criticized in some quarters—there was no such value in the Corporation. As a matter of fact, it held $700,000,000 or more of "water." To-day, however, no one who studies its holdings and assets finds any "water" in its estimates. A full billion dollars has been added to its assets. A glance at the increase in its properties and their values will make the most skeptical hesitate to accuse it of exaggeration.

In April of 1921, the Corporation celebrated its twentieth birthday, and its comptroller, Mr. W. J. Filbert, made to the directors and officers a report of its growth, showing enormous increases in all sorts of resources. Take the matter of iron ore. In 1901, it was estimated that the Corporation had some 700,000,000 tons; in 1921, it was believed that this had been increased to 1,100,000,-000 tons, and in the meantime more than 400,000,000 tons had been mined. There had been enormous increase in the holdings of coal lands. Its railroad tracks had been increased from 1,026 miles to 1,687. The actual performance of its fleet in transporting ore and coal had been increased by 90 per cent. There had been tremendous additions of all sorts—23 modern ocean-going freight steamers, nearly 3,000 by-product coke ovens, the immense development of the T. C. and I. in Northern Alabama, a development which not only from an industrial but an educational and social point of view is one of the most substantial contributions made since the War to the upbuilding of the South. And then there is Gary —a town built upon sand dunes—the most interesting and ambitious industrial town ever undertaken in any country.

How has all this been done? Judge Gary will tell you quite simply that it has been by "careful management, great foresight in preparing for future financial needs, never undertaking anything that could not be carried out."

This careful management is apparent wherever one turns in the Corporation. It extends to official quarters and to the expense accounts of officers, Judge Gary himself setting the example. He occupies to-day, at 71 Broadway, the offices that he took in January of 1899 as president of the Federal Steel Company. This is partly from association but largely from a dislike of ostentation. There are more pictures of eminent gentlemen of the business and political world on the walls of his office to-day, but the chairs, with their monogram of "FSC" are still there. It is outside, from the windows, that one sees the changes. In January of 1899, you could look from these seventeen-story windows to the north and on a clear day see Grant's Tomb, while to the south you looked to the Narrows. All that is changed. High buildings have shut in 71 Broadway, along with its nearest neighbors to the north, Trinity Church and its ancient graveyard. The river, however, is still open to Judge Gary, and here he still may view, as he did twenty-five years ago, the lively daily traffic, dominated by the outgoing or the incoming of stately ocean liners.

As for expense accounts, many a journalist on a hundred dollars a week, would feel that he was being cramped if he was as careful as a Steel Corporation official. They have been trained to this. It is Judge Gary's habit to counsel the presidents of his subsidiary companies in all sorts of matters which affect the Corporation and their relation to it. Always he insists upon the strictest economy. "We occupy positions of trust," he told them in one of these meetings. "We are expending daily money which is not our own. Our stockholders have a right to hold us to a strict account. The fact that the Corporation or any of the companies may be rich, or may be prosperous, or may have money in the treasury furnishes no justification for needless or extravagant expenditures. . . . I presume that some of you might be surprised to know how your individual expense accounts compare with those of other officials. I do not say this from the books. I am quite sure that many of you would be surprised if you should examine the expense accounts of the United States Steel Corporation. I know they are small.'' It was after one of these homilies that the president of a great subsidiary, leaving the room with his colleagues, said: ''Well, I don't know whether or no such talks help business but I know they ought to make us better men.''

This careful management in small things amounts to much, of course, in years, but it is more important because of the mental attitude against careless expenditures that it establishes. The great economies in the Corporation have come through its organization as was promised at the start. These are economies of integration. They are written on the face of the organization and its practices. There is the saving which comes in the moving of materials, raw, semifinished, and finished. To be near your base and where transportation is cheap and easy is a governing principle of the Corporation. It owns and controls much of its transportation, thus avoiding the delays that come from congested traffic, undersupply of cars, sidetracking because of the priority of perishable freights. Owning their transportation, they are able to lay in supplies against the interruptions the seasons bring, as in getting ore down from the Lake Superior region where for many months the lakes are closed by ice.

MASS OF MODERN STEEL BUILDINGS SURROUNDING OLD TRINITY CHURCH AND THE
OLD FIRST NATIONAL BANK BUILDING, AT THE HEAD OF WALL STREET, CORNER OF
BROADWAY. EQUITABLE BUILDING IN PROCESS OF CONSTRUCTION, SHOWING STEEL
FRAME WORK SEPTEMBER 4, 1914, THE LARGEST OFFICE BUILDING IN THE WORLD. ON
THE LEFT, TRINITY BUILDING; ON THE RIGHT, BANKERS TRUST BUILDING; IN THE
CENTER, AMERICAN SURETY BUILDING

The smooth and continuous operation that comes from controlling supplies is a great economy as is the ability to carry the hot steel from the producing mill to the finishing mill.

The unifying of departments has resulted in many substantial savings. Thus, before the Corporation was formed, each company placed with outside insurance companies such of its risks as it insured. Now, Judge Gary was a legal expert in insurance business, having for many years been general counsel for several companies and when made president of the Federal Steel Company, he at once introduced into its subsidiaries a plan under which they carried all of their own risks. This plan was extended to the subsidiaries of the Steel Corporation, when it was organized, with the saving literally of millions of dollars.

And then savings have come from the utilization of what were once waste products. The immense Portland cement industry of the Steel Corporation, one of its big money earners, has been built on furnace slag, once not only a waste but an expense to dispose of. Portland cement has become a great business, but there are many small businesses which have grown up, such as one in China, based on steel and iron junk. "The Chinese buy large quantities of discarded material," says Mr. Farrel, "defectives, we call them—defective wire, rods, defective nails, defective shapes. It is the great market for defective material. They shape these things up into various articles in a very clever and commendable way. They make a very good razor from a low carbon steel wire rod. They even buy old horseshoes." Wherever one turns in the Corporation one finds developments from waste, which have or will utimately become businesses in themselves—two blades of grass growing where there was one, or none, before!

This of course would have been impossible without large cash resources. Judge Gary says that one of the chief elements in effecting large economies has come from their money reserves. "The money we have in banks," he says, "which can be utilized from time to time at one point or another as necessities may require, enables us to get along with one half the cash that these companies, if separated, would require for carrying on their businesses successfully." The policy of keeping a great working capital makes it possible for them, too, to apply the new methods, processes, inventions which come out of the policy of keeping a large number of men in friendly competition. This friendly rivalry is in itself one of the substantial economies of the Steel Corporation. Mr. Schwab gave an example of this in the steel suit. "One of the things we did," he said, "was to send to each blast furnace manager each month the cost of each one of the hundred furnaces in the Steel Corporation, or ninety, to be accurate, putting the best furnace at the top, with the name of the manager and the conditions, and the worst at the bottom, with the name of the manager and the conditions, for the education and stimulation of the other managers. The result of this was that the first year we made a saving in that department alone of approximately $4,000,000."

In Judge Gary's judgment, one of the most important economies from large cash resources is that it enables them to provide workers with plant and living conditions which would be out of the question under other circumstances. He believes that there is not only a moral obligation on the Corporation to use its funds liberally for the benefit of labor but that it is the soundest of economic practices. Mr. Filbert, the Corporation's comptroller, in tabulating the economies which have been secured by consolidation and coöperation in the Corporation, includes along with the centralizing of the purchasing of raw material, the conservation of ores through grading and mixing, the utilization of low grade coals for coking purposes, etc., etc., "safety, compensation, welfare plans and pension allowances."

The working capital which Judge Gary finds so advantageous has very largely been provided from surplus. The Corporation started out in 1901 with $25,000,000 surplus, and each year since, after dividends and special appropriations have been taken from its earnings, the balance has been increased. This has piled up until, for five years now, its undivided surplus has amounted to more than half a billion dollars. Of this total of undivided surplus about one half, or $253,000,000, has been added to its liquid wealth, while the balance, $264,000,000, together with approximately $360,000,000 of earned surplus specially appropriated for additions and extensions, making a total of $624,000,000, is lodged in property and plant investments.

The holders of common stock look on this surplus with an envious eye; the critics of the Corporation with a hostile one. This surplus is popularly supposed to be one half billion dollars in the bank. The Interchurch Report, in criticizing the wages paid by the Corporation, intimated that the proper use of it, would be to double wages, that there would still remain $11,000,000, which could be used for working capital. The writer evidently did not consider what effect the distribution of this accumulation—the work of twenty years of careful financing—would have on employment in times of depression. This big surplus is a most practical form of unemployment insurance. That is, it makes it possible for the Corporation in slack times to carry on extensive repairs, to build costly plants, to pile up mountains of ore and iron and steel—all work which requires money, when money is not coming in.

The idea of many stockholders has been, in recent years particularly, that it was high time that the Corporation should "cut a melon." Judge Gary does not fully agree. One of the most useful of the institutions which he has established in the Corporation is the annual open forum stockholders' meeting. For twenty-five years he has never failed to preside at these gatherings. All stockholders are invited and any stockholder present can get the floor. Perhaps the most interested group that attends is from the ranks of labor. They meet their fellow stockholders on equal grounds, and their talk is frank and free. A few years ago, one of them suggested that he lead the meeting in prayer. Judge Gary acquiesced, and probably for the first time in the history of Big Business a stockholders' meeting bowed its head and listened to a prayer for its guidance.

The conduct of affairs is quite frankly discussed at these meetings and stockholders do not hesitate to ask Judge Gary's explanation of this or that situation. Last April, the question of the surplus was raised, "Would not the Chairman tell them why it was not distributed?"

"I am interested in that myself," the Judge replied.

"A large part of my income and the income of my two daughters and two grandchildren is derived from declaration of dividends on the stocks of the United States Steel Corporation. But, gentlemen, the best interests of the stockholder are always served, always protected, by first, a conservative management which is best calculated to save the corporation from financial harm, disaster or distress, whatever the business conditions may be or whatever emergency may arise. There are many in this room who have seen one corporation after another, railroads and other concerns, go into the hands of receivers, who have been obliged to borrow money from time to time, and who have finally come to the point where credit was not good, and they had to turn their properties and their business over to the courts for reorganization and refinancing, very much to the prejudice and sometimes the total loss of the interest of some of the stockholders."

And then he presented some facts and figures on the surplus, which were news to many of them. Particularly did he disabuse them of the idea that the surplus is a checking account. Here is the table he presented:

We have undivided surplus on hand..........	$517,061,308.00
From this amount there has been invested in capital, that is, new properties necessary to be built and established if we are to take care of our business and keep our position in the trade, not only in this country but in all other countries	264,070,646.00
Leaving a balance of net working assets......	$252,990,662.00

This large sum is found in the following accounts:

Inventories	$213,189,316.00
Receivables	29,362,252.00
Securities	36,506,508.00
Cash	79,197,290.00

Making a total of	$358,255,366.00
Less current and contingent liabilities	105,264,704.00

Leaving the net as above stated	$252,990,662.00

"Of course," he said, "if I were a speculator on the Stock Exchange, buying to-day in the hope of selling to-morrow or next month at a profit, I might be glad to have the management of a corporation take some action in the way of declaring dividends which temporarily advanced the prices of securities, leaving that management to shoulder the trouble if it came afterwards by reason of taking any action proved to have been improvident.

"Gentlemen, we do not manage our corporation for the stock market."

And thereupon a stockholder broke in with an anecdote:

"A man said to me, 'You know Judge Gary, don't you?' I said, 'Yes.' He said, 'Does he ever give you a pointer on the market?' I said, 'If Judge Gary had a son who was in the brokerage business and the Judge knew at three o'clock in the afternoon an extra dividend would be declared the son would not know it until the newspapers had it the next day.' I believe that is true."

It undoubtedly is true—it is one of those Gary policies by which the Judge has established the validity of his claim that Big Business can not only be made stable but can be profitably carried on without any practice unbecoming a "gentleman and a scholar."

In these twenty-five years he has inaugurated and led in a movement which has practically revolutionized the principles and policies of the iron and steel industry. When he began his work the industry was nearly, if not quite, the lowest in morale in this country; it has become the highest, the most self-respecting, controlled, responsive to public opinion. Compare the morale of the steel industry to-day with that of many other great industries, and the contrast is the evidence of the claim.

In 1901, the competitive practices of the steel industry were frankly brutal; its heroes were those who were most successful in putting their weaker fellows out of business. "Ishmaels, all of us," one of the honest ones once declared on the witness stand. Under Judge Gary's leadership the industry has been put on a basis of regulated competition which has revolutionized all its practices and brought it from a condition of chronically drunken prices to where its prices are as stable and, on the whole, as reasonable as those in any industry. Regarding the steel and iron industry as semipublic in character, Judge Gary has steadily worked to break down the defiant attitude of his colleagues in regard to what they called government interference with their operations—that what they did was nobody's business but their own. To-day a great body of the trade accepts his contention that the government should supervise iron and steel, though undoubtedly very few follow him in his willingness that the government should say what prices are reasonable and what unreasonable.

His task of breaking down his colleagues' defiance of the government was much more difficult because the government itself was often as militant in its procedure as the steel men. Its favorite method was prosecution. Judge Gary had always insisted that it was practical to substitute coöperation; and again and again in the last twenty-five years when the practices of the industry became oppressive under development, as in the case of "Pittsburgh Plus," or objectionable under the socializing and humanizing of public opinion, as in the case of the twelve-hour day, he has sought correction through conferences and education, rather than force.

As he sought to build up a machinery of arbitration as well as a peaceful attitude of mind toward the government, he has also sought to work out a labor policy based on peace instead of war, the replacing of points of mutual antagonism by points of mutual interest. Hence, 10,000 men are now continually serving on committees in the Steel Corporation, 60,000 are yearly buying stock, hundreds are borrowing money to build homes, 90 per cent of the executives come from office boys—day laborers.

His greatest victory has been, possibly, in bringing men in the industry to ask, unashamedly, the question, "Is it right?" and to refuse when they thought it wrong. There were few men, inside or out of his immediate business group in 1901, who listened to talks on ethics in business with anything but an irritated amusement. It simply "was not done." But Judge Gary has won man after man to his point of view. I have already quoted Mr. Schwab's manly tribute to him at the dinner given to him by his competitors in 1909: "I am glad of this opportunity to say publicly that with my bounding enthusiasm and optimism, I was wrong in most instances— indeed in all instances—and you were right. The broad principles that you brought into this business were new to all of us who had been trained in a somewhat different school—their effect was marvelous, their success unquestioned.''

Only the day before his death in 1909, Henry Rogers, who to the last was faithful to his duties as a member of the finance committee, followed Judge Gary into his office. ''Judge,'' he said, ''I just want to tell you that when we started I thought you were always wrong. I have learned that you were right, and I wish that I had learned it much earlier.''

The next morning at nine o'clock, the news came to Judge Gary that Mr. Rogers was dead.

Henry Frick was another that Gary finally won over. There could hardly have been wider differences at first than theirs in business points of view. Mr. Frick, like others, expected to use on the stock market advance information which he was accustomed to get from the management of corporations in which he was interested, and when Judge Gary flatly refused to allow him this information he was bitterly angry. Then, they disagreed absolutely on labor policies. Frick was as militant as the most aggressive labor leader, and Gary was a pacifist. Frick believed that Gary did not like him. It took considerable time for the Judge to overcome this feeling. One thing that finally led them together was their mutual interest in pictures. The Judge thought that the Frick collection lacked especially in one particular. He thought Mr. Frick should have a good Van Meer, but Frick knew little of the great Dutchman. Later, when he did acquire his marvelous example of that master's work, he wanted the Judge to share his pleasure and wrote him from his country home in Massachusetts: ''Have the new Van

Meer here. It's a beauty. Am anxious you should see it.''

One by one, those who at the start had withdrawn from the Steel Corporation Board, doubtful of the Gary policies, became reconciled to him. There was John D. Rockefeller, for instance, as shown by this last paragraph from a letter declining an invitation which Judge Gary had sent him to the dinner which, in 1921, the Iron and

JOHN D. ROCKEFELLER
KIJKUIT
POCANTICO HILLS
NEW YORK

October 21, 1921.

Dear Judge Gary:

*   *   *   *   *

With every good wish for you, and great appreciation of what you have done in these years of unusual stress in the administration of the momentous affairs committed to your charge, believe me, with high esteem and most kindly regard,

Sincerely yours,

Hon. Elbert H. Gary,
71 Broadway, New York.

Steel Institute gave to Marshal Foch—a letter of which Judge Gary is very proud.

Perhaps nothing better proves his unique qualities as a leader than the building up of the Iron and Steel Institute. Twice a year this body holds a meeting of from 1,200 to 1,500 men, and it is a remarkable fact that every man of them will be in his seat in the assembly hall to listen to Judge Gary's business forecast. Many of them have come to regard what he has to say as almost prophetic, but he claims no prophetic powers. He is an inveterate optimist in regard to American business, basing his faith on the country's fundamental resources. Depression never scares him, never shakes his faith. That is, he is no opportunist in business, and this steadiness and farsightedness has had for years now an extraordinary effect on this great group.

What are the qualities that have made the man the leader that he is? They are the qualities of the statesman. He would have lasted but a little while in the group where he found himself if he had not brought to its multiplied problems a highly disciplined mind—one that can be neither confused nor fooled. His mind is so trained that it quickly penetrates, selects, and lays hold of what is essential in the most voluminous report on the most difficult question. Almost every associate of Judge Gary with whom I have talked in preparing this narrative has spoken in admiration and wonder of his prompt mastery of problems. The present secretary of the Corporation, George Leet, for eleven years the Judge's private secretary, never has lost his sense of amazement at this power of quickly getting at essentials. Mr. Leet says that in 1911, when the Bureau of Corporations' bulky report on the steel industry was laid before him, the Judge spent four hours going over it, with numerous interruptions. "After he left," says Mr. Leet, "I looked over the books and I found, to my astonishment, that he had gone through them from end to end, marking paragraphs and even making marginal comments. 'How in the world did you do it?' I asked him. 'Did it photograph itself on your mind?' But he did not seem to think it was anything unusual. He had the habit of 'just getting the gist out of a book,' he said."

His associates all remark his interest in new knowledge, also his insistence that it be sound. "Are you guessing?" he will ask a man that reports something to him. "If so, I can guess as well as you can." "You will learn," one of them remarked, "never to go to him with anything unless you have learned all you can about it. He senses whether a man knows what he is talking about or not."

"I never saw anybody who could put figures together more quickly or more exactly than Judge Gary. Of course, he does not claim to be an expert in the details of steel making, but bring him a problem in manufacturing and he goes at it as a lawyer would at the problem of a client in a lawsuit. He will follow it from start to finish, get the gist of it quickly: not much gets by him" —this from one of his fellow directors.

"He is a wonderful leader," says one of his subsidiary presidents. "When you take a problem to him, he helps you to come to the right solution and then gives you all the credit; and if it is trouble with somebody, always says at the start, 'Now, what is the other fellow's side?'"

Along with his trained capacity for getting the gist of a problem, goes great patience. "His patience and his knowledge will wear down anybody that I ever saw sitting opposite him," a fellow finance committeeman remarks. And this patience is combined with a quality very unusual in a man of well-based and stoutly held views, and that is tolerance of opposing opinion, willingness to listen and consider what others think and say.

Mr. Lindabury, who for many years was general counsel and a member of the finance committee, considered his willingness to listen to other men, to listen to opposite

Copyright, Underwood & Underwood, N. Y., 1925

FINANCE COMMITTEE, UNITED STATES STEEL CORPORATION, APRIL 1925

LEFT TO RIGHT, SEATED: GEORGE F. BAKER, HON. ELBERT H. GARY, J. P. MORGAN. STANDING: W. J. FILBERT, PERCIVAL ROBERTS, JR., JAMES A. FARRELL, RICHARD V. LINDABURY

views, most unusual. "He is the only man of his class that I have known that has this characteristic," Mr. Lindabury told me once, "I have known John D. Rockefeller, Sr., the elder Morgan, Jim Hill, well—had business dealings with them—all of them were intolerant of opposing opinions—intolerant of those about them—expected to be agreed with. Judge Gary is never intolerant. He seeks the opinions of associates, listens to everybody. His mind is clear on what he thinks, but he is kindly toward those who oppose him in business, and he gives up when there is a majority against him, in a good-tempered and friendly fashion."

This tolerance has been marked in his dealing with public criticism of the Steel Corporation's practices and policies. Judge Gary has been bitterly assailed again and again for upholding what he was trying to remove, and many of his associates, knowing his efforts and his difficulties, have resented the attitude of his critics. His care, however, has been always to find out if there was anything in what they were saying—how far they really represented public opinion. If their accusations were false or ignorant, you could afford to disregard them, but if there was anything that was true and essential, then it was your business to heed it. "Have no fear of unworthy criticisms," he told his colleagues once, "and entertain no unjust prejudice."

Not many months ago a public attack was made on Judge Gary which an appeal to the documents in the case would easily have overthrown. "I could have smashed him," he said of his critic, "but I have no disposition to hurt him. I think it is not in my nature to hurt anybody —at least I hope that is so. I know that is my policy, I don't believe in it. Of course," he said reminiscently, "I am less aggressive now than I used to be. When I was in the public school and a new boy came, his place had to be settled, and I never shirked that!" There is a protective wisdom in this—Judge Gary has always had so many heavy campaigns on hand that he could not afford time or strength on small ones.

The estimates of the group of remarkable men who have been associated with him in handling affairs in the tempestuous history of the Corporation are always interesting. "Judge Gary has sagacity, intelligence and patience," I have heard George Crawford of the T. C. and I. say. "He is just and courageous, has great knowledge of the motives of men. He is one of the most truthful men I have ever known and he has had a broadening effect on all of us who have been associated with him."

A note that runs through all of Judge Gary's speeches and letters and through the comments of his contemporaries is his desire that things be fair. "He has a passion for exact justice," his old secretary, Mr. Leet, says. "He wants justice more than anything else in the world." As a matter of fact, Judge Gary does not think that anything but justice works in the long run in handling human affairs. He is a profound believer in the essential moral quality of the universe. To him the effort to do business without considering the moral law is foolish and stupid. I have never seen him more irritated than when commenting on that point of view. "You cannot separate them," he says. "Moral principles are at the base of all permanent business success—they go together. In the long run, every business question, every public question must be settled by what is right and what is wrong."

Nobody knows better than he, however, the difficulty of

saying just what is right and what is wrong in the complicated situations of life. That is, he has none of the vanity and intolerance of the ignorant and inexperienced in affairs. His repeated counsel to his associates has been that when it is not quite clear what is right, the benefit of the doubt should be given to what seems to be right. "Courage to do the right thing and fear to do the wrong thing," he told his executives once, "are of equal rank in every good person's determination." "Again and again," Mr. Lindabury told me in the interview referred to above, "I have heard Judge Gary say in a meeting of the finance committee, 'I don't know just why I am opposed to that, but somehow it seems to me wrong, therefore I am against it.'" That is, he holds that even seeming wrong is a sufficient reason for refusing a proposition.

It is right here that his most intelligent associates feel that he has made his greatest contribution. "I should not have cared to travel over the road of the Steel Corporation unless Judge Gary sat in the chair," said one of them. "He has put the Golden Rule in the Steel Corporation's business. It was a bloody battle ground before he did away with all that kind of work."

George Verity, the head of the American Rolling Company, which began business about the time of the Steel Corporation, believes that his leadership has been an incalculable benefit to the industry. "If a man of another type," says Mr. Verity, "harder, colder, less human, less committed to right dealing, less anxious that a higher ethical code should prevail in business, had come into the Corporation, it would have brought endless disaster. He is a man of character, and he has been able to make the contribution that he has because he is a man of character.''

Again, Judge Gary is a likable man, approachable, interested in everybody's problems. His personal qualities have made him acceptable when, if he had been dictatorial or pompous, self-seeking or vain, he would have made far less headway than he has. It is not that in the ease of approach he forgets his dignity. Indeed, he seems to have a very strong sense that it is due to the Corporation and to the iron and steel industry that he set a good example in his conduct and ways. He is fastidious in dress, meticulous in courtesy, refusing to see no one that has any excuse at all for coming to him. He is careful about where he goes and what he does, and this must be a bit hard on him at times because he has more or less of the sporting spirit. He loves horses but keeps no racing stable. It would not, in his judgment, be a good example. When he travels he has an enormous curiosity about what goes on in all ranks of human beings, but carefully refrains from following his desire to prowl around in the under as well as the upper world. He would like to fly and now and then, he confesses, he has broken over when a good excuse offered—as once in Uruguay, when he found it, difficult otherwise to meet an important engagement. But he was not so far away even there that the news of his exploit did not find its way to the finance committee, with the result that he was reprimanded—they did not want him to take any chances, they told him good-naturedly. All this is human and likable.

He is generous, particularly in what concerns the steel towns, the body of iron and steel workers. Hundreds know this, but the last thing in the world the public knows or that he would have it know, is what he gives. He has great concern always about the personnel of the Corporation—knows the men from top to bottom, in a quite surprising way, and looks out for them, foresees situations, and is constantly warning his executives to look ahead. Three years ago in a meeting of the subsidiary presidents, he reminded them that the time was coming when they, who had been working together for twenty years and more, would not be here. There was only one man on the board of directors and on the finance committee that had been continuously there from the start, he said. That, of course, was himself. He wanted them to be thinking now about how their positions might be filled by promotions from the ranks, and if there were nobody competent, then they should recognize this and train men. "I should like to be sure," he said, "that in our great industrial army, of which I may tell you I am very proud, no gap will be made that cannot be filled by promotion."

His pride in the steel industry has made his leadership particularly acceptable. Judge Gary is a man of fine loyalty—and something of a hero worshiper! His feeling for Roosevelt amounts to that. The Judge knew Roosevelt at his greatest moment—backed him in his attack on corporate crime, and never lost the elation of the fight. He would, I think, have liked to have seen Roosevelt back in the White House. It may be that this was in his mind when in December of 1915 he gave a great, but strictly private dinner, all the great financiers of the day being invited to meet the ex-President. It leaked out a few days later, and the newspapers were filled with speculations, much to T. R.'s enjoyment as the note on the following page shows.

This loyalty of his has been a large factor in holding

the men of the iron and steel world to him in the trying circumstances which have surrounded their industry through the last twenty-five years. Colleagues and competitors knew that he never lost sight of his responsibility

SAGAMORE HILL Dec 22ᵈ 1915

Dear Judge Gary,

I thoroly enjoyed the dinner; and I am immensely amused at the excitement it has caused. I hope you have'nt minded it! Believe me, I appreciated your friendly courtesy.

Faithfully yours
Theodore Roosevelt

to them—never failed to interpret *their* point of view, though often, as they knew, it was not *his* point of view. They had their side, they were the men upon whom the burden of production lay—they must stand the vicissitudes. Whatever their mistakes, their differences, Judge Gary did his best to present them fairly to the public.

They came to know that they were safe in his hands—that he would never betray them. They also knew that he was incessantly working to convert them! Sooner or later they realized that he was leading them to the water, though they knew he would not try to force them to drink until they were ready—or realized that they would suffer if they did not drink!

It was difficult for a considerable progressive element in the public to realize his strategy, to understand that probably he was moving as rapidly on the whole as was possible, and keep the line he led unbroken. He was not infrequently pelted with criticisms which were undeserved and which cut him deeply but which, because of his object—which was that of his critics—he passed without reply. A rare kind of courage!

Judge Gary's leadership in the iron and steel world is the logical result of a combination of fine qualities unwaveringly applied for twenty-five years to realizing a body of principles and policies always ahead of his day. He has demonstrated in practice the soundness of his code. He has made a lasting contribution to our difficult and often baffling problem of substituting in American business balance for instability—mutual interest for militarism—coöperation for defiance—frankness for secrecy—good will for distrust. No man in contemporary affairs has more honestly earned the high title of Industrial Statesman.

INDEX

357

(1)

THE END

BIOGRAPHY and AUTOBIOGRAPHY

THE LIFE OF ELBERT H. GARY

By IDA M. TARBELL.

> This is not only the life story of a great and powerful man in our industrial life, it is the story of the steel industry and much of the story of the country itself as well. $3.50.

DAVID WILMOT: FREE SOILER

By CHARLES B. GOING.

> An historical biography of one of the most intense personalties in the great Free-Soil struggle which culminated in the Civil War, the originator of the Wilmot Proviso. $6.00.

FORTY YEARS OF IT

By BRAND WHITLOCK.

> An autobiography—a record of real service in American life. A fine story and a fascinating account of forty odd years of useful activity. $2.50.

SAINTE-BEUVE

By LEWIS FREEMAN MOTT.

> The story of one of the most striking personalities of the nineteenth century—Charles Augustin Sainte-Beuve, the greatest literary critic of France. $5.00.

D. APPLETON AND COMPANY

NEW YORK   LONDON